Piers Dudgeon is a writer, editor
Born in 1949, he worked for ten
London and then started his own comp
a number of bestsellers with authors as diverse as
Daphne du Maurier, John Fowles, Edward de Bono,
Shirley Conran and Susan Hill. Since 1989 he has
worked as a journalist and written ten works of non-
fiction. In 1993 he moved with his wife and three children to a village on the North Yorkshire moors, where he
is setting up a residential school for writers and artists.

By Piers Dudgeon

Tactics (ed.)
Dickens' London
The English Vicarage Garden
Village Voices
Enchanted Cornwall (ed.)
The Country Child
The Spirit of Britain
Emmerdale
The Girl from Leam Lane
My Land of the North (ed.)
Breaking out of the Box
Kate's Daughter
Child of the North
Lifting the Veil
The Woman of Substance
Captivated
Our Glasgow
Our East End

OUR EAST END

Memories of Life in
Disappearing Britain

PIERS DUDGEON

headline
review

First published in 2008
by HEADLINE REVIEW
An imprint of Headline Publishing Group

First published in paperback in 2009
by HEADLINE REVIEW
An imprint of Headline Publishing Group

3

Cataloguing in Publication Data is available from the British Library

ISBN 978 0 7553 1712 7

Typeset in New Baskerville by Avon DataSet Ltd,
Bidford on Avon, Warwickshire

Printed and bound in the UK by
CPI Group (UK) Ltd, Croydon, CR0 4YY

Headline's policy is to use papers that are natural, renewable and
recyclable products and made from wood grown in sustainable forests.
The logging and manufacturing processes are expected to conform to
the environmental regulations of the country of origin.

HEADLINE PUBLISHING GROUP
An Hachette UK Company
338 Euston Road
London NW1 3BH

www.headline.co.uk
www.hachette.co.uk

Contents

———

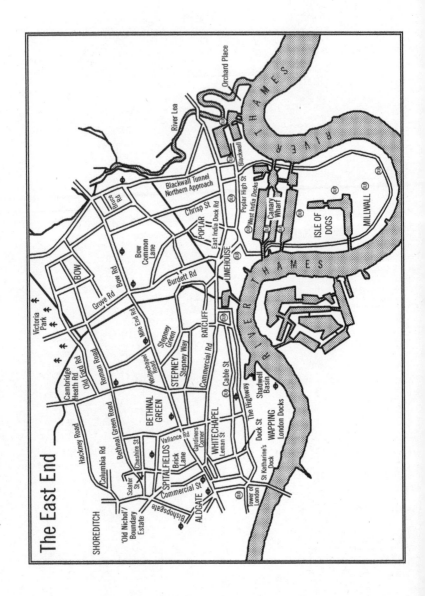

The East End

INTRODUCTION

Outcast London

In the spring of 1922 a young man of thirty-two returned to England from America, where he was fast becoming famous in the silent movies of the day. He was in search of his roots and stepped into a scene that the Hollywood dream factory could not have produced more touchingly.

> Children are playing, lovely children. I see myself among them, back there in the past. I wonder if any of them will come back some day and look around enviously at other children.
>
> Somehow they seem different from those children

with whom I used to play. Sweeter, more dainty were these little, begrimed kids with their arms entwined around one another's waists. Others, little girls mostly, sitting on the doorsteps, with dolls, with sewing, all playing at that universal game of 'mothers' . . .

I want to shriek with laughter at the joy of being in this same old familiar London. I love it.

It is all so soft, so musical; there is so much affection in the voices. They seem to talk from their souls. There are the inflections that carry meanings, even if words were not understood. I think of Americans and myself. Our speech is hard, monotonous, except where excitement makes it more noisy . . .

I leap into the taxi again and ride on. We drive around . . . I get out and walk along among the crowds.

People are shopping. How lovely the cockneys are! How romantic the figures, how sad, how fascinating! Their lovely eyes. How patient they are! Nothing conscious about them. No affectation, just themselves, their beautifully gay selves, serene in their limitations, perfect in their type.

I am the wrong note in this picture that nature has concentrated here. My clothes are a bit conspicuous in this setting, no matter how unobtrusive my thoughts and actions . . . I feel the attention I am attracting. I put my handkerchief to my face. People are looking at me, at first slyly, then insistently. Who am I? For a moment I am caught unawares.

A girl comes up – thin, narrow-chested, but with an

eagerness in her eyes that lifts her above any physical defects.

'Charlie, don't you know me?'

Of course I know her. She is excited, out of breath. I can almost feel her heart thumping with emotion as her narrow chest heaves with her hurried breathing. Her face is ghastly white, a girl about twenty-eight. She has a little girl with her.

This girl was a servant girl who used to wait on us at the cheap lodging-house where I lived. I remembered that she had left in disgrace. There was tragedy in it. But I could detect a sort of savage gloriousness in her. She was carrying on with all odds against her. Hers is the supreme battle of our age. May she and all others of her kind meet a kindly fate.

With pent-up feelings we talk about commonplace things.

'Well, how are you, Charlie?'

'Fine.' I point to the little girl. 'Is she your little girl?'

She says, 'Yes.'

That's all, but there doesn't seem to be much need of conversation. We just look and smile at each other and we both weave the other's story hurriedly through our minds by the way of the heart. Perhaps in our weaving we miss a detail or two, but substantially we are right. There is warmth in the renewed acquaintance. I feel that in this moment I know her better than I ever did in the many months I used to see her in the old days. And right now I feel that she is worth knowing.

There's a crowd gathering. It's come. I am discovered,

> with no chance of escape. I give the girl some money to buy something for the child, and hurry on my way. She understands and smiles. Crowds are following. I am discovered in Lambeth Walk.[1]

Lambeth Walk is not in the East End, it is in Southwark, on the south side of the Thames across London Bridge, but Charlie Chaplin had no doubt he was a cockney, and the street life and level of emotional understanding is redolent of the culture of the East End which we identify with being a cockney. Clearly, the East End of London is not only a district, it is also a condition of the mind.

> It is you; it is who you are; it is where you came from. Every day of my life . . . I am still aware of how it used to be. Inside I haven't changed a bit. My feet are firmly on the ground.

True East Enders *are* their environment and take it with them, wherever they venture forth. Their environment is an emotional one, as much as it is a bricks and mortar one. The East End is a place *and* it is a condition of the mind. 'You can take a boy out of the East End, but not the East End out of a boy.'

It is different to the Southwark cockney's condition, because this peculiar spirit was born out of an extraordinary history, which believe it or not is still continuing today. It did not stop with the Second World War, after which so many cockneys moved out. Nor did it end with the huge wave of immigration in the 1950s, nor even with the closure of the last of the docks – its window on to the wide world – in 1981.

Certainly the spirit was tested post-war when so many East Enders' houses lay in rubble and a tower-block solution to the Blitz made any kind of community difficult to sustain. But it did not burn out. The new immigrants were soon imbued with their own version of it, just as previous immigrant populations had been. And there are still people who can claim their families to be indigenous East Enders, like Tony Burns, who runs the Repton Boxing Club in Cheshire Street off Brick Lane, and whose family have been Bethnal Greeners for well over a hundred years.

The history of the East End is all about change, but within a deeply laid continuity. Whole communities come and go, and believe that it is over when they have gone. But it is not.

A cockney is defined as one who was born within the sound of Bow bells, which makes the geography of the East End even more uncertain. Are the bells in question of Bow, the community east of Stepney and Bethnal Green, or of St Mary le Bow in the City, the financial capital on the East End's western border?

In 1392 Dick Whittington is supposed to have heard Bow bells call him back to London to become Lord Mayor. For centuries St Mary le Bow dominated life in the City and the nine o'clock bell not only marked the curfew, but also the end of an apprentice's working day. Today's bells were cast at the famous Whitechapel bellfoundry in 1956, after having been destroyed by enemy action in the Second World War.

> They hang 100 feet (30 metres) above the ground in a bell frame made of Javanese Jang. The smallest bell weighs 5 cwt (285 kgs) and the biggest or tenor bell weighs almost 42 cwt (2135 kgs). Each bell has an inscription from a Psalm or New Testament canticle on it, and the first letters of each inscription spell D WHITTINGTON.[2]

But there is something about this romantic claim by the City of London upon the East End that makes for uncomfortable reading. For history tells us that the East End was always considered by those to the west as the land of the outcast, its streets 'full of coster-mongers' barrows and its mingled odours of unwashed garments and fried fish' attracting writers and reformers, such as Charles Booth and Sir Walter Besant, in number.

In the 1880s an anonymous penny pamphlet entitled *The Bitter Cry of Outcast London* was given great publicity in the *Pall Mall Gazette* and the *Daily News*, and in 1902 the American writer Jack London again described the East End as 'outcast London' in *The Abyss*, a short book based on his own experience as an East End down-and-out.

This word 'outcast' applied to East Enders incriminates the social group who rejected them, namely the industrialists and money men of London.

Nearly 400 years ago they marked the East End out as a pit by foisting its 'stink industries' on it – 'breweries, gunworks, tanneries, lime kilns, glue, soap and candle works' – principally because the dominant west winds would keep the smell of them away from fashionable, aristocratic and more civilised London.

Having established these and other industries, including, from 1800, the Docks from Tower Bridge to Blackwall, the industrialists and City men set about exploiting the East End's workforce, paying them just 5d. an hour to work in the docks in conditions barely humane, and rewarding, say, a finisher of boots 2s. 6d. per dozen pairs, or a female shirt-maker 10d. to 3s. for a dozen shirts, working ten and a half hours a day. The most celebrated case concerned the exploitation of the matchbox makers employed by Bryant and May, the lowest of the low, who were paid twopence-farthing per gross boxes and told to 'buy your own string and paste'.

It was certainly not wealth. It was not even survival. Strikes led to cases of starvation. Women workers were taken to court for attempted suicide.

> Oh, those trudges through the lanes and alleys round
> Bethnal Green Junction late at night, when our day's
> work was over; children lying about on shavings, rags,
> anything; famine looking out of baby faces, out of
> women's eyes, out of the tremulous hands of men.[3]

The Match Girls' Strike of 1888 stirred a few consciences, but it was not the first event to do so, nor would it be the last. Men like William Booth, who founded the Salvation Army in Whitechapel, the American George Peabody, who gave a fortune to house the rabble in East End tenement blocks named after him, and the Irishman Thomas Barnardo, who opened his first Children's Home for orphans and destitute children here, were already doing their bit. And even if, as we now know, many East End children were taken off the streets of Whitechapel, Bethnal Green and Stepney by Barnardo's and shipped to Canada and the Antipodes without parental consent, at least someone was trying to make amends.

Their concern had an extraordinary consequence. Soon, socially conscious undergraduates from Oxford University were coming to peer at East Enders in their dilapidated and often hopelessly unhygienic abodes, bringing with them nothing but a desire to learn. The people must have felt as if they were living in a zoo.

The question is, who was in the cage behind bars and who in front? Refreshingly, the man behind the initiative saw the East Enders as looking into the cage and the Oxford undergraduates looking out from theirs. The Reverend Samuel Augustus Barnett, vicar of St Jude's Whitechapel, was described by Beatrice Webb as 'a diminutive body clothed in shabby and badly assorted garments . . . small black eyes set close together, sallow complexion, and a thin and patchy pretence of a beard'. But he was quite a man.

Barnett had been told by his boss, the Bishop of London, that the parish of Whitechapel was 'the worst in the diocese, inhabited mainly by a criminal population'. Soon after he arrived he proved the bishop right by falling foul of the cockney art of 'shoot-flying' – he was knocked down in Commercial Street and relieved of his watch. In the days when men wore fob watches, 'shoot-flying', or 'blagging' as it was also called, was the most assured means to a meal. Three or four men worked it together, generally where the City toffs were – Broad Street, Finsbury Square . . .

Barnett wanted to wake the world up to the cockney East Ender's sense of community, which he understood as an academic concept and saw immediately his parishioners understood instinctively. The privileged young Oxford men barely out of their teens, whom he brought to gawp at the natives, in his opinion understood nothing at all, even though many of them were already earmarked as the coming men in the fields of politics, journalism, education and religion.

The headquarters for Barnett's initiative was Toynbee Hall in Whitechapel, a large building a short walk from Aldgate East tube, still as active today. Arnold Toynbee was a Tutorial Fellow of Oxford and the man who coined the phrase 'industrial revolution'. He had been a pupil of the philosopher T. H. Green, who, in the light of the hardship visited on the working man in the East End and elsewhere by the industrialists and money men of the City, first saw the need for what he termed 'active citizenship', the concept of community that every man has a duty to his fellow man.

This clearly fitted hand in glove with Barnett's thinking, and Toynbee was a frequent visitor to St Jude's vicarage. They became great friends. When Toynbee died at only thirty-three years of age, Barnett decided to name the initiative and its Whitechapel headquarters after him.[4]

A typical Oxford group of undergraduates addressed by Barnett in the early days – this one at St John's College – included Cosmo Gordon Lang, later Archbishop of Canterbury, J. A. Spencer (later a Liberal journalist), E. T. Cook (later Editor of the *Daily News*), A. H. D. Acland (a future Liberal minister), Michael Sadler (future Master of University College London and Vice Chancellor of Leeds University). He challenged them, as he did all his prospective volunteers or 'residents' of Toynbee Hall, to come and see the East End communities for themselves.

For better or worse, and one can see why they responded as they did, what came out of it was a new Socialist State. Key Toynbee residents included Clement Attlee, Prime Minister from 1945, and William Beveridge, whose *Report on Social Insurance and Allied Services* formed the basis of post-war social security legislation in Britain. Both maintained a life-long association with the Hall. In 1919, the national dockers' organiser, Ernest Bevin, who was to become foreign secretary in Attlee's government in 1945, cut his political teeth in the East End with a campaign to secure dockers' wages of 16s. a day for a 44-hour week, and was largely responsible two years later for the creation of the Transport and General Workers' Union. 'The Whites', as they were known on account of their white membership cards, were rivals of the Blues, the older National Amalgamated Stevedores' and Dockers' Union, and so fierce was politics in those days that marriages between the groups were 'disencouraged'.

Toynbee Hall has other socialist associations. The meeting that brokered the end of the 1926 General Strike happened there, and institutions of social reform, including the Workers Educational Association, one of the first Citizens' Advice Bureaux, and the Child Poverty Action Group, started there too.

The East End had always been a left-wing political cauldron. The first Labour Party Member of Parliament, Keir Hardie, was elected from West Ham (South) in 1892. The 5th Congress of the Russian Social Democratic Labour Party, forerunner to the Bolshevik Party, took place in Fulbourne Street, opposite the London Hospital in Stepney in May 1907. And prior to the Russian Revolution, led by Lenin in 1917, Bolsheviks (including Lenin) visited the East End frequently, as did Stalin, who stayed round the corner from Toynbee Hall at the Tower House in Fieldgate Street. Moreover, Sylvia Pankhurst had her headquarters in Bow.

How much help all these politicians were to the poor of Whitechapel and Stepney is difficult to say. From the 1960s, politics served to close the docks, the principal employer in the area, and it has been said that the welfare state took the motivation out of the working man. Certainly it is a fact that Tower Hamlets continues to be one of the most deprived boroughs in Britain today.

However, of crucial importance, because it was something to which the East End gave life, was Samuel Barnett's concept of community, of 'active citizenship'. It is a concept that is still unimpeachable, still with us in the East End today, and in the face of modern technology (television, the internet, etc.), which represents the opposite of community, it has never been more important that we understand it.

The East Ender was a community animal. He found something money can't buy. That is why he is still a talking point today. None of the children born within earshot of Bow bells had any doubt who they were, or the values they espoused.

PART I

THE COCKNEY SPIRIT

—

CHAPTER ONE

Mother London

―――――

> This was OUR place. We knew every nook and cranny,
> every little alleyway, every empty house (usually inside
> and out), and probably every cat and dog.[1]

The East End was a community in which its children
belonged and were free in a way that those up West,
who walked with their nannies in Kensington Gardens,
could only dream about. The first principle of the East
End way of life was that the mother was the source:

> Family life was closely knit, attached to mother, the
> linchpin of the family wheel. Nothing was done without

3

mother being consulted. Even her grown up sons bowed to her long after they were married. Her daughters when married would never live too far from her, so that mother was always on hand to help and advise; grandchildren worshipped her, paying regular homage and visits to Granny.[2]

Mum was the patriarchal figure in those days. She was responsible for the children in every respect. Father would only emphasise and support her discipline when necessary. His task was to work and support the family and make decisions upon family matters whenever he felt it necessary. Otherwise he would like nothing better than to be left in peace after a hard day at the workshop to enjoy a glass of tipple and settle down in his easy chair. The children were primarily Mum's responsibility from birth until they handed over their first wage packet. It was not the custom for married women to work in those days unless they were widows and obviously had to take a job to support their children; for many an unfortunate widow it was a struggle to maintain their families upon the somewhat meagre weekly pittance received from the Relieving Officer.[3]

Patriarchal indeed! Nothing could have been more feminine; she was often mother to more than half a dozen children. But she did also take responsibility in certain key areas, elsewhere deemed to be exclusive to men. For example, in many East End families the wife did work, and it was her working that kept the family above the breadline:

Mothers, young and old, sat outside [in the street] on kitchen chairs tending to piecework – hand-stitching hems, sewing on buttons, threading and knotting crochet lace collars and cuffs or whatever else would earn a few shillings. They gossiped or cracked jokes or sang old familiar songs while they worked to help the time go by. One of our neighbours, who took in washing, often stood outside her downstairs window on warm days, listening to an old-fashioned wireless from within as she ironed sheets. She always had two irons on the go: one warming on the stove and the one she was using to do the pressing.[4]

My mother was a forager. God bless her, she foraged all her life, that's how she brought us up. She got a good few bob off the people in the Mission. She would tell the hard-luck story so as to get herself in. Well it was a true story. The whole thing was having your poverty well known to the people who had the giving of charity. They noticed that mother was a 'dead' cripple, and that father was a loafer, and that she had children to bring up. And so she got on the list for any of the gifts which came from wealthy families, to distribute among the poor. They made out she was 'deserving'. They were always asking whether we was good children or not, and whether we were clean, and whether we went to Sunday school.[5]

She was nine times out of ten the dominant personality. Even if she was the victim of physical abuse from her husband when he came home from the pub on a Friday night, having spent the week's wages, she took charge whenever she could, falling naturally into the role. Arthur Harding's sister had a stall in Roman Road market, east of Bethnal Green, in Bow. But when their mother turned up, she would take charge.

> You've got to remember this, that young or old the
> mother was the top Johnny in the family. What she said
> was law.[6]

She was invariably the family exchequer. 'All the money you earned went to her and she would share it out.' In many households she also ran the 'family club'. Money was collected – say, 2s. 6d. a week – members could withdraw funds at any time, usually at Christmas.

> Every single family had to watch expenditure very
> carefully whether the family earner was a labourer,
> artisan, ganger or foreman. The eking out of the family
> income was Mum's responsibility and she struggled
> through her weekly task, often to her own detriment, in
> many cases by starving herself to feed the youngsters.[7]

Later Harding described what happened after his mother took up heavy drinking:

> Mighty [the sister] was now the mainstay of the family.
> She was the main breadwinner because she had a fixed
> job and she was earning money at the stall. But mother

was the paymaster – we were so obedient that we gave
her all our wages.

In turn, the mother depended on her mother, whose
house she and her husband lived in, to start with. It was
very rare, and a recipe for disaster, for a couple to set
up home in the husband's parents' house. And even
when wife and husband moved out, it would be to a flat
close by, and probably chosen for them by the mother,
after asking around.

One of the wife's sisters, Joyce, lives with her husband
and children in the same block, another of her sisters,
Joan, and one of the husband's brothers in the same
turning, and her mother and father in another nearby
street. Mrs Wilkins is in and out of her mother's all day.
She shops with her in the morning and goes round there
for a cup of tea in the afternoon. 'Then any time during
the day, if I want a bit of salt or something like that, I go
round to Mum to get it and have a bit of a chat while
I'm there.' If the children have anything wrong with
them, 'I usually go round to my Mum and have a little
chat. If she thinks it's serious enough I'll take him to the
doctor'. Her mother looked after Marilyn, the eldest
child, for nearly three years. 'She's always had her when I
worked; I worked from when she was just a little baby
until I was past six months with Billy. Oh, she's all for our
Mum. She's got her own mates over there and still plays
there all the time. Mum looks after my girl pretty good.
When she comes in, I say 'Have you had your tea?', and

she says as often as not, 'I've had it at Nan's.' It
appeared that, on average, the wives saw their mothers
about four times a week.[8]

The second principle of the East End was that family was
open to the community. George Bishop described Bethnal
Green as resembling 'a small country village. Many
people were related, and everyone knew his and her
neighbours, their jobs, their worries, hopes and dreams.'[9]

Everybody helped each other. You shared your troubles.
For instance, if there was an unfortunate occurrence in
the family, a death or an illness, and somebody was in
trouble through it over money, the list used to go round
the doors, there'd be a penny or tuppence put on the
list.[10]

Doors were never locked and we would be in and
out of one another's houses because we all trusted one
another and even when our parents fell out it never
affected the friendship of the children.[11]

Front doors on many houses had a hole through
them with a piece of string and a knot which was
attached on the inside to a latch so when we visited our
friends, we would knock on the door and pull the string
and go in, and nobody said you can't walk in my house
like that . . . It was friendly. If anybody was in any bother,
we would help them. If they were ill they got helped, if
people got themselves in trouble with the police, which
being very poor was not unusual, they were helped, so it
was a very strong community.[12]

One obvious fulcrum of the community was the corner shop, a particular kind of store, which could sometimes give 'tick' if funds were low, and which was a meeting place and relay station for news and gossip.

There was simply not enough money to buy in any quantity, and every little community had its corner shop where you could buy ha'pworth and pen'orth of commodities like tea, sugar and jam. For jam, the customer would provide his own container, usually a cup, which would be weighed before about one ounce of jam, taken from a 7lb jar, was scraped in with a wooden spoon. Tea was packed in penny packets by the wholesaler, but the shopkeeper would always 'make' a ha'pworth, sold in a square of newspaper twisted into a funnel shape with the bottom screwed up, sufficient to contain a couple of spoonfuls of tea. The smell of these shops stayed with their customers long after they ceased to exist. A mixture of candles, coffee, carbolic soap, corned beef, spice, jam, tea, etc . . . sawdust on the floor brought a whiff of pine and oak, but the catalyst blending them all was the resin on the bundles of firewood, stacked against the counter on sale at a ha'penny each.[13]

The shop was also a place to meet. 'Some days you see so many [people] you don't know which to talk to,' said Mrs Landon, who once kept a record over a week of all the people she saw in the street that she considered herself to 'know'. As Michael Young recorded in *Family and Kinship in East London* (1957), 'There were sixty-three people in all, some seen many times and thirty-eight of them relatives of at least one other person out of the sixty-three. Her story showed how she had built up a series of connections with people she had known in school, work or street, and, even more forcefully, how her mother and other kin acted as a means of communication between herself and the other people in her social world.'

Such connections meant that the street had a life of its own.

> Everybody knew everyone else's business. We all knew when Flo or Maggie was pregnant, long before it began to show. Like a jungle telephone news went from door to door. If you had a new pair of boots on the whole street turned out to have a look. The old women sat on their windowsills nattering for hours.[14]

It was a scene replayed daily, endlessly, year in, year out, throughout the East End:

> On a fine evening the women would enjoy a good gossip. The older ones would sit on chairs while the younger and fitter ones would stand but all had their arms folded. This practice took place all the way along the street – little groups involving the occupants of eight houses from each side of the road would enjoy these chats. If some interesting tit-bit was on the agenda, the groups would often overlap. Father hated my mother

gossiping and if a neighbour spotted my father coming home from work would call, 'Look out Mill, Scotty's coming', and Mum would make a hasty retreat indoors; however, if he caught her chatting on the doorstep he would call out, 'Hey, News of the World, haven't you got anything better to do?'[15]

Childbirth was an occasion when the community stepped in to look after the existing children or help in the birth itself. Charles Adams remembered:

When a birth took place, a woman in the road would be midwife and others would bring pieces of clothing and other little bits for the new baby. The other children in the family would be looked after and given a meal or two, and if the husband was working someone would make sure he had a meal when he came home at night.[16]

But skilled helpers who might have no professional training at all were also available to act both as midwife and, at the other end of life, as mortician. Mrs Mapstead, 'with her carpetbag and her slight air of superiority', was one of these.

She was the person you called upon to assist at home birth. She fetched and carried, and looked after the kids and generally took over whilst you were confined, and in cases of death, she laid out the corpse and got it ready for visitors saying their last farewells before the

undertakers removed it to their premises. Her motto was
'I gets them into the world and I sees them off!'[17]

This way of living first and foremost to help others also
brought out the best of some very special people, for
whom altruism was a priority even over the law.

Doctor Deacon was one of these. According to
Ralph Finn, he was 'the most loved person in the East
End'.

Deacon knew everyone in the Whitechapel community, and worked hand-in-glove with Father Gregory
in the Catholic Mission there. Deacon was, however,
like many others at the outbreak of the First World War,
a conscientious objector and being also a bit of a soft
touch for those who claimed to be conscientious
objectors too, he effectively helped many men avoid the
call-up. When he was found out, he was imprisoned and
struck off the medical register.

After the war he returned to his old patch and was
once more the first doctor everybody wanted to see,
because he was so caring and put his vocation and his
patients' needs before everything else, in particular
before his remuneration when someone in dire
financial straits needed his help. For this was before the
National Health Service.

Whenever there was a sensitive issue he came down
on the side of the community. One such issue in those
days was abortion. Without efficient contraception,
families were very large. Midwife Jennifer Worth
reported delivering one mother of a family of eighteen,

and having ten children was common. The physical, emotional and financial implications were disastrous for many. Abortion was, however, illegal, and a dangerous, backstreet option. Deacon would not perform an abortion, but he would treat any patient who had fallen foul of 'Hat Pin Bella', and he would not report Bella for bringing backstreet relief to the mothers of unwanted babies.

This attitude almost occasioned his second downfall. For Bella was taken to court and Doc Deacon was accused of practising without a licence. What in fact happened was a testament to the doctor and to the wisdom of the judge, as well as a clear signal as to the value of Deacon to the East End. Doc Deacon spoke up in court about the nature of the community to which he had dedicated his life, and his love for it, and the vocation he felt he had to serve it, and the need he felt the community had for such a service. The judge, while censoring him, took no further action against the doctor.

Legends are made of such as this, and the press hailed the unregistered Dr Deacon as 'The Saint of Whitechapel'.

CHAPTER TWO

Frontiers

—————

From today's perspective, where community is the factory, the office and perhaps the internet in a silent anti-social sort of way, the East End experience might sound a little overpowering, and there was indeed a tendency in these East End village communities to become inward-looking and isolated from the world outside.

As a boy, Cyril Demarne had a vision of what his own much-treasured community might become, taken to its logical conclusion, when fire ravaged Fowler's treacle factory east of Poplar in Orchard Place. This was a completely isolated community, where the River Lea becomes Bow Creek and, before it spills into the Thames, meanders in such a way as to create a tiny isolated peninsula.

Flames curling from the windows and roaring through the roof with a cloud of sparks streamed across Bow Creek . . . In conversation afterwards, my father told me of the close-knit group of families who inhabited the area. The entire population, numbering about 200 men, women and children, were members of no more than six families, among whom the Lammins, the Scanlons and the Jeffries were the most numerous. These families tended to marry within their own circle . . . The community had its own school, two pubs and a small general store . . . [they] worked in local factories [and] in the East India Dock or the adjoining Trinity House Wharf, but many of the locals earned a living from the river . . . 'toshing'.

Toshing meant salvaging timbers and anything they could find on river or river bank. The law was that such finds should be taken to Dead Man's Wharf at Deptford, to await claim, but most items quickly disappeared into the local community for processing. Following the fire, his interest sparked by his father, Cyril ventured forth to Orchard Place to see for himself:

I reached the site of the burned-out factory and stood gazing at the ruins. A few women stood at their doors

following me with their eyes and it was clear, from their
unsmiling faces, that they regarded me as a foreigner,
not welcome in their midst . . . People were readier with
their smiles in the streets around my home, but ours was
a more open community; we were used to seeing
strangers passing daily. Unlike the folk in Orchard Place,
we were not segregated, a situation which must have
coloured their outlook.

The East End was a conglomeration of little communities, which did not mix with each other, let alone the
outside world. This was never more apparent than
when thousands of East Enders went hop-picking in
Kent in the summer and bonded with other East
Enders from other districts, yet when they returned
home they would never meet up with the new friends
they had made, even though they lived but a mile or
two away.

There was also the feeling that if anyone left their
'village' they were not part of things in quite the same
way ever again. Ivy Alexander reported that children
who returned from the countryside open air school run
by West Ham council were quiet, well-behaved and
'posh' – they had had some of their East End corners
rubbed off by being outside it.[1] Others felt the same:

Nan always thought everyone 'posh' if they lived outside
a radius of two miles of Ducal Street. She had two sons
who married outside the area and she always said no
good would come of it and she was right.[2]

Nevertheless, children growing up in this extraordin-arily tight people-environment loved it, and there were obvious benefits:

> Us, as children, whatever street we went into, adults knew exactly who we were. We knew the adults. We were brought up that most of them we called them uncle and aunt. We never said Mr and Mrs so and so or whatever the name might be.[3]

And quite clearly the intensity of the community did not inhibit them at the time:

> The saving grace for me, even at the age of three, was that the world outside our home was a vast and wonderful playground full of adventures, imaginary or very real, like the mysterious old derelict and war-damaged buildings we kids loved to explore. We were at risk and courting danger and I heard of more than one child who fell from an unstable rooftop to cellar, but I suppose that was the furthest thought from any of our minds when we were running wild and free. We needed an escape from hardships at home and we found it in the streets outside.[4]
>
> There was always something going on. There was no traffic you see, hardly any traffic, Stepney Green was almost rural in a sense. One of my earliest memories was of a blacksmith, the smell of hooves burning. My mother remembered when cows were grazing. I don't know if you have been there, but there is a long park, so we

played in safety there. We had no distractions, we had
no television, the radio was usually for dance music or
something, even I remember the crystal set, but there
was never ever a silence, maybe in the middle of the
night. And only the middle, because with the kids going
up to bed (seven in two beds) there would be like all
these kids in one room, jumping on the bed and hitting
each other with the blankets and fighting and playing
football.[5]

Another piece of green, which knew no frontiers and
was the largest at that time in the East End, was Victoria
Park, east of Bethnal Green above Mile End and Bow.
Between the wars, Saturday mornings meant tennis for
Vicki Green, while Billy Scotchmer liked to sit round
the bandstand and listen to the uniformed band play a
medley of marches and ballads.

On Sunday mornings in the small lake by the flower
gardens strangely dressed men in long rubber waders
sent model motorboats careering at speed around a
centre pole in the middle of the lake. And on other days
in the summer if you wished, you could swim in your
birthday suit in the small lake.

Likely, Billy would have seen the unfortunate inmates
of Bishop's Way workhouse on the edge of the park,
who, all clad in their unmistakable workhouse clothes
would walk out on a Sunday morning, along with the
children from the Charity Schools, 'boys in green

corduroy suits and peaked caps, girls in green coats and white aprons and bonnets, coming home from the bread distribution at St Matthew's School with the loafs in clean white pillow slips.'

Some boys preferred their own street as their turf.

There was a square of asphalt. This was our skating rink, we called it the 'Ashey' and there was so little traffic about, which meant that after school was finished we could skate with very little risk of being hit by a vehicle. A pair of skates cost around 2s. 6d. and most children had them. You would have a key which operated a claw on the front of the skates, which clipped to the welt of your shoe. It often happened that the sole would pull away and you would be barred from using them by your parents until you obtained a strap which would take the strain off the claw.[6]

For some the 2s. 6d. was more than could be afforded. In which case,

The games we played were invented. One was with an empty tin can which we placed two sticks on and put in a circle. We would pick sides and toss for who threw first. The object was to knock the sticks off the can then put the sticks back on the can inside the circle without being caught by the other side.[7]

Our games were linked with the seasons. We had no apparatus except what we improvised for ourselves – coats down in the road for goal posts; the lamp post for a cricket stump; a rough piece of wood shaped for a cricket bat; 'tibby cats' fashioned from firewood; balls of pressed paper and string and glass marbles (called 'glarnies', four a penny). There were caps down for 'egg if I move'; spinning tops; iron hoops for boys and wooden ones for girls; cherry stones for 'bobs'; 'conkers' on string (proud was the boy who had a 'twentier' from his 'kills'); five stones and hop scotch chalked on the pavement for girls.[8]

If there were vehicles about, games would take a quick turn to the more daring:

We boys had several ways of getting a ride . . . or Hopping On, as we called it. The private cars, of which there were far fewer in those days, had bumpers which stood well out from the car and had a curly bit at the corners, where one could sit in some sort of comfort.

There were favourite places and suitable runs for this pastime. In our case it was from Brick Lane to Great Garden Street (later renamed Greatorex Street). The best spot to get on board was at one of these corners when the car had to slow sufficiently for it to turn. In this way we would ride up the street, alighting when the car turned the next corner, having to slow down again to do this.

The easiest vehicle of all to jump on was the horse and cart. These had nice tailboards, supported by chains at just about the correct angle for hanging on to. These were slow enough to make it very easy to get aboard for

the free ride, although not so exciting . . . [But] you very
often got other kids shouting out . . . 'Look behind you
mister!' At this, more often than not, out would snake
the driver's whip, catching one a nasty flick on the
fingers if you were unlucky.[9]

Leisure hours were spent roaming the streets of your
community in a gang playing tin can Tommy, knock
down ginger and hopscotch. Games came round in
cycles, everybody played spinning tops or gobs or
marbles, whichever was the rage at the time.[10]

Knock-down ginger was every boy's favourite game, the
aim to knock at a series of front doors simultaneously
and cause chaos when the householders appeared:

We selected a row of houses where the front doors were
adjacent and fitted with large, cast-iron door knobs.
These we tied together with a piece of stout cord,
allowing sufficient slack for either door to open [only]
about six inches.[11]

Skipping was popular with boys as well as girls:

Easter Monday was skipping day, the day when most
streets managed to procure a 50-foot length of rope,
two energetic lads took on the job of turning the rope,
standing on opposite pavements to leave the whole
width of the rope available for the skippers. The song
would ring out:

All-ee in together, cold and frosty weather,
When the wind blows we all go together.

And the skippers began to jump into the orbit of the
rope. The whole street turned out . . . Then the fitter and
more expert took over, shouting for 'bumps'!
Salt, mustard, vinegar, pepper, GO!
The rope rotated as fast as the turners could make it
go, the diminishing band leaping and gasping in the
centre. Then if you really wanted to test the assembled
throng, 'Double Dutch' used two ropes instead of one![12]

Although paying for entertainment was rarely possible
for most children, that did not necessarily discount the
cinema. Penny gaffs in public halls – the earliest
projected films – were shown publicly in this country in
1896.

It was the penny bioscope then. You sat on wooden
seats. The main entertainment was to see whether you
could hit the pianist with your monkey nuts. She would
sit playing in front and you'd sit at the back.[13]
A Mr Eagle who lived in Baxendale Street played the
cinema piano and it was his job to alter the tempo of
the music to suit what was taking place. If there was a
chase then he would play fast, and with a love scene
something slow and sentimental. The Picture House, as it
was called, had no single seats, everyone sat on a bench
which curved to the shape of the building. Upstairs, (the
gods) there was a front railing where the children sat on

the floor and dangled their legs through. The entrance
fee for the cinema was a penny which you put in a
bowler hat as you went in.[14]

After the Cinematograph Act in 1909 many new
purpose-built cinemas were erected and a number of
the old halls were converted to sole cinema use. They
had a number of very big luxurious cheap cinemas in
the East End; the age of the super cinema and the great
Hollywood epics began soon after the end of the First
World War.

We used to go to the cinema whenever we could. We
used to bunk in. There was a cinema in Bethnal Green
Road called Smarts, Smarts Cinema, and we used to
hang around the back. I was doing this from about the
age of ten or eleven you see, you could hang around the
back door and then when somebody came out of the
back you'd nip in quickly and then you'd sneak upstairs
to the gallery and sit in the cinema. The attendant used
to come round looking for kids and he'd say 'where's
your ticket?' and if you didn't have your ticket he'd
chuck you out you see.[15]

What a treat that was! The large room, for that was
all it was, was full of Yiddisher mammas and their
offspring, with practically no men. Most of the audience
had bags of peanuts, which constituted part of the
afternoon's enjoyment; peanuts in those days were not
peeled, as they are today, but had to be shelled. I
suppose that we were lucky that the films were silent,

because the continual noise of peanuts being cracked formed an artillery background to the show. To this was added the constant request of illiterate parents to their more literate kids to read out the words that flashed on the screen.[16]

Water naturally held a strong appeal for East End kids, both the Thames and the Grand Union Canal, which snakes above Hackney Road to the north, down past Victoria Park, through Mile End to the east, and south to the Thames at Limehouse. There is also Limehouse Cut, which strikes out north-east from Limehouse to the River Lea.

With no baths at home, it was nothing to see 'about a dozen kids on a Friday night in the summer, down in the canal having a scrub up. It was the only time the canal coppers – they were a private force employed by the Port of London Authority – stayed away.' The danger, dirty water and water rats never seemed to worry them.

As a matter of fact, we used to chase the water rats across.[17]

I remember going with a boy from Wimbolt Street, Bertie Asavado, down to the canal and playing on a moored barge. I looked round for Bertie and he was gone. I looked over the other side of the barge and he was struggling in the water. I shouted for help and a young fellow standing on the bank dived in and pulled Bertie out. He could easily have drowned . . .[18]

> Wapping children used to go swimming in the river –
> they weren't supposed to, so they couldn't ask their
> mums for towels.[19]

There was even a beach at Tower Bridge, opened by the King in July 1934:

> A haunt of the mudlarks. Who could forget the pleasure
> boats that paddled from here to Southend, Margate and
> Ramsgate. The Royal Sovereign, the Laguna Belle and
> the Golden Eagle?[20]

Some girls went, more demurely, for indoor games like pin-a-pic, which was literally, even a touch pathetically in those days when no one owned anything much, precisely what it said:

> We would cut pictures out of a comic. The comics were
> bought by one of my uncles who perhaps had a little bit
> more money than us, for his children and the comics
> would be passed right round the house and then we
> would cut the pictures out at the end and put it in the
> pages of a book and it was called pin-a-pic. You gave
> your friend a pin and they would put the pin in a page
> and if they won a picture (because not every page had a
> picture) then they would win the picture . . .[21]

Vicki Green couldn't remember where the book came from. She agreed her family couldn't afford books, although she did read them. The local Whitechapel library was a little haven. She would go there to do her homework, to get away from the continual noise of house and street.

Julie Hunt and her friends were just a little more daring:

> In the school holidays we used to go to a play centre
> and some of the time we used to go to the Jewish
> school, the Jewish centre in Henrika Street, which was
> very good. We, we used to say that we were Catholics,
> but we would like to learn about the Jewish faith and all
> the rest of it. So, anyway, er, we joined that and we
> learned how to make baskets and lights and all the
> different things they done.[22]

Willy Goldman, who was Jewish, went the other way, going to the Mission for the Conversion of Jews to Christianity:

> Good for a free bun-and-tea if you put on a pious face
> and joined in the singing of evangelical hymns.[23]

His mum had earlier taken him there for free medical treatment. The Aldgate Mission to the Poor was set up by the Catholic Father Gregory who had a vocation to convert immigrant Jews to 'the true faith'.

> As far as I know there was only one geshmutter, one
> apostate there, a smarmy, smooth-skinned Galician who
> lisped. Everyone called him Ginger Nuts . . . Ginger Nuts

went out into the market, set up an orange box, and began to preach. His fiercest heckler was Shlomka the Carman. Shlomka destroyed every meeting Ginger Nuts held. He attacked him with cries of 'Rubbish! Rubbish!' . . . Yet folk used the Mission a lot. Its medical section was superbly equipped and staffed by some very brilliant doctors. It was funny really. They went there, the orthodox Jewesses, with their shaitels, their wigs, on their heads and their children tugging at their skirts, and they sang – or pretended to sing, or mouthed Yiddish words to – religious hymns; they looked at the forbidden pictures and images all around and they bore the illuminated texts, the figurines, the oil paintings and the prayers with fortitude. It was the price they paid for free medical treatment.[24]

Cockney children were willing targets of religious missions if there was something in it for them in the here and now. The Docklands Settlement[25] entertained seven to fourteen year olds with cards, table tennis and dancing, as long as you'd been to church first.[26] It was subsidised by Sir Reginald Kennedy Cox from his own income.

Neither religion nor politics meant much to children, however, though they sometimes role-played the hypocrisies of their parents:

Immigrants have always been a feature of the area and we kids were a mixed bunch, many of us being first or second generation children of European or Asian

refugees. Sometimes we maintained a loyalty to the
foreign blood in our veins, at other times we tried to
hide it. I suppose it could be said that the Irish and the
Jewish stock remained truest to their origins and most
proudly proclaimed their roots. However, whatever our
forebears, we were certainly all one thing. We were
cockneys.[27]

Anti-Semitism in Willy Goldman's childhood was
nothing more than a game, but a good one, an
opportunity for tribal divisions and fighting, Yids versus
Goys.

It is only since getting into adult hands that positive anti-
Semitism in England has deteriorated from a sport to a
tyranny.[28]

Willy goes on to describe how, when he and his brother
went to an all non-Jewish school, they were originally
different and therefore picked on, but his brother was
such a good fighter that he became a stalwart of the
school's own force for fights against other schools, even
Jewish ones.

We all played together: Polacks (the children of foreign
Jews), Choots (the children of English-born Jews),
Gentiles, coloureds, boys and girls, the children of
bookmakers, prostitutes, stallholders, auctioneers,
gamblers, thieves, rabbis, shopkeepers, boxers, barmen,
touts, tallymen, washerwomen, chorus girls, furriers,

tailors, pressers, pimps, ponces, and unemployed. But
when the trouble began divisional unity took shape:
Polacks versus Choots, one school versus another, one
playground versus another. And trouble began easily. A
disputed goal, a torn comic, a lost ball, a burst balloon –
and we were at war. Fighting would break out. But it
was never vicious until the adults interfered.[29]

And how crazy some of these adults seemed, wonder-
fully crazy, picturesquely so, part of the imaginative
tapestry that made the East End, viewed from inside,
such an intoxicating friendly, but unusual show.

Joyce Ayres lived in Bethnal Green opposite Fakie[30]:

An old crazy Jewish lady. I think we tormented her
dreadfully . . . [but] she was well looked after in the
street: if anyone was making a stew or broth, some
would be put in a basin and taken to her – not like
today, when people would want to put her in a home.

Living here during the Second World War, the odd,
even the bizarre, became not commonplace, but comfortable to the child's imagination, as these memories
suggest:

During the air raids a bald-headed man came. He called
my sister and myself 'Buttercup' and 'Daisy'. He would
give us chalk. We were allowed to draw on his head.

Old man Dunkell was also a character, every market
day you could see him being helped up the steps by Mrs

Dunkell or one of the boys, or both the boys, and sitting in a wheelchair. All the local people used to swear that he wasn't a cripple, but if it was a ploy it certainly served the purpose. He would sit in his wheelchair looking grave faced and ill, he had a gaunt looking face with a stubbly chin and thin wispy grey hair, he used to wear a pair of greasy slippers, he never seemed to wear shoes. Suddenly either one of the twins or maybe Mrs Dunkell would push him up to the Roman Road market where he would take up position, cap would be on the ground by the side of him and he would open up his violin case and start fiddling. He never was much good but it gave him a good living anyway, he never seemed to complain about it and he always gave a rendering of *Nellie Dean*.

One of the things that I remember most vividly about my early childhood was a Gypsy woman. On Saturday nights she always got drunk and she used to have these long beaded earrings and she used to come down and you could see her earrings shaking in the gas light of the street lamps and she shouted out 'you killed our Lord, you killed our Lord'.[31]

Childhood for the cockney East Ender, like childhood for everyone, peaked at Christmas. Christmas made everything extra special, particularly the many markets, all of which put on some sort of show. Here was the concentrated essence of East End culture – the characters, the colours, the sounds, the eccentricities. And for Jim Stuart, an habitué of Chrisp Street market in Poplar, east of Limehouse, running north off East

India Dock Road, which straps the top of the Isle of Dogs, one Christmas in particular brought it home to him what being a child of the East End really meant:

Let me set the scene. Picture a typical pub in Poplar, not a stone's throw from the entrance to Blackwall Tunnel. The regulars, all merry and bright on the strong ale they supped in those days, have just collected their Christmas Club money, paid in coppers and tanners throughout the year to the man who always sat at a card table, just inside the door of the public bar. The bar is packed. Three of us: my friends, Dickie, Charlie and me with one foot in the doorway, gazing in . . .

We three East End harum scarums, just turned eleven years old, were out to cadge a few coppers from Dickie's Mum, always a soft touch when she had a few. Tonight was like striking gold; she coughed up sixpence for each of us.

Sixpence! It was a fortune. My whole week's pocket money never amounted to more than three ha'pence, if I was lucky! We were in high spirits, with our tanners burning a hole in our pockets. I tied mine in my hanky, for safety.

Now we were all set for that one bright light burning in the December night . . . Chrisp Street market at Christmas was like a fairy-land to the poor kids of Poplar. It drew us like a magnet; its smells, its lights, its jolly crowds. Stepping it out lively and chattering like monkeys, eager for the good things to come, we cut across the grounds of St Michael's Church. Back on the road and kicking a tin can along in front of us, we ran slap bang into a policeman. The can hit him in the shin. He beckoned us towards him, simply by crooking his finger. We gathered in front of him, quaking, while he gave us a lecture, and we expected at any second to get a whack from his rolled up cape. We were quite close to Hay Currie School and he asked if we went there. We were glad to tell him that we had moved up to Culloden Street School and into the Seniors. When he let us go we walked off with our arms round each others' shoulders, whispering, not daring to look back.

We soon forgot our brush with the Law, as we were caught up in the steady stream of late night shoppers making their way over the railway bridge, up the steps and down into the throng of Chrisp Street Market.

We briefly glanced into Old 'Ink's little shop at the front of the bridge, where trays of home-made Toffee Flats, twists of Paragoric, Barley Sugar and Acid Drops, all laid out on tin trays and finely dusted with a powdery sugar, tempted us to spend our fortune. But we were not tempted, and moved on.

From all sides came the cries of the stall-holders, shouting their wares under the glare of naked electric light bulbs, strung out on wires above the wooden stalls, standing in the gutter, along the length of Chrisp Street.

We watched spellbound at the eels being gutted and chopped up, seconds after trying to slither off the block. The man was too quick for them, but we stood and watched, hoping they would get away, but they never did: and he sang out 'All alive-o'.

Rabbits divested of their furry coats, dead of course. But not too long ago, judging by the blood on the woman's bare arms as she jointed, then chopped through the backs of their pink little bodies.

Goods were weighed, wrapped in newspaper and passed over to outstretched hands, with a 'Ta luv, g'night dear'.

Everywhere, a good-humoured banter between shopper and stallholder, a feeling of belonging, safe in the surging crowd.

A dark Indian man pouring something on a pile of orange rinds, on a plate, then set light to it. We three coughed and spluttered when we got a whiff of it, much to his annoyance, for the stuff in the bottles was supposed to cure coughs and colds, all for sixpence a bottle . . .

Familiar smells . . . sickly sweet honey-combs and rock, sugar bubbling in a pan ready for the flavouring to be added. Hot chestnuts – we stood toasting our cheeks at the wide smiling face of the vendor's fire. Sarsaparilla and other hot drinks from the Italian man, serving from a colourful little cart, his horse tied to a lamp post round the corner, eating damp cabbage leaves.

From a side street came the sound of a barrel-organ accompanied by the clickety-clack of the tap dancers, as they tapped and strutted on their wooden mat laid out on the road. One man kept the handle turning while another passed round the hat.

Music and cries were all around us, 'Aypers – all aypers!' a lady called, meaning that the cards of buttons, hooks and eyes, lengths of ribbon and every other handy thing on her stall cost one halfpenny.

'Salt Ma – don't forget your salt!' The man sawed through the great icebergs of salt with a hand saw, cutting pieces to your requirements.

'Your Army Greys at nine – a tanner a pair your Coloureds!' Army grey thick socks were three pence dearer than the thin coloured ones.

'Cheap Jacks' selling off crockery, crashing the plates together, making jokes to the ring of upturned faces. 'Now then, ladies – who'll make a bid for this gozunder?' which everyone knows goes under the bed.

The Pie and Eel shop smelled lovely. The cheery ladies behind the counter ladled out rich gravy, sloshing it over the mountain of potato set beside the steaming pies on the thick china plates of the fortunate customers. Either side of the marble top tables, set in pews down the wall of the shop, people were eating their supper while the milling crowds passed by outside.

We followed Prince Monolulu, the black tipster, he towered above the crowd calling, 'I gotta horse – I gotta horse!' We ran behind him, to touch his hand; he smiled down at us and ruffled our hair, with a cheery, throaty, 'Hullo boys'. The three of us stayed until the shoppers began to wend their way home and the stall-holders began to pack away for the night. Then, scavenging beneath the stalls, I found some speckled spuds and crushed cabbages, a few almost good apples and some oranges with soft patches in them. I rescued them all before the sweepers brushed them all into a big heap, to cart the rubbish away. I put them into a cardboard box and took them home to my mum.

That night, we were sitting round a cheerful fire, my two young sisters fresh and pink from the bath, Mum with a clean white pinnie on. She reached out her arms, gathering the three of us to her breast. My heart felt full, when I heard Dad say, 'Are you happy Lou?' and she smiled her apple-cheeks smile and nodded. I remember Dad as he laughed and said, 'That's us, hard up, but always happy!' I unknotted my hanky, and in a moment of pure generosity, I gave Mum my sixpence.[32]

CHAPTER THREE

Cockney
wide boys

————

We are often told that it was the poverty and
uncertainty of life, the insecurity that brought
people together into this mutual dependence of
relatives and friends and people they knew.

> People were marvellous in them days, we were all in the
> same boat.[1]

The obvious question is whether, if the community had
been relieved of that insecurity, the community values
of loyalty, 'active citizenship', and interest in your fellow
man, which translated into honour and decency but

also, so the legend went, identified the behaviour of its most outrageous criminals, would survive.

If the question was ever considered it was soon lost in the sheer fun that was had – for adults as much as for children. Here, in the East End, if a person had a piano they was rich!

One day my father pulls up in his van and says he's 'picked up a piana'. My father often 'picked' things up, but a piano? This was something different.

Bud, Tigs, Lu and I [the four sisters] gather round to admire the 'piana'. It's glossy and chestnut-brown, like a conker, with pearly keys.

Out in the street where it stands, Father sits down with the air of a real pianist and knocks off a couple of tunes. My mother comes out, he looks at her and starts to sing one of her favourite songs. My mother smiles; it's a rare sight.

Soon all the neighbours have gathered around, and before we know it, they're having a right old knees-up. The men have brought beer and the women are dancing. Cheryl's mum, still in black, weeps when my father plays 'You'll never walk alone' for her little girl.

We children dance round and round until we're sick and giddy from spinning. But still my father's fingers run up and down the keys, playing requests. I'm flabbergasted, I didn't know he was musical.

As it gets late, the men get drunker. When it's time to shift the piano, there's no one sober standing. The drunken men try to take the piano through the front door. I catch snippets of alcoholic reasoning.

'Shift the rear end, Ted.'

'To the left. No. No. To the right.'

'Up . . . a bit. No, down.'

''Ang on, 'ang on.'

Eventually, ''S no way. Not unless we knock the door frame in.'

'Let's knock the front door in.'

My mother and the other women, in uproar, intervene just as the men attempt a drunken charge at the door with the piano.

Finally it is agreed to leave the piano where it is and to shift it in the morning.

I fall asleep listening to the commotion and the magical music still ringing in my ears.

The next day I get up early thinking of the miraculous piana. The sun is still coming up over the roofs, but I can hear voices and cracking sounds from outside. I open the door to find some estate boys are bashing up the piano. They pull out its wooden innards and smash them against the wall.

My father, hearing the noise, runs out in his vest and drawers. But it's too late. The piano lies like a dead thing, its keys scattered all over the concrete like broken teeth. The estate boys run off; even they are too scared to face my father.

My father bends down to pick up a broken key. I expect him to swear and start making threats, but I'm astonished to see tears in his eyes.[2]

Cyril Demarne had a more regular 'ding-dong' at home:

> Saturday night was the traditional and an invitation, like life itself in the East End, was entirely devoid of frills. 'We're 'avin a ding-dong Sat'day night; bring yer own wallop.'
>
> The Marsh family, our downstairs neighbours, held parties and were generous with invitations . . . Alfie Marsh was the pianist . . . no musical education . . . but a good ear and nimble fingers . . . the latest music hall songs and all the old favourites . . . *Tipperary*, *K-K-K-Katy*, *Take Me Back to Dear Old Blighty* . . . Then came solos from budding Marie Lloyds and Harry Champions . . . Parodies were very popular and there was loud applause for the rendering of *Ta-ra-ra Boom de-ay*.

These were the days before karaoke, of course. The Mission Hall had a harmonium, and a few pubs had penny-in-the-slot ones, but the East End pattern of a Saturday night was first off to the pub, where they probably wouldn't sing, and then back home with a gallon or two of beer and singing and dancing to the accompaniment of a piano.

> The golden rule at such gatherings was that everyone had to do their best singing solo; no matter if we had heard the darn song a thousand times before no-one ever cribbed at hearing it again.[3]

Of course, during the Second World War, Vera Lynn, an East Ham girl and the forces' sweetheart, as she was known, famous for such patriotic numbers as *We'll Meet Again*, *It's a Lovely Day Tomorrow* and *The White Cliffs of Dover*, was everyone's choice.

Lucy Collard remembered how parties close to the docks had a special flavour:

> When I was in my teens, there was a family in the next street to where I lived in Grundy Street, and they were all lightermen and on a Saturday night there was always a party going on somewhere or other.

The job of the lightermen was to transfer goods between ships at anchor and the wharfs or quays aboard flat-bottomed barges called lighters. If ever there was any contraband going around, the lightermen knew about it.

> We used to go to these all night parties and then come home on Sunday and wash and change and go off and watch the lads training for the Doggett Coat and Badge race, you know, training with their sculling, and we'd just go along the river somewhere.

Lucy also recorded that street celebrations close to the docks were coloured by the various cultures that mingled in the area, and everyone would join in.

When I lived in Hind, which is now Hind Grove [near
Limehouse Cut], there was just about every nationality
down in that road, but everybody was friendly towards
one another. We shared in their feast days, the Diwali
with the Indians, and Chinese New Year, and the Pesach,
the Jewish, and it was just marvellous.

According to Sally Worboyes, the Catholic 'Procession
Sunday' was the biggest draw of the community feast
days. Early that morning men would go out with
buckets of whitewash and a brush to mark the route
round the streets of Wapping on the pavement kerbs.
Altars and grottoes were set up outside Catholic houses.
Pubs would do collections. People used to come back
from all over to see their old parish procession, and for
many children it was the highlight of the year.

The event that grabbed our interest was the preparation
for the outdoor procession for the veneration of the
Blessed Virgin Mary when bands from all over London
marched into Wapping on May Day, and my best friend
was going to be one of the Catholic girls dressed in long
white satin gowns and wearing beautiful headdresses
decorated with fresh flowers and pearls, just like a
bridesmaid. She was to carry a bouquet of flowers to
match and her black hair would be set in perfect
ringlets . . .
    Just about every one of us in the East End came out
to see those once-a-year processions, when the
pavements along Commercial Road were bursting with

> joyful crowds through which I would ease and wriggle
> my way to the front.[4]

Procession Sunday was part of the East End 'theatre of the streets', a big annual event, but related to the pantomime that happened every day in the markets, and, thanks to the street sellers, on almost every street you care to mention.

Sunday was always a colourful day, traditionally not so much a Saturday, as the huge Jewish population never traded or shopped on a Saturday, the Sabbath. Sunday markets didn't seem to bother the Christian population.

> Sunday morning always meant a walk down the Row, or
> the Lane. There was Club Row, Sclater Street and Brick
> Lane, through to Wentworth Street and Petticoat
> Lane . . . and although we had no money to spend, we
> got one hell of a kick from window shopping.[5]

From Bethnal Green down through Shoreditch to Brick Lane and Whitechapel was one teeming mass of people. Markets seemed to be in every street.

'The Row', Club Row, was the animal market off the far western end of Bethnal Green Road.

> Birds in cages sang everywhere. Dogs could be
> purchased from a shilling upwards, also cats and
> monkeys. You could buy almost anything down the Row.

Old Nichol Street, which cuts across the Row, was the

place to go for bikes. Further into this area on the edge
of Bethnal Green and Shoreditch was the flower market
on Columbia Road. Most of the stall holders were
locals:

> There was Stones, Gales and Swifts and many others I
> have long since forgotten. There was a cart that sold
> drinks, hot in the winter and cold in the summer. The
> drink was called sarsaparilla and tasted like today's Coca
> Cola.

Columbia market is still trading today. Mary Lester
remembers going a lot as a child in the 1990s:

> I loved hearing the man shouting 'Indoor, outdoor ivy' in
> a singsong way as if it was all one word, something like
> 'In-deraht-derivy'.

Lilian Hine remembered the costermongers with great
fondness.

> They were really great people. Often they were owed
> money, but took pity on anyone in poor circumstances.
> On the stall where they sold lovely home-made sweets
> they must have lost profits because they were always
> giving them away. The weather never seemed to worry
> them at all, and it could be very cold with frost and fog.
> They always had a coke basket alight and us children
> would stand around the fires warming our hands on the
> way to school and back.[6]

Among the Sunday crowds at Columbia Road, Daniel Farson noted more men than women – husbands 'returning home with a clutched plant pot as a guilt offering before the lunchtime session in the pub from which the wives were excluded'.

Far to the east, in Roman Road, Bow, was an altogether better class of market than you'd find in Bethnal Green, 'the respectable working class – the sort of people who went to church on a Sunday. Lower-middle-class people.'[7] Vi Short described Roman Road market as 'our Mecca', the centre of life in Bow between the wars. Children would call out: 'Oi'm goin' up Roman fer mi mum, cum wiv us?'[8]

> I would accompany my mum shopping on Saturday evening . . . In those days the shops and the stalls were operating until nigh on midnight. The brightly lit shops and the well-lit stalls with their sizzling paraffin carbide lamps coupled with the back-chat salesmanship of the stall-owners and the crowds of shoppers milling everywhere – the whole scene was characteristic of a carnival atmosphere. To the young mind it was an adventure to worm one's way in and out of the crowded scene. As soon as we arrived at Roman Road I would go into the pudding and pie shop and buy a slice of plum pudding to munch whilst mum would say that she would not be a minute as she had to see someone. This used to puzzle me at first until my inquisitiveness got the better of me on one occasion and I followed her to discover that she popped into a nearby pub for a glass

and was sitting talking to other shoppers likewise engaged. When after a few minutes she came out and discovered I was waiting outside instead of outside the plum-duff shops she nearly had a fit. 'Don't you dare mention this to Dad, if you do I'll kill you,' she said, and thereupon bought me another slice of plum-duff no doubt to seal my lips. I kept my word but often laughed to myself about the incident that evening.[9]

Back to the west side, a little beyond traditional East End boundaries was Hoxton market, where Ted Harrison remembers butchers would specialise, 'one selling only pork, another only beef. Some of them were quite small shops, just the front room of a house really. At the pork butcher's, for twopence, you could buy a couple of ounces of pork off a big boiled leg of pork they kept on the counter, or saveloy and pease pudding for a penny-ha'penny. No one had fridges in those days, so Sunday we got bargains: flanks of meat for a tanner, a pig's head for a shilling, lambs' brains for feeding the babies, at threepence a saucerful.'

South into Shoreditch High Street there was once what Arthur Harding referred to as 'our Champs Elysées, a prosperous market place with stalls and shops on both sides of the street'. It used to cater to thousands even in the weekday up to about 1910.

A few streets to the east bring you to Brick Lane in Spitalfields, and a market noted then for its fruit, and a few streets to the west, to Spitalfields market itself, where it all began.

The area of Spitalfields takes us back to 1197 and the founding of the hospital of The Blessed Virgin Mary Without Bishopsgate – for 'Spital' read 'ho-spital'. Otherwise known as the Priory of St Mary Spital, it was built on fields bounded by two Roman roads, Bishopsgate and Aldgate High Street, leading eastwards beyond the city wall.

Shortly after the priory was founded, a fruit and veg market began trading on the western edge of Commercial Street, off Spital Square, in what was in the twelfth century a field adjacent to the priory.

Originally, the market was the commercial end of the St Mary Spital scheme, an outlet and financial fillip for the priory's farm industry, and later a hugely important outlet for farms elsewhere in the East End and beyond the River Lea.

Walk down Commercial Street into Whitechapel Road and you will find what was once not only the biggest street market in London, but on a Saturday night a place of seriously unrefined entertainment – music halls, the Pavilion theatre for melodrama, raucous harmonia nights in the many pubs, and much, much more:

> Amidst the flaming naphtha lights can be discerned toys, hatchets, crockery, carpets, oil-cloth, meat, fish, greens, second-hand boots, furniture, artificial flowers, &c.
> Round every stall are eager women, bartering with the salesmen . . .
> But why is the man in that doorway jumping up and

down, backwards and forwards, shifting on to one leg and then on to the other, bawling himself hoarse, while another man a few yards behind him in the passage is turning a tune out of a barrel-organ? The man who is skipping about as if he were on hot bricks is dressed like a coachman, but the breast of his coat is faced with crimson satin, trimmed with silver lace. 'Hi, hi! only one penny! The Gallery of Varieties!' 'Walk in! Walk in! Now exhibiting! Only one penny! The best wax works in London!' bawls the lively man in the doorway. Inside, ranged round the three sides of an oblong room are a number of figures, which the showman assures his audience are all wax, and not, as stated, made of wood. 'This finger is broken off to prove it. And you will observe, on removing General Garibaldi's cap, that he is bald, on purpose to show that there is no deception; here it is, all wax,' feeling his head.

We were invited to step up stairs to the Chamber of Horrors, where, for one penny, we should see 'all the celebrated murderers of many bygone years, including that beautiful piece of machinery of a man in the agonies of death'. This was rather too bad; besides, as the invitation to go upstairs was given, the organ encouraged us with 'Down among the dead men'.

The farther the hours got into the night the busier the stalls and shops became. The Cheap Jacks and quack doctors put forth all their powers of cajolery. Certain cures for every disease flesh is heir to were to be bought remarkably cheap. The functions of the different parts of the human body were explained minutely with Latin

words of 'thundering sound'. Youngsters were shooting
away their halfpence at double-quick time for Barcelona
nuts. Men and women are thronging the public houses,
talking in loud keys over their beer and gin, as if to
drown their boon companions' voices at the same time
they drown their own sorrows.

Every Saturday night there are many shows.
Mysterious creatures exhibiting in enclosed square spaces
about six feet each way. Hairy men, hairless dogs,
gorillas, Aztecs, and giants. Beyond the Mile-end Gate
the young English giant is located. By his own account
he is 7 ft 4 in high, and has been presented to Queen
Victoria and the Royal Family.

If Spitalfields is where it all began, Whitechapel Road,
its frenzied attractions described in the late nineteenth
century shortly before the Ripper murders began, is the
dark heart of the legend. We see it in our imagination
in the swirling fog, a 'pea souper' that characterised the
area right up to the Smoke Abatement and Clean Air
Act of the late 1950s.

Walking in the 'pea souper' was a weird and
adventurous experience. To me it conjured the image of
being lost at sea; a tiny boat in the vastness of the ocean
utterly alone and shrouded in darkness. Suddenly, like
the mournful hoot of a nearby foghorn raising hope that
rescue was at hand, a voice, a looming figure on top of
you almost before you saw it; the cheerful
acknowledgment at encountering a fellow lost soul.

Stumbling at last on a main road to find the Conductor walking ahead of his bus, guiding it by torchlight, the driver following the inadequate beam as best he could, to be halted by the cry, 'You're on the wrong side of the road mate!' as another vehicle appeared ominously close. The fog, murky by day and even more menacing by night, engendered a spirit of camaraderie something like that encountered in wartime.[10]

But at night, in the warren of little streets off Whitechapel, it was menacing indeed:

Turn down this side street out of the main Whitechapel Road. It may be well to tuck out of view any bit of jewellery that may be glittering about; the sight of means to do ill-deeds makes ill-deeds done. The street is oppressively dark, though at present the gloom is relieved somewhat by feebly lighted shopfronts. Men are lounging at the doors of the shops, smoking evil-smelling pipes. Women with bare heads and with arms under their aprons are sauntering about in twos and threes, or are seated gossiping on steps leading into passages dark as Erebus. Now round the corner into another still gloomier passage, for there are no shops here to speak of. This is the notorious Wentworth Street. The police used to make a point of going through this only in couples, and possibly may do so still when they go there at all. Just now there are none met with. It is getting on into the night, but gutters, and doorways, and passages, and staircases appear to be teeming with children. See there in that doorway of a house without a glimmer of light about it. It looks to be a baby in long clothes laid on the floor of the passage, and seemingly exhausted with crying. Listen for a moment at this next house. There is a scuffle going on upon the staircase – all in the densest darkness – and before you have passed a dozen yards there is a rush down-stairs and an outsurging into the street with fighting and screaming, and an outpouring of such horrible blackguardism that it makes you shudder as you look at those curly-headed preternaturally sharp-witted children who leave their play to gather around the mêlée . . . How black and unutterably gloomy all the houses look![11]

The murders began on 31 August 1888, possibly earlier. The question is whether Mary Ann 'Polly' Nichols, her throat cut, her abdomen wounded and mutilated, was actually the first, or whether Martha Tabram's body, stabbed, according to the post-mortem, thirty-nine times on 'body, neck and private parts with a knife or dagger', was a victim of the same man several weeks earlier. Or indeed whether Emma Smith, a prostitute found 100 yards from Martha Tabram the previous April, her head, face and vagina terribly injured, was the first. For sure, the murders continued – Annie Chapman on 8 September, Elizabeth Stride, Catharine Eddowes, Mary Kelly, Alison McKenzie, then in February 1891 Frances Coles, though it was never clear where the murderer's guilt either began or ended. The absence of a criminal conviction and the morbid, taunting letters to the press, mocking the police – 'I gave the lady [Annie Chapman] no time to squeal,' signed Jack the Ripper – ensured that the extraordinary episode would pass into the mythology of the area.

Gardiner's Corner, Whitechapel, named after a famous clothing store with its clock tower, the junction where the five main thoroughfares of East London – Commercial Road, Leman Street, Aldgate High Street, Commercial Street and Whitechapel High Street – meet, was until a few years ago tacitly agreed to be 'the gateway to the East End'.

Charles Poulsen, born in 1911, remembered Whitechapel as 'dirty, noisy, smelly, a great wide, very wide, the widest main road in London actually carrying six lines of traffic each side going very fast east and west and off this great wide major highway opened a whole network of tiny, slummy, narrow turnings full of old Victorian tenements that should have been demolished before the century started and that was where the people lived.'

Long after the furore about the Ripper died down, well into the twentieth century the evening market and the great vista of Whitechapel Road was a popular venue for an evening stroll. 'People had a coffee in Lyons, strolling till 10 or 12 o'clock at night,' recalled Ivor Spencer,[12] born in 1924.

Sam Clarke made his first visit there in 1920 and remembered the Lyons Corner House in particular: 'Stepping into a luxurious bright decorative building with fitted carpets . . . it was beyond anything I have

51

known. It was a great feeling. Thank you Mr Lyons!'[13]

From 1927 there was another novelty and magnet of interest for strollers. Boris Bennett, born Boris Sochaczewska in Ozokoff, Poland, in 1900, and later a famous West End photographer, opened his first shop here. Couples would make a bee-line for his smart, well-lit, and highly organised studio. 'It was an instant success,' recalled Ivor. 'The studio emulated the glamour of Hollywood photography, and was able to photograph up to sixty bridal couples on a single Sunday – the traditional day for Jewish weddings. Crowds would often gather outside to witness the scenes.' Having your photograph displayed in Boris Bennett's window 'was like being in the papers', said Ivor.

Nor was Bennett popular only among young marrieds. It was everyone's desire to have him photograph the family and appear in the window of 150 Whitechapel Road. Vicki Green remembers how one photograph he took of her family was copied and handed down through the generations. 'Everybody in the family eventually had a copy of this photograph. My eldest uncle had a large framed picture and my cousins got all these photostats made. Recently two or three years ago, one of my cousins died and his wife had this picture out, and it was a second marriage and the children of this cousin came to the Shiva and said "Who's who, who were all these people on this picture? We'd like to know more about it." And they said, "Ask Aunty Vicki because she'll remember it all."'[14]

After the Second World War, Whitechapel was still a

huge draw. People would 'go to Aldgate' to visit the jellied eel and coffee stalls, all night cafés, and the famous Jewish salt beef restaurant, Bloom's. Alf Stuart recalled that in the 1950s,

> It was a very lively place . . . Every Saturday evening, all the families used to 'parade', as they used to call it, walk along from the Pavilion, which was on Whitechapel and Vallance Road, up to Mile End Gate. The big treat in those days was United Dairies, believe it or not. That was where all the boys used to go and pick up girls. United Dairies had a little shop and the treat was – they couldn't afford anything else – to go there and get a glass of milk. That was a big thing!

It all came to an end in the early 1980s, when the Greater London Council constructed a one-way system at Gardiner's Corner and destroyed its character for ever.

There is, nevertheless, much still that speaks of continuity in the area, not least that other legendary market, Petticoat Lane. The name ceased to denote a street in 1846, when it became Middlesex Street. Today the market is still held between Middlesex Street and nearby Goulston Street on Sundays, with a smaller market open on Wentworth Street from Monday to Friday.

> Petticoat Lane was the place where you could have your silk handkerchief nicked at one end, and by the time you got to the other end you would have bought it back.[15]
> Originally the Lane was the market place for the

Jews, which is why it was closed on Saturday.
Completely emptied. Not a soul in sight. We had two
shops in the Lane. Occasionally one shop ran out of
something and Dad would take a tray across the road.
One day he lost his watch. We knew more or less when
he would have lost it, and we knew who took it, and
definitely where it would be taken to. There was a man
in New Street (near Liverpool Street station). We'd go
there in the late afternoon and buy it back for half a
crown. He was a fence. Pickpockets used to sell it to
him. Dad warned him: 'If you pick my watch again you'll
never come into the shop again.' He said: 'I'll pick your
watch every week until you apologise.'

You could see Dad with his watch threaded through
his waistcoat with his jacket buttoned up and scarf
round his neck, and his overcoat on, and still they would
get his watch. They were artists.

They used to come into the Lane and we used to
give them a room upstairs and there they'd put
everything that they'd nicked during the day and put
them all on the table and they'd bid amongst
themselves. The money would go into a kitty and each
would get what they had bid for successfully and then
the money would be divided amongst them afterwards.
It was another world.[16]

Around this time, the famous travel writer H. V. Morton
made a journey to Petticoat Lane and was fascinated by
the skills of the costermongers. He recorded his
experience in *London* (1940):

I saw a neatly bearded woman, whose brown coat
looked as though it was draped over a barrel, go up to a
fishmonger, standing beside two gigantic codfish and a
number of smaller fish.

'How much?' asked the woman, indicating a group
of still life.

'Six shillings,' replied the fishmonger, with a keen
glance from small, black eyes.

'One and ten,' remarked the woman, reflectively
turning a plaice upside down and prodding it with a fat
finger.

Whereupon a singular change took place in the
fishmonger's aloof attitude. He was insulted, outraged.
Suddenly, picking up a plaice by the tail, he said with a
threatening gesture, 'I'll wipe it acrost hey face!'

The customer was not outraged as a woman
would have been in Oxford Street; she just shrugged
her fat shoulders, as she would have done in Damascus,
and moved away, knowing full well that before she
had retreated very far she would be recalled – as indeed
she was. After a brisk argument she bought the fish
for two and fourpence and they parted the best of
friends.

I have seen the same drama played out on a carpet
in Alexandria.

Morton also commented on the beguiling beauty of the
Jewish girls, while remarking on their extraordinary
integration into the East End culture:

A young girl with eyes like the fish-pools of Heshbon sits on an upturned crate outside a butcher's shop. Her fingers glitter with rings, and when she laughs she throws her fuzzy head back, exposing a plump, olive-coloured throat, as Moons of Delight have been doing throughout the history of the Orient . . . Were I a sultan, swaying above the street in a litter, I would roll a lazy eye in her direction, make a minute movement of a jewelled finger, and, later at the palace, would address her: 'Moon of Great Beauty and Considerable Possibility,' I would say, 'wither comest thou, O Radiance, and who is thy father?'

Whereupon she would spit at me with her eyes and reply: 'Cancher see'm respectable . . . cancher? You're a nice chep, you are, sitting up there, dressed like a dog's dinner an talkin' like thet . . . lemme go . . .'

For though her eyes are the eyes of Ruth among the alien corn, her larynx is that of Bill Sykes.

On leaving the East End, Morton wrote: 'I caught a penny omnibus back to England with the feeling that I might have spent two hundred pounds and seen less of the East, less of romance, and much less of life.'

Alf Stuart might agree with him. Alf was born Alfred Schwartz in 1915 at 312 Barking Road on the East side of the Lea in East Ham, a fairly good area with relatively little poverty. Jewish by race if not religion, Alf changed his name, so he says, 'because I had a hard time in Germany during the war as Schwartz.' His father, Harry, had a dress factory and 'wasn't short of a pound'. The family lived above the shop at first and had a couple of retail shops, one in Greengates and another in East Ham High Street.

Alf was sent to school in Whitechapel – 'a private school, you had to pay for it' – and he hated it. He played truant most of the time and left as soon as he could. His father wanted him to be a cutter and designer for the family firm, but Alf had other ideas:

> I thought I might be a barber when I was 14, so I went to a barber's shop and the first day I was there the governor said, 'Help lather out this fellow.' And I was lathering up and he was blind drunk, and he retched right in my face. I got the lather brush and I pushed it in his mouth and ran out the shop! That was my one day of working.

His father then sent him to a textile merchant he knew in Queens Road, Upton Park. They employed an auctioneer at weekends to do business outside the shop.

> It became a busy market at weekends, similar to Petticoat Lane. One day the auctioneer was going to lunch, and the manager of the shop saw some material sticking out of his jacket. So he put his foot out, tripped him up, pulled the material and the fellow rolled the whole length of the shop. It was a roll of white satin he was pinching. Now this fellow's name was Harry Feldman, he had a son called Marty, who was an actor

with big eyes. You remember him? Harry got the sack
right away, but he built up a business after the war in a
very big way in dresses. He became a very big
wholesaler. I used to supply him with material, and he
always paid on the dot.

Anyway, the whole thing was these merchants
haven't got an auctioneer any more. Now I was already
15 and had started there at £1 a week. Then it went up
to £1.50 week, so I said, 'Well, I can do what he was
doing, I can auctioneer.'

So they said, 'You, fifteen years of age, you can
auctioneer?'

And I said, 'Course I can. I know how to do it,' and I
was always quite a big fellow.

So he said, 'Go and try it on the weekend, go and try
it,' and I got up there, and they saw this young fellow,
and I had a very, very good day. From £1.50, I got £4.50
a week the next week, my wages went up right away. I
worked there for about two years, till I was about 17,
and I'm going to lunch one day, walking to lunch, and a
fellow taps me on the shoulder and he says, 'I've been
watching you for a long time, how would you like to
come and be my manager and work for me?'

So began Alf's trading career. In his younger days, as a
market auctioneer, he came as near as anyone I spoke
to, to being one of those East End wide boys who lived
on their wits and knew better than you apparently what
you needed to transform your life and realise your
dreams.

Often, one imagined, the street trader sailed close to the wind in his endeavours. He was not part of the vicious East End culture traditionally represented by Isaac Bogard, Arthur Harding, the Sabinis, and the Krays, although he would almost certainly know them (or they him).

Alf was the epitome of what we understand by the cockney trader, slightly fly, effortless, very quick on his feet. He might be found in any of the street markets, either with a pitch of his own, or as an independent working for someone in business there, or roaming the many markets on his own, and never in the accepted sense doing a day's work in his life.

With a pitch on Petticoat Lane, Alf was in his element:

> It was very busy, a very, very busy area. To get a stall on Petticoat Lane you had to be a magician; it's all dropsy, do you know what I mean by dropsy?

Backhanders?

> Yes, backhanders to get a stall there. I only worked it for about six months altogether because I found better markets than that, but when I came out of the forces I didn't know what to do, so I bought chalk figures. Do you know what chalk figures are? For the home, vases and everything, dolls, figures, and they looked like they was china, the way they were finished.
>
> So, I'm working Petticoat Lane with these chalk

figures one day and I see two men walking down with about a thousand people following behind them, and I thought, I wonder who they are?

Now, when I started there was a fellow there called Bill Strong, who sold real china in the Lane. He said, 'Alf, you won't take nothing here, because I've got such a busy business.' In fact, I did take a few bob, but I wasn't taking a fortune, until the day these two men were walking along with all these people following them.

I thought, they must be celebrities, so I got off the stall and I went to speak to them. I said, 'Excuse me, do you mind telling me who you are?' One said, 'That's Olsen and I'm Johnson.'

'Ole' Olsen and 'Chic' Johnson were a zany comedy team of the 1930s and 1940s, and a big part of the entertainment scene for nearly half a century, the masters of 'anything-goes-mayhem', their most chaotic conglomeration of comedy routines created for the stage smash *Hellzapoppin*, which opened at New York's 46th Street Theatre in 1938. The show consisted of two acts with twenty-five scenes, during which the audience was bombarded with eggs and bananas. Then when the lights went out, the audience was besieged with rubber snakes and spiders. A woman ran up and down the aisles shouting out in a loud tenement voice for 'Oscar! Oscar!' Meanwhile, a ticket salesman began to hawk tickets for a rival show (Rodgers and Hart's *I Married an Angel*). The Broadway madness ran for a record breaking 1,404 performances. Then, in 1941, Universal

Pictures made a screen version of *Hellzapoppin*, a terrible flop, as it happened, but it was that film that was doing the rounds in England when they wandered down Petticoat Lane market that Sunday and Alf Schwartz was selling his chalk figures . . .

I said to them, 'I wonder if you're not too proud to come and stand up on my stall and as I auction a figure you autograph it, autograph the article that I'm auctioneering.'

They said, 'Course we will.' They came over and I sold out within half an hour. Bill Strong was standing with his mouth open, he couldn't believe it! When they left, I said, 'Thank you very much you have made my day,' and one of them said. 'Here's two free tickets, come and see our show' and he gave me two front row tickets to come and see Hellzapoppin, to see the film. Anyway, that was Petticoat Lane in those days.

Before that, Alf had sharpened his wits in a different field altogether.

I got to know a man called Halprin, governor of the Houndsditch Warehouse Company, which was a very, very big store. When I came out the army I got my gratuities which was £365, that's how much I got – £365 gratuities for being four years a prisoner of war. I got the money and I thought what shall I do with it?

Now, in those days, £365 was a lot of money, and I said I know what I'll do, I'll go and speak to this man at the Houndsditch, he might give me an idea. I go to him, and I says, 'I've got my gratuities through from the army and I wonder if you could help me. What would be a good thing to earn a few bob?'

So he said, 'I'll tell you what to do, I'll sell you stuff,' he said. 'Ladies' combs.'

I said, 'Is there such a big demand for ladies' combs?'

And he said, 'Colossal! You couldn't get them during the war, you could not buy a comb. Now, I'll charge you 1s. 9d. for the small ones, and 2s. 3d. for the larger ones, and you sell them at 3s. 6d. and 4s. 6d. You'll find you're making 100 per cent and they will go very quickly.'

So I thought, I'll spend £200, and I bought £200 worth of combs and a big suitcase, got on the train and went to a place called Ashford market. I get there and I had printed a big banner, a lucky banner: 'Ladies' combs, 3/6 and 4/6'. Anyway, I opened up there and I'm taking money for these combs – people couldn't get enough of these combs – and all of a sudden a Rolls Royce pulls up not fifty yards away from me, and a fellow gets out in uniform. He was a chauffeur. He gets out a little table and puts combs on it, two pence halfpenny each! Now, what do you do? I could not believe it! So I run over to him and says, 'How did you get these? How many have you got of these?'

He says, 'I've got a gross.'

And I says, 'Well, I'll have the gross,' and I bought the gross off him. Then I said, 'But how did you get them?'

He says, 'My governor is in the car there, his name is

Mr Hogan of the Combined Optical Industries of Slough,' which were Halex, they were a well known make, Halex. They had the whole of Slough, it was a big place, and now they had diversified into combs. They had only started that week, and he wanted to see if they sold, so he had come to Ashford market and they were putting them out at the manufacturer's price, at two pence halfpenny each. But I'm paying 1s. 9d., 2s. 3d. for my combs!

I said, 'I wonder if I could speak to your governor.'

And the chauffeur said, 'He's a charming fellow, Mr Hogan. Go and knock on the door of the car and have a word with him.'

So I knock on the door of the car.

'Yes son,' he says.

I said, 'I hear you are manufacturing combs Mr Hogan.'

He said, 'That's quite right. Come inside a minute.'

So I get in the car and he starts talking. He says, 'Well, we started this week manufacturing combs and we wanted to see if they would sell, I think they will be a very good seller. We are gradually cutting down our manufacturing of optical frames and we are manufacturing combs instead.'

I said to him, 'I'm interested in all your combs, how many can you turn out?'

And he said, 'As it happens we have just manufactured three thousand gross.'

So I said, 'I'll buy that, I'll buy the three thousand gross.'

And he says, 'It comes to £3,000. Could you sell all those combs?'

I said, 'I could sell millions.'

'Where have you got your places?'

So I mentioned every market in England. I mentioned everywhere you could think of, every market. I told him, 'I've got places all over,' which I didn't have. I said I could sell them anywhere.

Anyway, he turned round to me and said, 'Well, if you could be at my place tomorrow early in the morning, you can have the first consignment of combs that are turned out.'

I said, 'I'll be there.'

I had no idea where I was going to get £3,000 from. But I had done very well with the combs I had, I'd sold those out, so I thought I'll ask my mother-in-law, maybe she's got £3,000 hidden away. In 1945, that must be £250,000, must be, must be . . . Anyway, so I go home and I said to my mother-in-law, 'Mum have you got £3,000?'

'Are you mad!' she said, '£3,000! Never heard of it.'

I thought, well, that's just one of those things, and she said, 'Do me a favour, go round to Stoney Lane and get me some oranges. 'Now, you had to buy oranges on the black market then, everything was on the black market, oranges and grapes, and bananas and everything. Anyway, I went round to Garcia's, who were in Black Lion Yard, off the Lane, and Mrs Garcia [a Jewish lady] she said, 'Oh you look under the weather, what's the matter?' And I told her the story.

What Alf didn't say, but I knew to be true from others, was that Black Lion Yard was something of a centre for money lending, and indeed gambling, and that the Jews were traditionally pre-eminent in both.

Mrs Garcia said, 'On one condition I will lend you £3,000, that you take my son in as a partner. I will loan you the money, but don't let him hold the money. I'd been going to Mrs Garcia since before the war, she knew me very well. I went up to her flat, she gets out a brief case, counts out £3,000, puts it in the brief case, calls her son over and again whispers to me: 'Don't let him hold the money, you hold the money.' And we shook hands. In those days you didn't have to do more – no signing, I could have run away with the £3,000, no signing no nothing; we shook hands and we were partners.

So I says to her son, 'Now you go up to Ilford and get a 3-ton lorry here. At 7 in the morning, we are going to Slough.'

We get to Slough and I couldn't believe how big this place was. Halex, it's a well known name, and Mr Hogan was the managing director, and we get there and there is a commissionaire on the door!

'I have come to see Mr Hogan,' I say.

'Oh hold on. What name?'

'Mr Stuart.'

'I'll phone up and see if Mr Hogan is available.' He phones up.

Hogan says, 'Oh, send them up, send the boys up,'

and as we get upstairs he says, 'Have you had your breakfast yet boys?'

I says, 'No, we came early.'

We are in his board room, he phones and gets breakfast sent up for us and we have breakfast there! I count out the £3,000. He says, 'I like the way you do business. We'll have a very, very matrimonial affair; we will go on from strength to strength,' and he shook hands with me and that was that.

I buy the £3,000 worth of combs and they load them on and as they load them on, I say, 'What are all those combs doing in the side there?'

There were about 10,000 combs laying there with half a tooth broken. When they manufacture them they make a few mistakes at first and they were just lying there, and I said, 'What are they doing?'

And Mr Hogan said, 'You want them? You can have those for nothing.'

I took them. Well, this 3-ton lorry, an open lorry, it was down on its springs.

We get back. Where am I going to sell them? I go to Halprin of the Houndsditch Warehouse Company, he's the one who sold the first batch to me. He says to me, 'Well, how did you do with the combs?'

I said, 'I done very well, but I've got a lot of combs to sell you.'

'How many have you got to sell me?'

I said, 'Three thousand gross.'

He said, 'What! Three thousand gross!' He thought I was kidding. 'How much are they?'

So I told him, I told him well under his price, and I sold him the 3,000 gross of combs, and we made nearly £10,000. In one day, from £3,000 I got £10,000.

First thing I do, I go to the woman who gave me the £3,000, give her the £3,000 back and £1,000 for herself. Then we share the rest between us but before we share it we take off £3,000 for the next week's delivery. And this went on for months. Not only did we sell them to Halprin, but we sold them to everybody in Petticoat Lane. They were all buying the combs from me, everybody was buying the combs, queuing up for them. Oh, and by the way, Hogan said, 'You must let two particular firms have some of these combs.'

I said, 'Oh yes, who's that?'

'Timothy Whites and Boots Chemist. You have got to let them have a gross of combs every week, one gross.'

So I used to send them in a gross too.

Anyway, this went on for about a year and a half, but I didn't realise that after about a year so many combs were about that I flooded the market. Then I started getting letters from purchase tax people. Now, I didn't know anything about purchase tax. And in the meantime my partner, Garcia, had introduced me to the horses. I had never gambled in my life, and the money was coming in – such a lot. I was going to the races, Newmarket, or wherever. Five hundred pounds, a thousand on a horse meant nothing, and I was losing the money every week.

After being a PoW for four years, the world is your oyster and you don't care what happens. If I went and lost £1,000, I used to come back to my wife and say, 'Here you are, I've won £500,' and I used to give her £500 even if I'd lost £1,000. That went on until I had nothing left hardly, and they came onto me for purchase tax, and I get a subpoena to come to the purchase tax office in Bloomsbury.

I get up there and I'm shaking like a leaf, because I didn't know about purchase tax. Too late I asked people about purchase tax [like VAT] and they told me it's been going for quite a while. Anyway, I get up there, get in the boardroom, and there's about ten people sitting round a table, and at the top of the table was my CO, who I was prisoner of war with. I was a PoW with him!

I look at him like mad, and he looks at me. He says, 'Gentlemen, I'd like to take this case in camera,' which means he would like to take it on his own. We got into another room and he said to me, 'Well, what have you been doing? You owe all this purchase tax.'

And I said, 'I didn't know about purchase tax. I bought stuff and sold it.' (I didn't tell him how much I earned and gambled.) 'I bought it and sold it. I didn't realise. I never charged purchase tax to anybody.'

So he said, 'I tell you what I'm going to do – I accept that you didn't know what you were doing. I am tearing this up in front of you. You will never hear about this as long as you live. This is completely finished.'

And he tore it up in front of me. That was that, £500 I didn't have to pay! And that was the end of the combs!

The East End wide boy has now largely disappeared, or so we are led to believe. In fact, I discovered, he shifted operations a mile or so to the West, into the City of London, one of the chief banking centres of the world.

Twenty-five years after Alf was selling his combs in Petticoat Lane market, the Burns family was part of a Sunday ritual as sacred as any in Brick Lane market. Violet Burns, the matriarch of the family, had one regular pitch, and at the serious money end of the market Uncle Charlie had a stall that was more of a small department store.

Burns territory is off the top end of Brick Lane in Bacon Street. Harry gave a picture of the family's roots back four generations in this same street.

I was born here and we was brought up here, 26 and 28 Bacon Street. That was our removals yard next to it, we used to have ponies then, and every building down there was a small business. There was a tailor, a second-hand shop, there was Izzy Smith with the pickles, there was a diamond merchant, everybody was a small business. There was one woman had a tobacconist, she used to take the bets and her name was Muddle, and when the police raided her, they said, 'Mrs Muddle is in a muddle for round about £1,500,' which was a fortune in them days!!

There used to be look-outs [for the police] at the corner by one of those posts [bollards] in the road. One time the look-out had nothing to do, so he wrapped the post up in brown paper, put string round it, like it was a parcel, and says to a fellow, 'Give us a lift with this, will you?' Anyway, the next day the bloke comes back, hits him right in the chin and says, 'That's another lift you've got!' It's all comedy round here.

Across there during the war there was a tailor's shop, and one thing led to another and during the night he got robbed, but who robbed him nobody knew, only that there was a horse and cart. I said, 'Marcie, who did this?'

He said, 'I don't know, but we've got a description of the horse!'

Harry's son Tony, after working for his father for fifteen years, set up his own office removal business nearby, with his own son, nephews and cousins working for him. But before long, the son, Tony Jr, was moving in a world that his father and grandfather could only dream of . . . in the City, the financial centre. The transition was seamless. Said Tony Sr:

When he left school he came to work for me and then went into the money market which he became very, very successful at and he has now moved out to the suburbs, but he will always be an East End kid.

Pretty soon the two worlds met again in boxing, a feature of Tony Sr's life, almost from the off.

When I was in my teens, the only thing you could actually do in the East End of London really, you either kicked a ball or you punched someone on the nose, you know. My dad boxed, my uncles boxed, all my brothers and cousins were in boxing so I went along there and took it up. I didn't particularly like it when I first went into boxing, I don't know why, I just didn't like it at all for the first couple of years, but it was the done thing.

Tony packed in boxing at the age of 28, when his wife decided he'd had enough and suggested he take up coaching at the Repton Club. He found he loved it and was very good at it. Repton Boxing Club began in the nineteenth century, when Repton public school in Derbyshire decided to open a mission for the under-privileged youth of the East End. Learning the noble art, it was thought, would keep them off the streets and out of mischief.

In the amateur boxing world the name Repton is famous. Over the years the club has attracted and tamed many of the East End's wilder young men. Few hard men in the area have not been associated with Repton at some time or other, including the Kray twins. One of the most important financial sources of support for the Repton has been the City. With the special 'in' that the son availed them, they ran fight nights, where rich City folk would be invited to dine and watch a series of bouts.

Most of the people who have now started supporting us are kids from the East End who have gone on into money markets and financial markets and the stock

exchange. A fight night is a good night out for the
family. We take clients, they enjoy it, we enjoy it.

As I write, Tony is still running the Repton, and his
uncle – Harry's brother Charlie, in his nineties – is still
managing his department-store operation out of Bacon
Street, the family seat, a stone's throw from Tony's gym
in Cheshire Street.

Characters like Harry, Charlie and Tony Burns, and
Alf Stuart make the East End what it is in actuality and
in imagination. They are, in that sense, artists in life.
They play their roles in the theatre of the East End,
which is the original street theatre.

CHAPTER FOUR

Behind
the scenes

———————

G one now, but operating up and down almost every street at least into the early 1950s, was a colourful parade of tradesmen. First to arrive were –

> Bakers' boys calling hot rolls at 7 o'clock to 8 o'clock, then a procession of men with fish, vegetables and fruits, chair menders, scissor grinders, sweeps, ragmen, women with watercress and lavender, and in the evenings, up to about 10 pm, vendors of hot pies and baked potatoes.

Early on a Sunday morning came a bagel seller, 'a little

old man who carried a basket or sack containing the bagels'. On Sunday afternoons came the muffin man, carrying a tray covered with green baize cloth on his head ringing his bell and shouting, 'Muffins! Muffins!' The tray was heavy and carrying it gave the muffin man a distinctive lop-sided gait, as he lifted the shoulder opposite the one that carried the hand that supported the tray. And winkle sellers, who also dispensed Gravesend shrimps, and shouted, 'Shrimps and winkles – all fresh and lovely – come and buy!' Or just 'Alive, alive-o!' which they were not. People could get almost whatever they wanted on their own doorstep. Cows were even driven down the streets and milked into a jug at 2d. a pint. And there was the regular appearance of a cat's meat man – a man bringing literally skewered meat for cats. He would come along the street shouting, 'Meeeeeeet! Meeeeeeet!' And everyone had the same story of his leaving a skewer of meat behind a knocker and some local kid always eating it.

Also part of the parade was: –

The barrel organ, followed by a troupe of colourfully dressed painted ladies in flowing gowns and fetching bonnets. When the procession stopped, a crowd formed around them as the organ was wound into tuneful life by the operator turning and winding the key-like handle. The ladies, responding to the music, spread out and burst into lively song and dance. To my astonishment, in spite of the dresses and heavily rouged faces, I learned they were men and not really women at all.

Then too there was the rare wonderment of a
bearded and turbaned Indian peddling his wares from
door to door, displaying his goods, silk scarves, ties etc,
from a large and battered suitcase. Every call was looked
on with awe by the inevitable band of following
urchins.[1]

Most popular in summer was the ice cream seller, from
an Italian family based in Brick Lane. The father was
known as 'Padrone'. In winter, just as welcome, the
same men would sell chestnuts and baked potatoes.

Another rare source of entertainment that held us
spellbound was a travelling balancing act, provided by
an Italian-looking muscular trio. The highlight of their act
usually performed outside the local public houses came
when the strong man of the three would first balance
the whole frame of a bicycle to a pad on his forehead.
Not content, he would then follow this by balancing a
partial frame with a single wheel and saddle only.
Breathtakingly, a second member of the trio would climb
and mount the precarious saddle, meanwhile the third of
the trio would pour out soulful music from a series of
haunting whistles – a tune I readily remember them
using was, again, 'Sleepy Valley'.[2]

Then there was the Indian toffee man, with a metal box
strapped to his waist containing not toffee from India,
but something just as good.

This Indian toffee was like candy-floss, only heavier, and was always sold by an Indian, never anyone else. It cost 1d, and you didn't get much for your penny, but what you did get was delicious.[3]

Then, in winter, as dusk fell, the lamplighter would appear to turn on the street lamps, which cast their eerie glow across the darkening, foggy streets.

But behind the scenes of this colourful street theatre and the community it served was a background of sometimes quite terrible poverty. Many East Enders were on the breadline in the first half of the twentieth century.

Things were hard . . . So what used to happen, in order that we got fed as children, we'd go out in the morning with a mug each, or a cup – a cup was a rare thing, it was usually a mug, and in fact some instances it was the condensed milk tin used as a cup – and we'd go to a coffee shop in the high street opposite Hermitage Wharf . . . and we'd have a mug of cocoa and a couple of slices of bread and jam. And that was bread and jam, not bread butter and jam: bread and jam. Well that would be our breakfast and we'd be off to school. Then at midday we'd go to another coffee shop, in Turks Court, we used to go to, and we'd have a bowl of soup and a couple of slices of bread. And that would be fried bread. But that was accepted, that was – that was our normal diet in most cases. Then in the aft – when we came from school at four o'clock, we'd go to Ben's

Chapel in Old River Lane, and that was run by social
workers, and we'd have a mug of tea and bread and
jam again. So we got by fairly well.[4]

Cyril Demarne was born in Poplar in 1905, the eldest of
five (two brothers, two sisters). His father was a clerk in
the City until he fell ill and lost his job. Thereafter he
addressed envelopes at home for 1s. 6d. per thousand
(these were the days when there were 12 pence to a
shilling, and 20 shillings to the pound).

Sometimes we sat in the dark, for there was no penny
for the gas . . . We lived in three rooms and a scullery [a
small room for washing and storing dishes] on the first
floor of a small house for which my parents paid seven
shillings a week rent. This was considered ample
accommodation for a family of four, there were larger
families living in similar flats in our street . . . Our scullery
had room for a table and kitchen sink as well as the
cooker. The lavatory was in the back yard and shared
with the family downstairs . . . There was no bathroom
of course. Like most people we had a large galvanised
bath, which normally hung on a nail in the back yard
and this was used to bathe the children. My parents
used the public baths in East India Dock Road, opposite
Chrisp Street.

There were levels of poverty, and the Rose family, where
the father was 'a master painter, hanger, decorator' and
often out of work, hit rock bottom.

> In 1924 when I was fourteen, things were so bad at
> home money wise, we were actually starving, and I used
> to go to school with no shoes or socks on – in bare feet,
> in frost. Not snow, but in frost and that is a fact . . . and
> the atmosphere at home was very bad.

The Griffithses never sank that low, but confirmed that
others did, and that boots and shoes were always the
sign.

> I remember some children went to school without
> shoes at all, shoes or socks, just bare feet. I remember
> that very vividly. And I remember when all us kids were
> sitting on a wall once and we were sort of swinging
> our legs saying, 'How long have you had your shoes?'
> And one said they had six months or a year or
> whatever, and this one boy said I've had mine twelve
> years and when we looked down to his feet he had no
> shoes on at all. He said I've had these since I've been
> born.[5]

Mrs Carrington went one further perhaps with her
memory of an example of extreme poverty at school.
Mr Bernstein, the teacher, was stern but kind, as he
proved one sultry summer's day.

> It involved a boy called Cornelius that we called Connie.
> He was a dreamer, forever gazing into space and paying
> no attention to the lesson. He had incurred Mr
> Bernstein's wrath and was summoned to the front of the

class. In the midst of ticking him off Mr Bernstein became aware that Connie was not only wearing a heavy tweed jacket but had a muffler tucked into the neck. 'No wonder you are half asleep,' roared Mr Bernstein. 'You are too hot, remove your jacket Cornelius.' A slow flush mounted Connie's face and he backed away. 'No, no I'm not too hot sir,' he said. 'Of course you are,' contradicted Mr Bernstein. 'Remove it at once lad.' And he fixed Connie with a stern glance. Slowly, Connie undid the jacket and removed it to reveal his pale white torso with only his braces to prevent its total nakedness. Connie hung his head. There was a moment of stunned silence. There was not one in the room could boast of his or her own attire, but here was poverty indeed. Before there was even the beginning of a titter, Mr Bernstein flashed an eye of terrible rage upon us and hissed between his teeth, 'The first to laugh will be thrashed within an inch of his life.' No one laughed and Mr Bernstein tenderly buttoned Connie back into his jacket.[6]

The final degradation was being flung out of your house, your flat, your rooms. It was not an uncommon event at this time to see:

The bailiff's men piling on a single cart the few shillings' worth of sticks and crocks which represented the sum total of these people's worldly goods, while the man and woman thus dispossessed stood by to watch them go with no other show of emotion beyond a sullen

indifference or at most a futile defiance. Nor could I ever
grow sufficiently hardened to pass unmoved the
melancholy spectacle of an elderly couple standing
dejectedly outside the pawn-shop, staring with reddened
eyes at some precious article inside.

'When they're old like that,' it was explained to me,
'and their home's gone, they haven't much hope of
redeeming the things again.'[7]

The pawn shop was the vital facilitator of cash flow.
Every Monday morning the father's best suit would be
exchanged for five bob, to be retrieved the following
Saturday. One or two smart ones would buy sheets,
bedclothes and the like from the tally man – a door-to-
door salesman who sold on a hire-purchase arrange-
ment – paying the man a shilling a week, but hocking
them to the pawn shop for a lump sum. If the
repayments were missed the tally man was left to take it
out of 'the knocker'!

If it came to eviction, where would the evicted go?
The workhouse? There was no welfare state, no health
insurance. The workhouse was the pits, and adding
to their burden they were made to take in 'lunatics',
mentally ill children and the physically sick. Guardians
displayed their patronising attitude by lumping their
charges – 'idiots and lunatics, bastards, venereals, the
idle and dissolute' – together. Jack London gained
admission to an East End workhouse in 1902,
masquerading as a vagrant:

Many hours passed before I won to sleep. It was only
seven in the evening, and the voices of children, in shrill
outcry, playing in the street, continued till nearly
midnight. The smell was frightful and sickening, while
my imagination broke loose, and my skin crept and
crawled till I was nearly frantic. Grunting, groaning, and
snoring arose like the sounds emitted by some sea
monster, and several times, afflicted by nightmare, one
or another, by his shrieks and yells, aroused the lot of us.
Towards morning I was awakened by a rat or some
similar animal on my breast. In the quick transition from
sleep to waking, before I was completely myself, I raised
a shout to wake the dead. At any rate, I woke the living,
and they cursed me for my lack of manners.

In the hard winter of 1903, the *New York Independent*
reported: 'The workhouses [in Britain] have no space
left in which to pack the starving crowds who are
craving every day and night at their doors for food and
shelter. All the charitable institutions have exhausted
their means in trying to raise supplies of food for the
famishing residents of the garrets and cellars of
London lanes and alleys.'

The system was abolished in April 1930. After that
there was the dole and coupons for food, but getting it
was not easy. If anyone was desperate enough to seek
State aid, they received a visit from 'The Men' (means-
test investigators from the Welfare Board), who would
make an inventory of all your possessions and suggest
you sold the lot before bothering them again.

More likely than the workhouse, the destiny of anyone on a flit would be the kiphouse or dosshouse, a common lodging house – perhaps there first, and then a room in a Bethnal Green tenement, which were cheap and where terrible conditions appertained. A report by Miss Sydney K. Phelps in 1924 described the near disastrous state of affairs:

> Bethnal Green has been described as London's poorest slum, and I do not quarrel with the term. It is a very dreadful place. Hollybush-place, Green-street, Pleasant-place, and other neighbourhoods, which now consist of ruinous tenements reeking with abominations, were outlying, decent cottages, standing on or near plots of garden ground, where the inmates reared prize tulips and rare dahlias in their scanty leisure . . . before the present main road was formed to supersede the old Bethnal-green-road, which lies nearer to Cambridge-heath, this district was but a sort of country extension of Spitalfields.

These were probably the worst and most dangerous tenement slums in the whole East End. An article in *The Illustrated London News* described the Old Nichol Estate, between Columbia Road and Bethnal Green Road, as follows:

> Skirting the station of the Great Eastern Railway in Shoreditch, and traversing Club-row – the Sunday morning resort of pigeon and bird fanciers – the earnest

visitor has only to cross the road and turn up Nichols-
row, to find himself in as foul a neighbourhood as can
be discovered in the civilised world (savage life has
nothing to compare to it), and amongst a population
depressed almost to the last stage of human endurance.
Should he have started with an impression that report
had exaggerated the misery of these dwellings he will, if
he have the heart – and, let us add, the stomach – to
inspect them, prove that no allowable strength of
language could do more than adequately express the
condition of the dens which surround Friars-mount . . .
The miserable rooms are underlet and teeming with
inhabitants to an almost inconceivable extent. The water
for some fourteen or fifteen houses is frequently
supplied from one tap in a dirty corner, where it runs for
only a short time every day; and the places are mostly
undrained. Add to this the decay of vegetable matter,
the occasional evidence of the presence of pigs from
adjacent houses which have back yards (these have
none), and that sickly odour which belongs always to
human beings living in such a state, and the result will
represent a score of places extending over Bethnal-green
parish for more than a mile in length and half a mile in
breadth.

A stranger wouldn't chance his arm there . . . The
Nichol was a place on its own, you didn't go into other
territory.[8]

The police would never venture in there, never
venture.[9]

Nor was this the only Victorian tenement that should have been condemned. In the 1920s Emanuel Litvinoff moved from Christian Street in Stepney to Fuller Street Buildings between Bethnal Green Road and Cheshire Street:

We had two rooms and a small kitchenette. There were toilets in the yard. There were three toilets in the yard. Altogether there must have been about eighty to ninety people living in the whole block who shared these three toilets and there was a communal dustbin, and the place was foul. People used to stand on the toilet seats to avoid sitting on them. There were newspapers of, you know, saturated with urine all over the place. The dustbins used to overflow. It's a miracle that everybody didn't die of some dire disease there although we seem to have grown up pretty healthily. The rooms themselves were small, they were gas lit – electricity I think had certainly not been introduced into the East End, certainly not into most of the tenements and the gas was . . . you had a gas meter which used to take shillings and if you ran out of shillings or ran out of money then you just couldn't have any lights and you couldn't have gas for cooking, you see, so it was a vital thing. There were, let's see, there was a large bed in the bedroom and a child's cot and a sofa which we used to open in the sitting room, or the living room as we called it, in which four of us used to sleep, head to toe, you see. Actually I and my . . . the brother who was younger than me by thirteen months, my brother Pinny, were the two in the family who wet the bed, so we had to sleep in the cots and we were very tall kids and I remember that my legs used to stick out of the bars of the cot quite a lot, you know, about half of my legs were sticking out, and sometimes of course we just slept on the floor.[10]

These 'dark fortresses' towered above street upon street of the little terraced houses that most of us associate with the East End of this period, like Mr and Mrs Banton's four-roomed house in Minton Street in the middle of Bethnal Green.

The houses are nearly all alike in plan; on the first floor two bedrooms, and on the ground floor a living room, a kitchen and a small scullery opening on to a yard which has a lavatory at the end of it and a patch of earth down one side. Many of the yards are packed with clothes hanging on the line, pram-sheds, boxes of geraniums and pansies, hutches for rabbits and guinea-pigs, lofts for pigeons and pens for fowls. The only difference between the houses is the colour of the curtains and doorsteps which the wives redden or whiten when they wash down the pavement in front of their door in the morning. Dilapidated but cosy, damp but friendly, in the eyes of most Bethnal Greeners these cottages are the place . . .[11]

Overcrowding in houses and tenements was a big problem. Landlords cottoned on to the fact that they could make more money by squeezing more than one family into even the smallest of terraced two-up-two-down. In 1911 one out of every three people in Bethnal Green lived more than two to a room. In 1931 it was one out of four.

That, as an average, indicated serious overcrowding in the worst tenements, which should have been demolished before the twentieth century began, as this one in Frying-pan Alley:

A spawn of children cluttered the slimy pavement, for all the world like tadpoles just turned into frogs on the bottom of a dry pond. In a narrow doorway, so narrow that perforce we stepped over her, sat a woman with a young babe, nursing at breasts grossly naked and libelling all the sacredness of motherhood. In the black and narrow hall behind her we waded through a mess of young life, and essayed an even narrower and fouler stairway. Up we went, three flights, each landing two feet by three in area, and heaped with filth and refuse.

There were seven rooms in this abomination called a house. In six of the rooms, twenty-odd people, of both sexes and all ages, cooked, ate, slept, and worked. In size the rooms averaged eight feet by eight, or possibly nine. The seventh room we entered. It was the den in which five men 'sweated'. It was seven feet wide by eight long, and the table at which the work was performed took up the major portion of the space. On this table were five lasts, and there was barely room for the men to stand to their work, for the rest of the space was heaped with cardboard, leather, bundles of shoe

uppers, and a miscellaneous assortment of materials
used in attaching the uppers of shoes to their soles.

In the adjoining room lived a woman and six children.
In another vile hole lived a widow, with an only son of
sixteen who was dying of consumption. The woman
hawked sweetmeats on the street, I was told, and more
often failed than not to supply her son with the three
quarts of milk he daily required. Further, this son, weak
and dying, did not taste meat oftener than once a week;
and the kind and quality of this meat cannot possibly be
imagined by people who have never watched human
swine eat.[12]

The Reverend W. N. Davies, rector of Spitalfields, took
a census of some of the alleys in his parish.

In one alley there are ten houses – fifty-one rooms,
nearly all about eight feet by nine feet – and 254
people. In six instances only do two people occupy one
room; and in others the number varied from three to
nine. In another court with six houses and twenty-two
rooms were 84 people – again, six, seven, eight, and
nine being the number living in one room, in several
instances. In one house with eight rooms are 45 people
– one room containing nine persons, one eight, two
seven, and another six.

It is commonly supposed that such places ceased to
exist by the 1920s and 1930s, but it was not the case.
Some survived even the Second World War. The most

notorious post-war tenements in the Whitechapel area were in Flower and Dean Street, immediately east of Aldgate Pump.

The name of the street derives from its two builders, John Flowers and Gowan Deane, who were Whitechapel bricklayers and built the original street in the 1650s. It must have been one of the meanest looking streets in the East End of London, a dark cavern of decaying tenement blocks, nearly all of them six storeys high. These effectively shut out much of the light and it is probably true to say that the only growing things were the many children of the neighbourhood.

These six-storeyed tenements had rather grand titles. There was Nathaniel Buildings, and Rothschild Buildings, and my own buildings. I don't think these had a collective name but the blocks in Flower and Dean Street were Irene House and Ruth House. These were not blocks of flats in the true sense of the word but were separate stairways in one huge block of flats, the 'houses' each being named and having four flats on each of its six floors. I lived in Ruth House, on the top floor, at number 25.

This brick canyon we called The Flowery connected Brick Lane and Commercial Street, and at both ends the road narrowed to a single width, making it somewhat self-contained and forbidding to outsiders to enter. It was seldom used as a throughway by strangers. It was said that in Victorian times policemen were forbidden to enter it alone.[13]

Occasionally the police had to enter. The midwife Jennifer Worth describes one episode when she found two women fighting over a man:

> It was dark, but light from some of the windows illuminated the scene sufficiently to show that both women had their blouses torn off and were clawing, hitting, punching, biting and kicking each other. One had long hair that was a great disadvantage to her, as it gave her adversary something to grab hold of. Literally hundreds of people were in the courtyard, men women and children, shouting, jeering, cheering, egging them on. I wondered if one of the women would grab the skirt of the other and pull it off, so that she would be virtually naked. That didn't happen, but the woman with the long hair was forced to the ground, the other on top of her, banging her head on the cobblestones.
>
> Just as I was thinking, Dear God, someone's got to stop this, I heard the piercing sound of police whistles and two policemen rushed into the yard, blowing their whistles and wielding their truncheons to show that they meant business. Thank God they came when they did because the woman on her back otherwise would have been seriously concussed, if not killed.

This highlights too the ubiquitous nature in those days of the police on the ground, on the beat, not in cars, but on their feet, and with no radios, only whistles, torches and truncheons. If help was required, the drill was:

Blow three short blasts on your whistle or call on private persons to assist. At night time, if you do not wish to raise an alarm, signal with your torch in the direction in which another Constable is likely to be. The signal should be answered in a similar manner.[14]

The health hazards from overcrowding in tenements, flats and houses, and from vermin were enormous:

I have very vivid memories of lying in bed listening to the rats scuttling about in the roof. One of the delights of summer was the bug-hunt, when my nana and I would strip the beds and search for bedbugs and proceed to drown them.[15]

There was also an abundance of bugs at number two hundred and ten, not all of them behind the wallpaper, but tear a strip of this from a corner of the wall and you would expose columns of the things, like an endless red/brown army . . . They got into the bedding too; promiscuous buggers they were, not fussy whose bed they slept in, or who they slept with and lovingly bit.[16]

Led by my mother we turned out en masse to engage the Enemy in single-handed battle. Paraffin was our heavy artillery, but this was employed only as a last resort, for the smell of it in the stifling heat turned the youngest of us sick and made even the hardier ones blench. We would usually have to fall back on it all the same – which would lead to a stampede not only of the invaders but of the defenders.[17]

It is easy to see that people needed at some point in the year to get away from the claustrophobic elements of the East End, and they did, even the poorest. Sometimes it would be 'a beano' organised by the local pub, who would hire a charabanc and everyone would make for the beach – Southend perhaps.

> Us kids would like it better when it was all women going on the beano as the old birds were more generous wiv their moldies. Moldies is all the loose change that they would have in their purses. Sometimes the guvner of the boozer would hand out about two pound in pennies an 'apennies. And just as the charabang moved awf, all the kids would shout out, 'Frow out yam oldies,' and the old birds would wind down the windows of the charabanc and frow out all the money.[18]

But the big tradition – hop-picking in the summer in Kent – was possible for even the poorest, for you were earning in the fresh air of the countryside while you were holidaying. The farmers put people up in specially built, amazingly Spartan tin huts on the edge of a field. Henry Warren, whose father ran the local shop at Mereworth (pronounced aptly Merryworth), used to watch and marvel at the invasion each summer of aliens to his way of life, who turned the accepted order upside down.

> The first of them came on foot, a dreary vanguard pushing perambulators heaped to twice their height with

bulky bundles, a kettle and a saucepan clattering away somewhere underneath, and a tin bath piled on top.

Some came in wagons, singing. Perhaps I was playing somewhere in the lanes, between the hedges bright with changing maple. I would hear them approaching along the woodland roads, scattering the quiet with their raucous voices: and I do not know whether I was more filled with excitement at the novelty their arrival portended or with vague fear at the sudden intrusion of their loud ways . . .

Not many came in wagons: the majority, numbering several hundreds all told, came in trains that disgorged them at the next village, some two and a half miles away . . . in trains that boasted no cushions and obeyed no time-tables and spent the rest of the year patiently rotting in obscure sidings.

The new-comers tended to be irritable at first, wearied by a journey that had taken them the greater part of twenty-four hours and irked at finding themselves allotted insanitary huts with only straw to lie on and not even a fire to call their own.

There was, for instance, Mrs Grunter – Eliza, as everybody called her. She would roll into the shop like a gargantuan sack, tied not too securely round the middle. She oozed laughter. She had little black eyes that shone out of the deep folds of her face, always brimming over with tears. On the day of her arrival she wore a black satin coat that came down to her heels, and her hair, screwed into a tight 'bun' at the back, was surmounted uneasily by a bonnet that waved a purple osprey plume as she laughed. But from that day onwards, she discarded bonnet and coat, and appeared in an old shawl, one corner of which was always trailing along the ground, while her 'bun' perpetually escaped in an untidy tangle of tails down her back. Like the rest of the invaders, Eliza looked upon the country as a place to unbutton and relax in.

'Ere we are agen, ol' dear!' she would say. 'An' ain't you sorry to see us: not 'alf you ain't! Rattlin' in the profits faster than we can rattle 'ops off the bine. Oh, don't tell me! Now, 'ow much is that bit of fat bacon over there? Gawd! You don't 'alf shove the prices up when you see me comin' – AND you don't need a telescope, neither.' Turning to her companion, a newcomer, she continued: 'Still, 'e ain't a bad ol' dear, take 'im all round – all round, I said!'

Or there was Long Tom, who stood six feet four in his almost soleless boots and was as thin as a hop-pole. Rags fluttered from him as from a scarecrow. He stuttered painfully and wrung his hands all the while. With every word he would roll his tongue round his lips, whistle, and seem to be trying to tie his jaw into knots. Fortunately, he spoke very little, but would reach a lean, dirty hand over the heads of the other customers and give in his order on a slip of paper. The writing was almost indecipherable. 'What! Another billy-do?' some wit would call out, as my father held the crumpled scrap up to the light. 'Come on, mister! Don't keep us 'ere all night: there's duck an' green peas waitin' for us back at the 'uts!' But my father persevered, and at last Long Tom was served and allowed to thin away through the crowd like a ghost . . .

Once the strangers (as we called them, to differentiate them from the home pickers) had settled themselves in their huts and tents, they took complete possession of the place. They were respecters neither of persons nor things . . . they roamed about at will, breaking branches off trees, soiling everywhere, and scattering their refuse over the countryside. The local policeman was quite unable to do anything about it . . . But when it came to stripping bines there were few home pickers who could beat them.

At length the special train with cushionless seats carried back the Londoners to their homes, singing:

'Oppin' is all over,
Money is all spent,
Don't I wish I'd never
Come 'oppin dahn in Kent –
Wiv a tee-ay-ay, tee-ay-ay, tee-ay-ee-ay-O!

Charles Booth, the author of *Life and Labour of the People in London*, laid the blame for poverty in the East End not only on unemployment and low wages, but on the husband, who spent his wages on himself in the pub, and contributed to the overcrowding problem by being 'callous in sex', forcing the wife to undergo 'a trial of unwanted pregnancies' in the days before the Pill or any effective contraception.

In all these studies the villain is the man, the woman is
presented as struggling bravely on although worn out by
her children, loaded with hardship and old before her
time, sharing a home but not a life with a figure
pictured as neither a loyal husband nor a dutiful father.[19]

Stan Rose would not have argued with the reports:

I've known my father go missing on a Friday when he
had drawn the labour money, that was the dole money,
plus the er, the other thing for the food, and he never
came home till the Monday with nothing. And on that
Sunday, I will never forget this, my mother had to go to
a local shop in Lawrence Street where we were living,
we lived there for twenty odd year, and she had to buy a
pound of dates, tuppence, for our Sunday dinner with
toast. That was my Sunday – I remember. I mean that's
why I said he's no good. He could have looked after us
but he was a bad man. And there, and I used to go to
school with no shoes on, naturally old trousers with
holes in them and you were living oh a hell of a life, hell
of a life it was.[20]

He only lived for himself . . . Father was a bully. He
used to knock my mother about, so I was told.[21]

'The arch enemy was drink,' agreed Grace Blacketer,
but added that quite often women were drinkers too.

Pubs opened on Sunday from 1 pm to 3 pm and
6 pm to 10 pm, or 11. On weekdays from early morning
until 11 pm, or on Saturday till midnight. Beer and ale

cost 2d. per pint, and it was strong. 'Reeling men and women, singing one minute and fighting the next, were everywhere.' Organisations like the Blue Ribbon Army, the Salvation Army, the Band of Hope, and the Temperance Societies worked hard to stem the tide.

Stan Rose's dad became a busker to facilitate his addiction. He'd play the banjo, but when he got the money he spent it in the next pub he could find:

> There was fights – this is typical of the 1930s, 'specially weekends – there was fights with my mother, and my mother used to sell beetroots in Bow to get some money to give us some food . . . My father was a no good man.

Some in retrospect saw pubs as an invention of the industrialists to keep the working classes poor. It is a fact that dock companies did own pubs, just as the mill owners of the North of England owned their workers' favourite drinking holes, so that, in effect, a large part of the wages simply circled back into the parent company via the bar. Indeed, some East End dock companies at one time even paid the men their wages in the pub!

The need to get hold of some money must have got through to the children, for they engaged in a spontaneous war on want, educating themselves in stratagems that were useful then and formed the basis of a dodgy approach to life later:

> It was important for a child always to have a penny or a halfpenny or whatever it was to go on some of these

things and to spend a bit of money. If ever we had
visitors I would always get them to sit down on the
settee and hope that some coins would fall out of their
pockets, and I was for ever searching underneath the
couch to see if – and I would put my hand, slither it
down into the leather – in the hope that I would find a
coin, and I would always get sixpences and things like
that, and gradually, gradually would get enough to go to
the cinema or whatever.[22]

Boys from the tenements in Flower and Dean Street
would make Spitalfields market their target.

Anything was fair game and we would collect as much
loose fruit and vegetables as possible, putting these into
our sacks which we had slung over our shoulders. Later,
the contents would be sold, as and when we could
dispose of them. It would be a matter of gathering
around a cart that was being unloaded, about three or
four of us along each side of the vehicle. As the sacks
and boxes were taken off there was sometimes a tear in
a sack or a small breakage somewhere in a crate.

Young Arthur Harding also targeted Spitalfields, but
for firewood, knowing that he had a ready market
because everyone did their laundry in a copper, a large
water container encased in bricks and heated underneath by a wood fire.

There were heaps of old orange boxes all piled up [in the

market]. You'd tie them together and drag them home,
tied together by a lump of string. An orange box would
sell for a ha'penny or even a penny a bundle, selling it
around the houses as firewood.[23]

George Renshaw did the same, and the price he got for
the wood was the same, a ha'penny a bundle. But there
were other, less dignified, stratagems in his neck of the
woods, where children 'had to be enterprising in order
to survive'.

Many children would make Grottoes using sea shells
from shell fish. They would be laid out in a pattern on
the pavement, chalked around with coloured chalk and
after other stones and trinkets had been added would
look a work of art. A tin can would be held out and as
people passed by they would be asked to remember the
Grotto. Although this may seem like begging, hours of
work would go into the Grotto's construction, making
those few pennies justified.

Others even stooped to walking along the gutter and
picking up fag ends, then re-rolling them in new skins
and selling them at school.[24]

Among adults, the women especially, money was
made to stretch in a variety of ways. Clubs were set up
for Christmas and for other foreseen expenditure, a
way of self-enforced saving on the principle that the
group's will power was stronger than the individual's.
The clubs were often made up of extended family or

pub regulars, but were also popular among young women at work, who, when it was their turn, could draw several weeks' wages in one go and buy something expensive, like a pair of shoes.

There was pride in particular in what you could achieve even without much money.

> That was my home, shabby and indeed often untidy but always clean. By fair means or foul we always had enough to eat, wore an odd assortment of second hand clothes and rarely had money for extras but we were loved and that was sufficient.[25]

And any way of 'making do' would be considered.

> Having all your teeth out saved money on dentists' bills in the long run.[26]

Inevitably, this war on want led to petty theft, to pinching clothes at church jumble sales, where it was easy for a poor woman to justify that she should not be paying for the clothes anyway.

> Three or four of them used to go, it was a sort of holiday. Didn't cost anything because they used to pinch the clothes and they might get 5 or 10 bob out of it. Mother would get a good big load and fetch them out and I'd put them in the sack outside. They used to sell 'em to the wardrobe dealers down the Lane [Brick Lane] – in the old clothes market.[27]

The poor wages and lack of prospects inevitably drove men to crime too, and their children to a criminal mentality, but one of the strangest criminal mentalities imaginable, where the values of loyalty and honour and truth to one's own mingled with the most unutterable violence, extortion and murder, as we will see.

CHAPTER FIVE

Genesis

Really to understand how the East End came to this dire pass, we need to go back to the beginning, to where it all started, to a time when Aldgate was green fields and the market at Spitalfields was serviced by farms nearby. We need to get inside the economy of the area.

The basic geography of the East End is clear enough. The western boundary of the rectangle is the City of London, the financial capital, through which Bishopsgate, Shoreditch High Street and Kingsland Road run. Along the northern boundary run Hackney Road and Cambridge Heath, leading to Victoria Park,

Roman Road and the River Lea, which is the eastern boundary, as surely as the Thames – Wapping, Ratcliff, Limehouse, Poplar, the Isle of Dogs and Blackwall – is the southern boundary.

Returning to the western boundary, the gateway to the East End is Aldgate, Whitechapel – the old Gardiner's Corner, that exciting meeting-place of streets which I have described. Moving northwards is Spitalfields, Brick Lane, at the top end of which is Bethnal Green Road. But Stepney also pushes east towards Stepney Green – four big roads, Whitechapel Road into Mile End Road, below it Commercial Road, and below that Cable Street and The Highway.

A particularly significant step forward for Spitalfields market was made in 1682, when Charles II granted the right to hold it on Thursdays and Saturdays to one John Balch, significant not least because Balch was a silk thrower, a man employed in the silk weaving industry, twisting silk into yarn, and for the next hundred years, silk was to bring this part of the East End to its greatest ever glory. We have always been led to believe that the Huguenots brought the silk weaving industry to Spitalfields from France after October 1685, when the Catholic French King Louis XIV made the practice of their religion – they were Calvinist Protestants – illegal, even in the privacy of their homes.[1] But clearly there were silk weavers here already.

The huge influx of Huguenot immigrants did however make all the difference. They came to the East End with 'their fine crafts of silk weaving, but also with the mulberry trees on which the silk worms feed', and the character of Spitalfields was changed from a rural to an industrial community almost overnight.[2]

Fifty thousand Huguenots came to London, 15,000 of them settling in Spitalfields, which represented a huge increase in the overall population of the East End (all told, about 250,000).

The Huguenots were wealthy asylum seekers, refugees from political/religious oppression. Indeed, the word 'refugee' ('réfugié') was introduced into England with them. Their long-term impact was impressive. They helped set up the Bank of England, the first Governor of which was a Huguenot, and they brought huge changes to Spitalfields, which astutely they saw suited their purposes: trading just outside the city walls they avoided the restrictive practices of the city guilds, which made it illegal for foreigners to ply their trade within.

Sir William Wheeler had begun to develop the area from fields to terraced streets from 1650, but with the arrival of the Huguenots the process gained new momentum.

Spending freely of their wealth, which the French king had allowed them to retain, they built large and distinguished brick houses in the area of Commercial Street and Brick Lane. Into their prettily planted gardens they imported mulberry trees, the silk worm's natural host, the first species native to India and Pakistan to find Spitalfields to its liking.

Names of certain streets, like Mulberry Street and

Fournier Street, which connects Commercial Street to Brick Lane, return us to this time.

Today, one Huguenot house in particular commands our attention. No 19 Princelet Street. One street away from Fournier, it is a time capsule for two and a half centuries of the history of this area, and opens its doors to the public on certain days of the year. Built in 1719 by Samuel Worrall, its first occupant was the silk-weaving Ogier family. There is an elegant, wood-panelled spaciousness, which marks it out as a gentleman's residence, and the splendid, light-enhancing sash windows make it a gentleman weaver's delight.

These French weavers were custodians of a great artistic tradition. The beautiful gold- and silver-threaded silks, with their intricate floral designs, seemed to reflect the cultured weave of their own lifestyles, which were delicate, rich, not at all like those of the rough rural weavers of the north of England, for example.

Soon French was as commonly heard in the streets of this part of the East End as the clicking of looms and the heart-rending lament of the songbirds they kept in cages to entertain them while they worked. The East End tradition of keeping birds started here. Thomas Oakey recalled in the 1930s –

> Pegging for chaffinches was a favourite Sunday amusement, and the captive songsters were waged against each other in public houses – a cruel sport, in some cases involving the quenching of the birds' eyes with red-hot wire to stimulate their singing . . . The

> district was settled in former times by a colony of the
> thirteen thousand Huguenot refugee silk weavers exiled
> by the Edict of Nantes . . . The French name of the street
> where my dame school was situate [Fleur-de-lis Street]
> and the older houses in Quaker Street, with their
> characteristic broad windows built to accommodate the
> silk-weavers' looms, were evidence of the status of the
> early immigrants.

The Huguenots also spread north, beyond Brick Lane into Bethnal Green. They are credited with founding Bethnal Green 'as an industrial centre'.[3] The silk upholstery trade spawned the furniture industry, both here and in Shoreditch. By 1950, there were between 8,000 and 10,000 furniture workers in the East End. Curtain Road in Shoreditch and Gossett Street in Bethnal Green were the hub.

But it was not all a bed of roses. From 1775 the silk trade began to decline, owing to competition from abroad. As local weavers felt the pinch, they rose against the French. Newspapers of the time reported –

> The Spitalfields weavers do conspire and intend to
> petition to his Majesty the purpose of which is in
> opposition to the French weavers in their neighbour-
> hood. Others say that if they can get a sufficient number
> together they will rise.

Hordes of men declaring themselves to be East End weavers stormed into Brick Lane and the surrounding streets. Attacking anyone and anything French, they broke 'all their materials and defaced several of their houses and greatly disturbed the City'.

The downturn had other effects. In the face of adversity the Huguenots showed themselves to be sound East Enders, doing everything in their power to promote a benevolent community spirit, providing charity (food, clothing and money) for their people through their churches, like L'Eglise Neuve, now the mosque on Brick Lane. In 1797, a Huguenot soup kitchen, known as le Soup, was also opened in Brick Lane.

At No 19 Princelet Street, the attic windows were altered to let in more light for lower-key multiple weaving workshops. The industry and the area were changing. Huguenot residences were divided into smaller-scale apartments and workshops, often to be turned over to other crafts and practices. As 'some of the last of the old French refugees dozed away the evenings of their lives in pretty summer-houses, amidst flower-beds gay with virginia stocks and creeping plants'[4] in Bethnal Green, the whole area was becoming 'a region of small makers'.[5]

A love of gardening would remain a feature here. 'Flowers were everywhere. Most front windows displayed such plants as fuchsia, trained on a wood frame, geranium, India rubber plants, etc,' recalled Lilian Hine of the 1930s, remembering in particular 'little two-roomed cottages with land', which had 'flowers everywhere, and pumpkins, and even grapes'.

There were hand loom weavers in the area until 1939, 'and the last Huguenot silk firm closed its lofty weaving rooms in 1955',[6] but during the nineteenth century, as the silk industry waned, Bethnal Green was flooded with labourers, hawkers, furniture makers, general dealers, shoemakers, washerwomen, sawyers, and costermongers, the lifestyle of some of which couldn't have been more different to that of the cultured French silk weaver.

> Costers didn't live in homes. They lived in lodgings, where they dossed down for a bit, and then moved on. The lodgings were always unspeakably squalid and cheerless, because costers and their women were hardly ever in them. Life was lived in the streets, the markets, the pubs, the penny hops, the penny gaffs, the race tracks, the bawdy houses. Life, with all its richness, was lived outside. Costers went back to their lodgings only for a few hours' kip, before the next day dawned and the markets opened.[7]

In time, the neighbourhood was swelled by a rough bunch of impoverished and discontented natives availing themselves of cheap lodging on the edge of the city, including a scattering of Caribbeans and Africans bought out of slavery. Also, immigrant Irish labourers came to find work in the emerging East End docks and were themselves set upon by rioters when it became known that they were prepared to work for lower wages than were the norm.

As an East End vicar, the Reverend G. C. Daw, recalled:

After the fall of the Huguenot silk weavers, their fine
houses in Spitalfields were largely let out in tenements,
whereas a generation or so earlier they were all occupied
by good families. Now, the weavers are all gone, and
with them the old glory of the place has departed. We
have one or two silk factories in the parish, but they are
quite modern; and factory life at the East-end of
London, even under the best conditions, is not what we
should like it to be. You asked me what class our people
belong to. We have a good number of factory hands,
and of respectable artisans, but we have still more of the
lower classes, such as market porters, dock labourers,
costermongers, and the like. Single rooms are a special
feature of this part, and frequently we find a whole
family huddled together in one room, the rent of which
ranges from 2s. 6d. to 3s. 6d. a week.

By the 1930s vast numbers of out-of-work furniture
makers could be seen in Curtain Road every day, and
the cottage industry was vulnerable to market changes.
There were no warehouses; even large workshops were
few and far between.

There was nothing safe in cabinet-making – you'd got to
be a first-class man to work for people like Maple's or
Harrod's. Otherwise cabinet-making was no bloody good
at all – too much hard work, slave labour, kids wouldn't
stick it.[8]

Other small-scale industries also struggled – sawmills, caster-making, locks, hinges, dowels, glass, organ-building and all the other little trades of the district. There were, as well, the breweries, Mann's and Truman's, and the railways, but hundreds of small masters employed a few men in residential houses, 'thereby saving their employers factory space and any responsibility to their employees . . .' recalled Lilian Hine, 'Little children worked with their mothers many hours into the night, all to earn about a shilling a day.' She also recalled 'men with big baskets of boot uppers', boys and men with 'clothes in a black cloth cover going to the tailors. Barrows laden with goods made at home, such as furniture, brushes, etc.'

Sam Clarke described houses in Bethnal Green where the families lived in the lower storeys and the upper rooms were used as tailoring workshops. Tailoring was another large industry in the East End, but again, although a cutter-out was better paid than other sorts of tailoring work, unless you owned the business there was little to be made out of the sweatshop regime of high yield and competitive pricing. The work was also seasonal.

Tailoring wasn't actually a well-paid job, no. In fact a tailor was one of the poorest jobs in the game. Yeah it was very poor. In fact we used to make a garment . . . we used to get a shilling for every coat we made, like tailored, it was a shilling and if you were on £4 or £5 at the end of the week you was lucky 'cause it was not bad wages at that time. So, of course in those days the money went much further than today. I mean you could do a hell of a lot with £5. You could live a whole week for that money, which you can't do that today.[9]

CHAPTER SIX

Tailors, bakers and furniture makers

———

Some East Enders did get rich out of tailoring however, as they did out of furniture-making and out of all sorts of other mini-industries in the East End, and in particular out of renting space to the little workshops cum living quarters with which increasingly the East End was identified. But the profiteers were not your indigenous cockney.

As to the Jews and their skill in getting possession of houses, it must be owned that in many cases they deserve them, for they have keen sight and swift judgment. A few years ago I should not have thought that Poplar was a favourite Jewish hunting-ground. Even to-day if you look at the names above the shops you will see more Browns and Smiths than Birnbaums and Israelvitches. But I am told by many independent witnesses that the number of Jews in the borough is increasing fast; and it has been pointed out to me that a new synagogue has arisen on the site once occupied by Church schools. An old soldier, who complained bitterly that he could find no house, said: 'There was one I would have liked, only I hadn't the "ready". There was a bit of a shindy a year or so ago, Chinese riots, and so on; the crowd broke down the doors and windows, and made a bonfire in the street. Next morning, when the owner was looking at the wreck, along comes a Jew, and offers him £200 down for it. He gets it, and has to spend £80 putting the place together again. Now he lives in it, with his family and some workpeople – they make clothes – and some of them sleeps whilst the others works, and then they take it turn and turn about. Coining money he is.'

The article, about Poplar, appeared in a magazine written in April 1924. It ended:

But it doesn't do to go against the Jews. It's Bible, or something. If you go against them you don't prosper. That's why Russia went to pieces; they weren't very kind to the Jews there.

It is true. The 8,000 to 10,000 furniture workers in the East End were in fact Jewish managed. The Jews also owned the tailoring sweatshops and many of the houses in which people lived and from which they operated their workshops. But relatively few of them were in Poplar.

There had been a Jewish settlement in the East End on and off since William the Conqueror welcomed them in the eleventh century for their particular facility with finance, as he sought to get the British economy on its feet. The Jews were then expelled by Edward I in 1290, but from 1649, during the period of the Commonwealth, Sephardic Jews (of Spanish, Portuguese or North African descent) settled both in Spitalfields and a mile to the south, around Goodman's Fields and Mansell Street in Whitechapel. The families of those we met were a further influx, however, hastened by oppression and massacre in Eastern Europe. This time, from the 1880s, Ashkenazi Jews came from Russia, Poland, and Lithuania in particular, fleeing from the pogroms, and settled in a neighbourhood just north of the Mansell Street settlement, where the famous Petticoat Lane market became their own and they set up more than a thousand tailoring workshops. In 1888 the social reformer Beatrice Webb reported:

> In this quarter thirty or forty thousand Jews of all
> nationalities and from all countries congregate, and form
> in the midst of our cosmopolitan metropolis a compact

Jewish community. Judisch [Yiddish] is a language of the streets, and Hebrew characters are common in shop windows and over doorways. Overcrowding in all its forms, whether in the close packing of human beings within four walls, or in the filling up of every available building space with dwellings and workshops is the distinguishing mark of the district.

The pogroms[1] meant the systematic destruction of the Jews, their property and religious and commercial buildings and interests by the Russians. Vicki Green was born into a Jewish family in the East End of London in 1916. Her parents had fled the pogroms:

Most of our contemporaries came from parents who were immigrants from either Russia or Poland. They left home in their youth to get away from the pogroms and the Cossacks who would ride through their villages pillaging and destroying people's humble homes. They left their parents fully realising they might never see them again.

These Jews, the parents of Jewish cockneys like Vicki, spread throughout Whitechapel and Spitalfields, up to the top of Brick Lane, but rarely beyond into Bethnal Green; they also spread east from Whitechapel into Stepney. In 1896 Henry Walker wrote that the Jewish settlement was so numerous that it was superseding the lower class of Londoners.

And of course family and community, Samuel

Barnett's active citizenship, the concept that every man has a duty to his fellow man, was as natural a concept to these immigrant Jews in the face of their appalling persecution, as it was to the indigenous East Enders in the face of theirs. Indeed, probably more so, for the so-called indigenous East Ender was often not far from being an immigrant himself and under pressure only from himself:

> My own people, who I once thought of as East Enders back to when Adam was a lad, I discovered came from rural Essex around the Billericay area.[2]

Being thrust into the Whitechapel ghetto intensified the spirit of Jewish togetherness and community, and became the model or prototype for East Ender togetherness:

> My parents couldn't afford to entertain, but in those days in the East End you wouldn't wait for an invitation you'd just walk in. The room was always full of people, women who would come in to talk to my mother. They'd make a cup of tea and talk for hours and hours.[3]
>   When the temperature rose a bit everybody took their chairs, ordinary kitchen chairs like these, outside and spent their leisure and spare time in the evenings when they weren't working, on the pavement outside and that engendered a great community because when you walked past, there were all your neighbours sitting there, including the people who lived in the same block

as you and you exchanged greetings and gossiped and ruined each other's characters of course. It was very much a community.[4]

And not only did they form model street communities, they led the way in instituting social and commercial infrastructures. Theirs was the energy behind the start up of countless East End businesses. The Jews created the rag trade, the shoe trade, the furniture trade. And they had a great safety net. No one was allowed to founder within the community. They set up the social, industrial, religious and educational infrastructure that ensured it rarely happened.

One group from Poland formed the Loyal United Friends Friendly Society to help newcomers set up, find a job and a place to live. Another converted the church in Brick Lane, L'Eglise Neuve, into a synagogue, and soon there were Jewish free schools on every corner. The community soon dominated Spitalfields, White-chapel, and further east, into Stepney.

The East End was full of Jews. Every turning we had a Jewish School there. In our school I don't suppose there were more than two non-Jewish boys . . . In those days people were very very religious and you wouldn't think of lighting a fire on the Sabbath. Before the Sabbath you'd lay the fire and have a non-Jewish woman come round on the day and light it, and come round two or three times that day and put coke on it.

Not all were as committed to Jewishness, however. Ralph Finn points out the distinction between the second generation Dutch and Spanish Jews in the East End (the Choots – [pronounced Hutz]) and the newer immigrants from Poland, Russia, Lithuania etc. The Choots were less observant of religious practices, they drank, they gambled, and they ate traife (forbidden foods).[5]

> The Choots rapidly became cockneyfied. They spoke in the broad vowel sounds of the true East Ender. Like them, they were brash and warm and vulgar and extrovert and funny and stout hearted and loyal to their friends and though they did not wear their hearts on their sleeves as openly as the Polacks, they could be sympathetic and compassionate . . . in an English sort of way.[6]

Among these, some sought further to integrate with the host nation by anglicising their names.

> See my father's name was Maurice Mogolovski, so you put your name on the shop and you have to put Maurice Mogolovski, but all of a sudden, he had a brainwave, he was looking at his passport and he had Mogolovski M. Mogolovski first and then Maurice, so what he did was he didn't change it he just put M. Morris, and that's how we traded, M. Morris. He was no fool the old man, he knew the score.

Others were less successful at becoming part of the larger East End community –

> My parents were foreigners and remained foreigners.
> They spoke broken English as well as they could, [but]
> none of them were citizens of 20th-century London so
> to speak, none of them knew what it had to offer or
> anything, just this little, completely isolated ghetto
> existence, like a bit of Holy Russia of the 1890s plonked
> down in Whitechapel, that's what it was like.[7]

This is not to say that they mistrusted or disliked the British. The same parents, refugees from Tsarist Russia, born in Riga and in Grovna, both parts of the Russian Empire, were proud to live under the British flag –

> The first thing my father did when he got here was to
> wait all night in Ludgate Circus so that he could cheer
> Queen Victoria when she drove to St. Paul's on her
> Diamond Jubilee, that was 1887 I believe, yes. He was,
> he became a great patriot, he realised the privilege that
> Englishmen enjoyed which he didn't enjoy . . .[8]

This was a common reaction on arrival in Britain –

> My mother said that as she came along the Thames she
> saw Tower Bridge open and she thought, 'Ah, it's like
> the arms of a Mother welcoming me. So she felt a sense
> of security.'[9]

But these Jews were much more pragmatic than the East Ender. For them, the East End was a means to an end. They created their community, and then left with it, moving out to more salubrious areas as soon as they could.

> The Jewish people, as they prospered, wanted to get out of the East End. They had suffered and that suffering united them. Once they began to prosper they moved out. We were no exception. We followed the Jews that left because they were our market. Stoke Newington, Kingsland Road, Stamford Hill, Clapton, Kilburn, Golders Green.[10]
>
> Why do you think the Jews moved out of the East End? It was because they started doing much better. They all started to do much better. I mean a lot of the Pakistanis have moved out as well for the same sort of reason, they wanted to get out.[11]

So, this was the great difference. The Jews were there on sufferance. There was none of the loyalty to the East End we associate with the war-time British cockneys, who 'would rather camp in the kitchens of their uninhabitable blitzed houses or sleep in public shelters than accept accommodation in another area of the Borough'.[12]

The Jewish East Enders were, first and foremost, pragmatic, and *productive*. At home, the Russian Jews had not been allowed to trade in any way at all. So, if they wanted a chair, they had to make it themselves or go to another in the ghetto who made the furniture. Right from the start when they came to the East End they were employers. They employed labour, and often they got started thanks to the help given to them by their own kind in the ghetto, and by organisations set up by the community for the purpose.

My father's name was Aaron Newman, but everyone called him Alf for short. He was born in the East End. His father came from Poland, and I think he came over about the turn of the century, as a result of the pogroms. It's funny, my son is a Rabbi, and he was at a synagogue in Commercial Road taking a service about three or four years ago, and that synagogue called Congregation of Jacob in Commercial Road was where my grandfather came when he came to London in 1900 or thereabouts. At that time there was no social security, you couldn't sign on and get unemployment benefit. What amazed me, when they came over they couldn't speak English, so what did they do? Other Jews got them jobs or houses. My grandfather was a machiner in a factory, in the clothing business. My other grandfather, my mother's father, was named Marks Gershonwald, he was also in the profession. He was a presser and my mother used to tell me he could take a piece of cloth and make himself a suit which must have been fantastic, hand-made. He was a very strong man, he had been in the Russian army. At that time, Jewish boys of about fourteen were dragged off the street and put in the army. A very, very tough life. He used to tell

me they'd stand outside the sentry boxes and they had
to be given vodka to heat themselves up, as it was so
cold in Moscow, a terrible life. We lived in a block of
flats called Evelyn House, which is still there, in Old
Montague Street, just off Brick Lane.[13]

Tailoring may have seemed to the workers 'one of the
poorest jobs in the game', but there was no shortage of
staff, and huge profits were made, as Willy Goldman
recalled:

The tailoring workers were a class on their own. They
even looked alike. The majority were small, round-
shouldered men with an eternally weary air, who
appeared from their houses startlingly spruce and clean-
shaven every Saturday afternoon. By Monday they would
be their old selves again. They were weekend Cinderellas.
    Their habits were identical too. They smoked a lot
and sat outside their doors in summer. They were the
most solid, dependable strata in the rock of our street
society. Most evenings would find them with their family.
Even a call on a relative was a rare adventure. Apart
from the seasonal vagaries of their trade they were
regarded as model husbands by the women.[14]

The Newmans' sweatshop was just off Brick Lane. It
specialised in ladies' coats, and soon took off.

The business was doing very, very well, so much so that I
remember there were three directors and they went out

and bought three Humber Super Snipes to offset against their tax. It was a big thing at that time. I can still remember him bringing home a lovely shiny new car. It was good, we were kids. At its peak they were maybe making 1,500 to 2,000 garments a week. I can still remember going into the factory and the majority of the employees were Jewish, mainly women, and the noise was terrific. The sounds of machines, the women chattering away gave you a buzz when you walked through.

Having a loathing for living in the East End, Andrew Newman's father moved to the coast, to Westcliff-on-Sea in Essex. His son Andrew was only too pleased to get out of it.

I don't know how people could live in the East End. My parents moved to Westcliff-on-Sea – wide open, with the sea front and the beach, that's the reason why I could never live in the East End.

Another factory owner, Alf Stuart's dad, Harry Schwartz, left due to pressure of work.

My father had a factory manufacturing dresses. Originally he came from Piotrykov, a textile centre and one of the oldest cities in Poland. He left there when the pogroms were on and he went to South Africa, where he opened up a business selling ready made suits in a place called Kimberley, at one time the centre for diamond mines. He was right by the side of the diamond mines. At 24 he came to London, took a large shop in East Ham and at the back of the shop he built on a factory. He had about seven workers at the time, two women but mostly men, because not only did my father make dresses, he made coats as well. He was there till he had Sir Herbert French come to see him one day and said, 'Mr Stuart, you've got to get out of this place and take it easy.' Sir Herbert French was the top physician in London in those days, he was the Queen's physician. My father had duodenal ulcers, very very bad and he was told he should only eat boiled eels, and he wouldn't eat them you see. The doctor also said, 'I want you to move to Southend-on-Sea,' because its very healthy in Southend, the air is very good here. So we moved, and we had a big house.[15]

Young Bernard Kops was shocked by what he saw of the sweatshop where his sister Phoebe worked. Later in life he wrote a play for Radio 4 called *The Lost Love of Phoebe Myers*, 'a lot based on my sister, about working conditions':

Well, the sweatshop, you can still see it, it's still there, Bangladeshi kids are there now, but if you go down to Brick Lane you will see it. I suppose it was the amount of people crowded into a small room . . . And the sounds, the clatter and the girls chattering all the time above the sounds of the machinery and being very somehow happy, you know, a sweatshop, well it was sweaty. But I mean there wasn't despondency in any way it was just people crowded into this very noisy atmosphere. Yes, and it went on all day and they were laughing and joking about boyfriends and things like that, but totally, totally claustrophobic, and the boss walking around and making sure that everything is alright.

Nobody got work in those days, there was so much unemployment and suddenly one day my big sister Phoebe, she was older than me, she came and said 'I've got a job, I've got a job' and nobody could believe it – my Mother went 'Thank God' sort of thing, and then 'How did you get the job?' and she said 'Well, I saw Improvers Wanted, so I went in, the boss said OK you can start Monday'. So the following Monday, my mum makes sandwiches for her and we all got up and watch her going off to work – one wage would help tremendously – so she goes off and Mum is all day looking and saying, 'I hope she'll be alright, I hope she'll be alright.' Anyway, home time we are all looking over the railings to see her coming home and we see her coming and she doesn't look up or give a wave or anything, and when she comes upstairs she's crying. She rushes into her room and my mum says, 'Leave it to me, don't you dare say a word.' And she goes in and we can hear my sister crying her eyes out.

Apparently what happened was that the boss took her on because he liked the look of her and he had called her into the office and started to get fresh with her and it was called, not interfering, though yes, he was sort of interfering with her, and my mother said,

'She's not going back there.' But my father said, 'She's got to, because we need the money.' And then they were rowing on this level of terrifying need for money. And morality!

The Monnikendams arrived in the East End and set up a bakery business in Petticoat Lane in Whitechapel, taking advantage of situations as they arose, as J. Monnikendam recalled:

I was born over the shop. I used to deliver on a bike. He had bought the shop where he used to work – Harry Joseph's. Harry was a bit of a gambler, used to run across the road and have a bit of a bet. Got into financial trouble. Dad took the business over from him, and Harry started working for him.

At the start father would be baking in the cellar. Mother would serve on the ground floor. Father was bemoaning one day that he didn't have the money to buy tables and chairs and make tea rooms upstairs. Mother said she would give him the money. She had been keeping back one gold sovereign from the takings every week . . .

Why he prospered was that he introduced into his shop the kind of pastries that they ate on the Continent, which were more or less strange to the people of London. People used to come down the Lane on Sundays. The pastries were a penny each, thirteen for a bob, and they could buy pastries they had neither seen nor heard of outside the East End. The Lane was originally a food market. It relied on the English people coming into the Lane to buy things like olives and Dutch herrings – I think, even smoked salmon – that few had heard of.

The Herreras started up in similar fashion. Luck, it seems, favoured those who took a chance:

My parents' life is fifty times more interesting than my life, because mine, whatever it is, all these modern things and everything, it's easy, and they had a hard life. They both came from Poland and one day they were walking along and they saw a shop, a barber's shop, but it was in Stepney Green which wasn't built then, nothing was built except this row of houses, because it belonged to the brewery, Charingtons, you see. My father said that all the animals used to graze on the grass. So, he got into this barber's shop and said to the man, 'Can I have a job – I've been a fishmonger in Poland – will I be able to do barbering?' And the man said, 'Yeah, I think you will. If you can cut fish you'll be able to cut hair!'! Anyway, the following day when he came into work he found the man dead on the floor. He had dropped dead! He'd had a heart attack and nobody was in the shop. Well, my father got a bit panicky, because here he was an immigrant, and here he was left like that! Anyway, the police knew all about it and they didn't blame my father. So the landlord come running – he was a Jewish man, Mr Rosen – and he said to my father, 'Well, if you want it, keep the

shop.' And that's how they started off their life in
Stepney Green, he was there fifty years.[16]

Playwright Bernard Kops was born at Stepney Green
Buildings in 1926, the youngest of seven children of
Jewish immigrants, and gives the clearest picture of how
completely the Jewish community took over the East
End.

There were about 250,000 Jewish people in the East End
in my childhood. The only world I knew was the Jewish
world. I didn't know any other world. There was the
Yiddish newspaper, Yiddish signs – even boxing matches
and wrestling matches were written in the Hebrew script
– and at the heart of this Jewish world was Brick Lane.
Brick Lane embraced the whole community because
everything you needed was found there. You could have
your hair cut there, then there was Lou the
shoemaker . . . Further down the road you would hear
cluck, cluck, cluck, cluck, you know that sound that
chickens make, obviously they were coming towards the
end of their cackling, and out would come the men to
have a smoke in their aprons, their white aprons covered
in blood.

There was a Mr Katz, long gone, but not so long
ago, his was the last Jewish shop in this area. He was a
string maker. I mean a sort of amazing occupation –
what do you do for a living? – I make string! I string
them along!

Then there was Esther the sweet woman who was a

bit mad, everyone said, and she used to do quite well selling sweets outside secondary school, and all the kids used to rile her and shout at her and all the rest of it, it was like football crowds making monkey noises. She was Jewish.

Then there was the bagel woman. On the corner of Brick Lane, near Bloom's and I can still hear her saying (high voice) 'Bagel, bagel, bagel, bagel!' She sounded like some bird, some weird bird chirping away and she had a mad, well we would say a mad daughter.

Yiddish was *the* language of Whitechapel and Spitalfields in the first half of the twentieth century.

Whitechapel in those days was exciting. It was all Jewish! The whole East End was Jewish. Yiddish was spoken in every home; Yiddish was spoken in the streets; the shopkeepers spoke Yiddish. We had three daily Yiddish newspapers! Daily! Three! Yiddish books were printed here. There were always two Yiddish theatres in the East End of London.[17]

Everybody spoke Yiddish, as this was the heartland of London's East End ghetto. In fact, I don't know how I managed at school, as I didn't know a single word of English. Indeed, many years later, when I was about nine, I was shown a picture of a bowl and said it was a 'schissel' – I had never even heard the word bowl.[18]

Non-Jewish people living in the East End often spoke Yiddish and certainly understood it. It was a concoction

of German and English and Hebrew. I can't speak
Yiddish, but I can understand it. I can go to a play and
understand it. My grandfather and grandmother spoke
it. My mother and father could understand it, but not
speak it. There's no other language like it. A real mixture.
And sometimes you'd hear a cockney speak it.[19]

Ralph Finn recalled his mother having great fun 'yiddishing' the English language, especially people's names:

Paddy Rourke 'yiddished' into Paddy Footbollick and
Morry Lesher into Morry Sorry. She called the local
roadsweeper, whose name apparently was Alfie Moss,
Mossy-ossy-shit. She was not being vulgar. Yiddish has
the peculiar quality of taking words for natural functions
and using them naturally. Zaida's Pish-ooskie and Mossy's
ossy-four-letter-word can be uttered in the politest
Yiddish speaking company. In fact, you've only to say
'Ich bettach dir tzoo far-zeihen' – 'I beg you to overlook
this' – and you can then come out with a string of four
letter words that would do credit to the Chatterley
gamekeeper or Joyce's Bloom.[20]

Finn also remembered a non-Jewish market trader 'who'd learned a few words of Yiddish and called in a Billingsgate accent: 'Veiber, veiber, vehr kohft?'[21] 'Verh kohft' means 'Who's buying?'

The Jewish Mamma was of course also the mythic original, going way back in history, and prototype for the matriarchal figure that ruled the British cockney East Ender families. Vicki Green recalls hers:

> She was a typical Yiddisher mother. She cared for us, she would take the food off her own plate and put it on to our plates. In those days we had open coal fires with an old-fashioned grate to protect us from the fire and in the morning she would light the fire before we wakened and hang our vests and knickers on the top of the grate so that they would be warm ready for us to put on. She would bring in a little stool and a bowl of hot water where we could wash in front of the fire because there was no heating, certainly no central heating and we always had a good meal and after our dinner because we were so very, very poor we either could have a ha'penny, a half old penny, which we would spend with the old lady who had a perambulator outside the school with toffee bars and sweets; we could either have a ha'penny or sun. Now you'll ask me what was sun. Sun was a piece of fruit but it wasn't a whole apple or a whole orange, our parents couldn't afford that, they would go to the market across the road towards the evening and buy what the greengrocer had left on his stall which was perhaps a little bit bad and they would bring it home and cut off the bad part and give us the rest of the fruit. We ate well although it wasn't a moneyed home but we always had a good meal and a good bed.[22]

Many Jews lived, like Bernard Kops, in tenements built especially for the London Jewish poor.

We lived right at the top. When I was a kid it was like, miles high, can you imagine seven kids in that one small flat? The place always smelled, especially of cabbage, you know the smell of boiled cabbage is about the worst smell in the world, but you know cabbage was one of the staple foods of our time, and lentils and butter beans, everyone was farting you know, you live on beans you fart a lot. My mother would like stagger up, like preparing for the ascent to base camp, and every time she got up a flight she would stop and she would, 'Aah,' she would sigh. It's the Esperanto of the Jewish world, sighing, they sighed all the time. Sometimes my father would look at the wall, and, 'Aah,' and in that sigh was this whole discontent that the hand fate had given him.

These were set up by the East End Dwelling Company, these flats for families so that the rent was pretty low. A lot of these buildings, like the Rothschild Building, all round the East End there are these flats for families. The floor was covered with lino [linoleum]. Lino was around in the Edwardian times. I remember that there were great areas that weren't covered, so we were on to the floor boards. There was no bathroom. They had a communal wash house on the end of a block. There was a lavatory and a zinc bath, one living room and two bedrooms, and most of the children slept in one bedroom, seven to two beds. Mind you, we used to play cricket and football. We had what we called 'the airing', an area downstairs, a space for hanging out the washing and for kids to play.

It took a woman like the midwife Jennifer Worth, with daily contact with women living in these places, really to empathise with their problems.

> When you consider the physical effort required to carry all the shopping up those stairs: coal and wood in the winter, paraffin for stoves, or rubbish carried down to the dustbins in the courtyard; if you consider the fact that to take the baby out, the pram had to be bumped down the stairs, one step at a time, and then bumped up again to get home, often loaded with groceries, as well as the baby, you might begin to understand how tough those women had to be. Almost every time you entered the tenements, you would see a woman bumping a big pram up or down. If they lived at the top, this would mean bumping about seventy steps each way. The prams had big wheels, which made it possible, and were well sprung, which bounced the baby around. The babies loved it, and laughed and shrieked with glee. It was also dangerous if the steps were slippery, because the whole weight of the pram had to be controlled by the handle, and if the mother missed her footing or something happened and she let go, the pram and baby would go cascading down the length of the steps. I always helped when I saw a woman with a pram by taking the other end, therefore half the weight, which was considerable. The whole weight, for a woman alone, must have been tremendous.[23]

Meanwhile, No 19 Princelet Street off Brick Lane was entering another phase of its existence. After the Jews moved into the area, the Polish-Jewish Loyal United Friends Friendly Society took a lease on the property, dug up the garden where the Huguenot Ogier children once played, dug down more than a floor's depth at the back of the house, and built a glass-roofed synagogue, which can now lay claim to being the second oldest in London. The wood panels of the ladies' gallery high above the synagogue floor still carry written records of donations from the faithful. And deep down beneath it, there is a secret meeting place, where plans were laid to fight the fascist foe in the 1930s.

I liked the view from Princelet Street because you overlooked the rooftops and saw the soaring steeples of Christ Church, Spitalfields. Incidentally, on a Sunday I was always charmed because there'd be a carolling of the bells, and it would be whacked across the skyline. In fact I wrote a poem because of that. Also, the chanting on Sunday there used to come from Hebrew classes in a Brick Lane Talmud Torah. They would be reciting by heart you know, some Hebrew, and it whacked across and it would blend with the sound of the bells.[24]

When Bernard Kops was six or seven, his father lost his job, and his family was thrown on the mercy of the Jewish community:

The boss came up to my father one day and said Mr
Kops you look tired, you need a holiday. My father said –
really? – and he said I think you must pick up your
wages and that's the end of it Mr Kops. And that was it
for the rest of his life. I mean, he was forty five. He was
very very bitter. He was very naïve as well. But he had
one great gift that he somehow acquired probably from
his forebears and that was a love and a knowledge of
music. He passed that on to me, I think. He took me to
Aida, and it opened my eyes. I mean, without that it is
quite possible that I wouldn't have gone into the
theatre, gone this far.

**With the loss of the family income the struggle to
survive was even greater, but the ghetto had a safety net
ready made for the Kops family.**

Meals consisted mainly of us going to the Jewish soup
kitchen in Whitechapel and coming home with a saucepan
full of soup and black bread. That was often our main
meal in the evening. I can't remember the day time thing.

There was always a queue here, they were always in
business. Business was very brisk and the smell the same
every time you came. You would queue and you would
shuttle in and you would come up to the long table and
the soup was in great urns and it was ladled into your
saucepan and you would grab bread. The soup was
nearly always the same. It was thick green pea soup. It
was a meal. And black bread, chunks of black bread.
There was a funny sort of eroticism about it for a boy of

ten years old who was just stirring into the beauty of female flesh. There was that lovely smell of their scent and a place of otherness. Where did they come from? They weren't like ladies from the East End at all. Their bosoms heaved.

The Jewish Board of Guardians provided clothing. And you would go up the stairs and there was this enormous room stinking of camphor. Racks and racks of clothes of different kinds, like the biggest charity shop. Although they were too long or too short, they were all in very good condition. You realised that these clothes came from rich houses, made of marvellous material, but the fit, why should it fit? That's what your mother would say. Going home I always remember my father never wanted to go down the main road, he said he didn't want to be seen so he would shuffle along all the back streets. Being poor in this country was an embarrassment, but everyone in this area was poor so there was a strange sort of pride you had in being helped, you didn't want to be helped but you couldn't help yourself, so you had to accept it.

My father had his dreams, my mother had the reality of survival and she took on all the anguish and worry. She borrowed money from a money lender trying to survive day by day, so it would be like five shillings or ten shillings from a money lender, paying back he would come round with a book. When things got too much for her she would sing, and songs like 'You die if you worry, you die if you don't, so why worry at all? It's only worry that killed the cat, anybody can tell you that.'

The Jewish community was especially strong around the
New Road, Cannon Street Road area of Stepney, where
Jack Mogolovski's dad had a baker's shop.

> He made all the Jewish stuff. I was a pretzel maker,
> onion pretzel . . . my pretzels used to go all over London
> on a Sunday morning. All the Yiddisher people stuck
> together like, I mean they really stuck together, it's not
> like that now. Stepney was Israel!

On Philpot Street and Varden Street they set up a
Bakers' Union, with a club house where men would sit
around playing dominoes until a baker came in and
offered them work:

> All of a sudden Ross from Ross Bakers would come in
> and say, 'Who's free tonight?' Ginsberg would stand up
> and say, 'I'm free, I'll come in, what time do you want me
> to start?' And Bernstein would stand up and say, 'Well
> Ginsberg is a friend of mine, I'll go with him, two mates.
> We'll come in tonight.' Maurice would come in and say, 'I
> need a jobber for Friday night.' Friday night, no, no, and
> he would say, 'I'll give you another ten shillings extra, I
> need someone Friday night bad.' Marty would stand up,
> he was a bloke with a trilby hat and spats, dressed to kill
> with a gold walking stick, and he would say, 'I'll be there
> Maurice,' and Maurice would say, 'Don't come with your
> gold walking stick, I want a worker!' And they would
> leave the cards and when they came back they would
> pick the cards up from where they left off, playing the

same bloody game! And they would be left there, you
know, everything would be left there.

Goodman Schneider's father was a foreman baker
at Gradinsky's bakehouse in Berners Street in Whitechapel, and remembers that the union 'had a label
to show the public that if a loaf didn't have it they
shouldn't buy it'. Schneider recalls the hours his father
worked were excessively long and ill-rewarded:

> He would start work at four o'clock in the afternoon and
> come home at midday the following day. On Friday he
> would work 24 hours a day because the women would
> bring their cakes to be baked . . . a special dish for
> Saturday. He would earn 28 shillings a week in those
> days. If they went on strike for one week, which they did
> for many weeks, my mother would cry for him to go
> back to work . . . We couldn't live on 28 shillings a
> week. Nobody earned more than them. That was top
> wages. Nobody earned big wages in those days, and of
> course there were no pensions.

Goodman's mother was well educated, could speak a
few languages, and though she had five children she
managed to start a shop 'to help things along', running
the enterprise out of their house. Once again it was the
community that helped to set it up:

> She opened a little shop selling pinafores, blouses, to try
> and sell things to teachers. She got a loan from the

Jewish Board of Guardians to buy the material. She'd
hang up things in the window and the teachers [from
the school opposite] would come in and buy things. No
shop just front window – private. They'd come into the
front room to buy. And my father used to make bagels
in a figure of 8, the only ones you would see in London
at that time. He used to bake them in the kitchen and I
would push the barrow with him sometimes on a
Sunday morning. He was out all day long Sunday, selling
those bagels.

In Hessel Street, not far from the union, was a wonderful market, full of Jewish shops, delicatessens and so on.

You know where Hessel Street market is? That was a real
ghetto place, all Yiddisher stalls.[25]

At the end of that street, into Langdale Street, was a row
of more colourful tenements, with an artistic element,
called, naturally enough, Langdale Mansions, where
Martin Leonard grew up:

It was a very very famous block of tenement buildings, a
big square – Langdale Street, Wicker Street, playground
in the middle . . . Ted Lewis the heavyweight boxer lived
there, Albert Sumner the violinist lived there, his sister . . .
There was many many people who ended up solicitors,
musicians and actors. And I don't know if you have heard
of him Miles Tzelinker, Anna Tzelinker. Miles Tzelinker
was a personal friend of my brother-in-law, he lived in

Langdale Mansions and I went to his son's bar mitzvah.

We were in very poor circumstances. My father was a machiner for Savile Row, Burberry's. He worked like a horse and when he came home of a night time to help feed his children, he used to go as a night watchman to the Grand Palais, where the Jewish Theatre was upstairs. It was all done in Yiddish, and they used to have lovely musicals with dancing and everything and they used to love it every week there. They had top actors, and everybody used to go there. Marvellous.

In 1936 a new Yiddish theatre was opened, and Miles Tzelinker was asked to run it as actor-manager, as his daughter Anna recalled:

But what theatre? It was the beginning of the war. All theatres and cinemas were closed. They were frightened of too many people in one place in case any bombing took place. But the first year we had no bombing. So after a few months, they allowed the cinemas and theatres to open. And we played matinées to begin with. Then gradually, evening performances as well.

And there were two Yiddish theatres. The big Pavilion Theatre in Whitechapel and the Grand Palais in Commercial Road. And we were always playing against each other.

I'll give you an instance about this 'opposition' business. In the war, we had a play which made history in the Yiddish theatre. It was called *The King of Lampedusa*. Lampedusa is a tiny island at the toe of the

Italian peninsula. It's still there today. In 1943 a British pilot flew his plane over the Mediterranean and saw his petrol was running low. So he either had to crash or land and surrender.

So he swooped down and landed. The islanders who had been bombarded by the Americans and by the Russians and by the English (because there was a German base on that island) had heard of an impending invasion by the Allies. And when they saw this British plane swooping down they thought this was it!

They got hold of white flags and ran towards the plane to surrender. When the pilot said, 'I surrender!' the commander of the island said, 'No, no. I'll sign a piece of paper. Take it back to your base. We'll give you petrol. We are surrendering the island to the Allies.'

This British pilot happened to be a Jewish boy called Sidney Cohen from Hackney. Now, a friend of my father's, who was a journalist and a playwright, thought what a wonderful story. He wrote a play but then he turns it into a dream to make it theatrical, where everybody from the East End lands up on the island of Lampedusa! And the pilot is crowned king!

This play became such a tremendous success. Everybody who was anybody knew about it. All the papers wrote: 'Tremendous!' And we played it for eight months, until the doodlebugs started coming . . . But for eight months we played *The King of Lampedusa*, ten performances a week. And to this day, they talk about it.

During that period the phone rang and a cultured English voice said to the cash box lady would she please reserve four seats for Winston Churchill and company who want to see *The King of Lampedusa* that evening.

Well! You can imagine. It spread like wildfire all round the East End. By the time the evening arrived the theatre had been washed and scrubbed and cleaned, and everybody in the East End knew that Churchill was coming. The theatre was packed and outside the traffic couldn't go by for the amount of people waiting to see Churchill arrive. It was only when a policeman walked into the theatre and asked what all the commotion was about and said, 'What are you talking about? Whenever Churchill goes anywhere we are the first ones to be notified. We've had no such notification. It must have been a hoax.'

Which it was. Played on us by one of the opposite theatres! They were so jealous of the wonderful play.

Besides theatre, the Jewish community financed youth and sporting clubs.

You've heard of Basil Henriques? He was a massive man, about six foot seven inches. Well, in Berners Street was the Oxford and St George's club, which most of us belonged to, a mixed youth club. It was every day of the week. There was a big gymnasium there and everything.[26]

The Oxford and St George's Settlement Jewish Youth Club was founded in 1914 by Basil Henriques at 125 Cannon Street Road, dedicated to improving the lot of young Jews in the East End. Rose Loewe founded a similar club for girls in 1915, and in 1917 they married and were known as 'The Gaffer' and 'The Missus'.

In 1929 the club moved to a former school in Berners Street in Whitechapel, which runs parallel to Backchurch Lane and has now been renamed Henriques Street. There were 125 rooms equipped for welfare work and recreation. All sorts of games, skills and arts and crafts were available to Jewish East End boys and girls. The famous welterweight boxing champion Harry Mizler coached the boys' boxing team.

> The Jewish boys of those days who had not done well at school found in boxing the way to make a living. Many of them fought at the old Wonderland and later at the Premierland [in Backchurch Lane] for a cup of tea and a bun. The greatest of them all, Kid Lewis, a world champion, started that way.
>
> The Kid fought any weight, took on any opponent, was fast, skilful and ruthless. He was not only the greatest of the boxers to come out of the East End, but one of the greatest lightweights of all time; and the world of boxing remembers him too. Not as a Jew but as one of the great British boxers of all time.
>
> I remember when The Kid won his fights, the East End would make merry. He would ride down Whitechapel in an open car flinging handfuls of silver . . . Kid Berg was perhaps next in line to greatness . . . a two-fisted non-stop all-action hammer-away fighter who

didn't know the meaning of the word defeat.

Harry Mizler belonged for a while. He won a British title and everyone was proud of him. A nice boy Harry. Quiet, undemonstrative, sporting, popular. I knew him well. He was a member of the same boys' club – the Oxford and St George's founded by the late Sir Basil Henriques – as I was.[27]

This was not the only sports club run by and for the East End Jewish community.

All the clubs belonged to the Jewish Athletic Association. My brother went to the Victoria Boys Club, Foreman Street, off New Road [Whitechapel]. He was very good at all sports, at boxing, at cricket . . . and in 1912 he won the C.B. Fry Cup for being the finest sportsman. He started work as a cabinet maker when he was fourteen, was apprenticed by the Jewish Board of Guardians, a four-year apprenticeship. The boss used to get drunk and after he'd been working about a year, he refused to work there anymore. But he had an agreement. He went along to the Boys Club and told the managers there and they told him not to go back to work anymore. I know they broke the agreement and found him a job with the *Evening News* and he used to go out and report on sports matches, cricket, boxing.

CHAPTER SEVEN

Docklands

———

The Jewish settlement in Stepney in the late nineteenth and twentieth centuries was very effective
and a model East End community, in its own way,
except that it had no intention of remaining, none of
the loyalty that was, you might say head-in-the-sand
central to the East Ender.

East out of Bethnal Green Road into Roman Road,
you came to what Arthur Harding referred to as 'the
upper working class . . . the respectable working class' –
the sort of people who went to church on a Sunday.
'Lower-middle-class people.'[1]

Today, a green corridor, going south and connecting

all the broken patches of grass between Victoria Park and the Isle of Dogs, takes you down nearly all the way to Limehouse on the Thames. To the east of it lies Bow and then southwards Bow Common and Poplar; to the west is Mile End, Stepney Green, and then Limehouse.

Memories of the area around Grove and Burdett roads, which run down the east side of this green corridor, are of smells, the factories and breweries which, however obnoxious, provided reliable employment.

By sniffing, the cardinal points of the compass identify themselves faithfully by a particular smell: west, horseflesh (for dog-biscuits); north, sulphur-fumes (for matches); north-east, fish manure; and due east, the pungent stench of a paint-works, with gas thrown in for good measure. A certain bridge over Limehouse Cut, in fact, was known as Stink Bridge; few names were better deserved, and I never heard or knew that it had any other.[2]

I turned about and crossed the Mile End Road. Breweries. The smell of spilled beer, barley, hops, horse-manure and piss. Acrid, pungent. Unmistakable. There were still granite setts across the road. Then, and in the fogginess I could hear the horse-hoofs of heavy beer-drays urging back to 'home'. The odour of full-cask and empty-cask, quite different in quality, hung about in the fog, at the brewery entrance. Each smell seemed to carry the weight or the loss of weight of content . . . at the brewery entrance, the smell was one impacted from the techniques of earlier centuries: horse-dung and urine, stale beer and beer-impregnated woods . . .

> Breathlessly I ran back along the Mile End Road . . .
> past a broken necklace of barrow and pushcart, the
> evening straggle of pedlar and commercial pusher, the
> odour of ripe fruits and greengroceries, fustiness of cloth
> bolts and heaped old clothes for sale, the dry, hoarse,
> dustiness of ancient shoes and unlaced boots awaiting a
> depressed custom, an old phonograph hauled past me,
> held in a baby's creaking broken-down perambulator, the
> turn-table winding down to a permanent halt . . . 'South
> Am . . . er . . . ic . . . aaan Jo . . . oo . . . e'. The smell of
> barrelled, brined, schmaltz herrings, splinter-wood boxed
> kippered herrings laid out in greasy rows, their artificial
> varnishings staining the boxes with a smelly, oily excess,
> these and piquant, pickled cucumbers in glass jar or
> small barrel, overpowered all the aromas.[3]

Rows of terraced cottages in Bow Common Lane, Tryphena Place, and Lawes Street, later Sherwood Street, were the remnants of a village that had been there in living memory. Recalled Harry Salton:

> My gran used to talk about green fields in her child-
> hood, and around Whitehorn Street, Frances Mary Buss
> House, part of that building used to be a dairy farm. The
> big hall used to be the cow shed, apparently, and the
> rings were still situated in the walls where the cows were
> tethered and the hay loft, which overlooked Whitethorn
> Street was turned into a library.

In Bow Common Lane, nearly opposite the Sherwood

Arms on the corner of Sherwood Street, was a little cottage all on its own, where Harry remembered an old lady lived 'with her twin sons who must have been 45–50 years old'.

> I never ever knew their names but they were always referred to as the Sand Dancers because they looked the image of the music hall act of that name. Next door to them was a firm that used to cure fish, smoked haddock and kippers etc. The brothers often used to be seen carrying a big tray of large cods' heads which they collected from the fish curers, and it was said they used to cook and eat them.[4]

Farms in these areas will have supplied Spitalfields and other markets. By the second decade of the twentieth century, you would have to ride out further east to find as rural a scene, as Cyril Demarne was wont to do with his mate George White along the Barking Road, through West and East Ham, across the Rippleside crossing to Barking and the verge of Dagenham marsh (in years to come, the site of the massive Ford motor works). As houses and street lights became fewer the two boys would stop and sit by the Chequers pub singing songs and 'drinking in the nectar of the countryside'. And they'd watch the carts laden with produce from the surrounding farms rumbling past, bound for Spitalfields, the carmen invariably asleep, having rigged the front of the cart to allow the horses to plod on without guidance.

Draymen kept the feel of the countryside alive in Bow Common during Harry Salton's childhood. It could have been a million miles away from the Old Nichol:

> The most traffic that we used to see was when the horse and carts of the Wiseman's Stables returned after a day delivering. They used to be parked outside in the road until it was ready for the drivers to take them in the yard and be unharnessed. It was a pleasure for us children to stand and stroke these gentle beasts, who were generally feeding from their nosebags, and every now and then they would throw their heads back to get the last bit of oats or chaff at the bottom of the bag, which made dust go up their nostrils, when they would give a loud snort to clear them again. There was one drayman, Harry Knight, who used to take one of us kids up on his seat, whilst he drove the cart into the stable. It was certainly a thrill for the chosen. I was lucky several times because I lived right opposite.[5]

And so we come, at last, to the Thames and Docklands, and the major industry that drew so many into the East End, both from abroad and from elsewhere in Britain. The docks were the major employer, but also the major exploiter, and the real reason why so many families in the first half of the twentieth century knew hardship.

The first wharf was built in Ratcliff, between Limehouse and Wapping, in 1348, but boats didn't dock to disgorge their goods directly onto land until the nineteenth century. Before that it was the job of lightermen to transfer goods between ships at anchor and such wharfs or quays, aboard flat-bottomed barges called lighters.

Few know where Ratcliff is today, it has all but disappeared, but it used to be the disreputable sister of Limehouse, herself no model of moral purity. The Highway, the belt above the belly of Wapping, link road today between Limehouse and Whitechapel, was once *Ratcliff* Highway, and had a reputation for being the most notorious, villainous and exciting area of dockland.

With the business Ratcliff brought to this neck of the Thames, the hamlet quickly grew, spreading north along Butcher Row, the main route to Stepney and Hackney. From the sixteenth century the shipbuilding industry also took hold at Wapping, Limehouse, and Blackwall. And when the East India Company (chartered by the British Government in 1600 to trade in the East Indies) set up shop at Blackwall Yard, further to the east, a new river community sprang up on this north-bank strip of the Thames east of Tower Bridge, with extraordinary consequences, as Walter Besant described:

> The whole of the riverside population, including not only the bargemen and porters, but the people ashore, the dealers in drink, the shopkeepers, the dealers in marine stores, were joined and banded together in an organised system of plunder and robbery. They robbed the ships of

their cargoes as they unloaded them; they robbed them of their cargoes as they brought them in the barge from the wharf to the ship. They were all concerned in it – man, woman, and child . . .

Of course the greatest robbers were the lightermen themselves; but the boys were sent out in light boats which pulled under the stern of the vessels, out of sight, and received small parcels of value tossed to them from the men in the ships. These men wore leathern aprons which were contrived as water-tight bags, which they could fill with rum or brandy, and they had huge pockets concealed behind the aprons which they crammed with stuff. On shore every other house was a drinking-shop and a 'fence' or receiving shop; the evenings were spent in selling the day's robberies and drinking the proceeds. Silk, velvets, spices, rum, brandy, tobacco – everything that was brought from over the sea became the spoil of this vermin . . . [and] they shielded each other. If the custom-house people or the wharfingers tried to arrest one, he was protected by his companions . . . The people grew no richer, because they sold their plunder for a song and drank up the money every day. But they had, at least, as much as they could drink.

Sailors, on shore for a few weeks while their boat was in dock, were regarded as a similarly legitimate object of plunder. The case of Charles Riley, Mary Robinson and Mary Williams at the Old Bailey is typical. The two women were said to have pulled a young sailor to a house at Salt-petre-bank, but not being strong enough to rob him, they called in Riley, who 'with a naked knife, threatened to cut out his liver if he did not deliver the money'.

The whole area catered to the huge and constant influx of transient sailors, immigrant settlers, as well as brave night-owls from up West in London, all flocking to the taverns and opium dens off Cable Street in Shadwell, to the Railway Tavern in Poplar, which specialised in prostitutes, and to the Chinese gambling and opium dens of Limehouse Causeway and Pennyfields. But it was Ratcliff in particular that really rose to the challenge, as a nineteenth-century commentator recorded:

Up and down Ratcliff-highway do the sailors of every country under heaven stroll – Greeks and Scythians, Lascars, Chinese, bold Britons, swarthy Italians, sharp Yankees, fair-haired Saxons, and adventurous Danes – men who worship a hundred gods, and men who worship none. They have ploughed the stormy main, they have known the perils of a treacherous sea and of a lee shore – but there are worse perils, and those perils await them in Ratcliff-highway.

Every few yards we come to a beer-shop or a public-house, the doors of which stand temptingly open, and from the upper room of which may be heard the sound of the mirth-inspiring violin, and the tramp of toes neither 'light nor fantastic'. Women, wild-eyed, boisterous, with cheeks red with rouge and flabby with intemperance, decked out with dresses and ribbons of

the gayest hue, are met with by hundreds – all alike
equally coarse, and insolent, and unlovely in manners
and appearance, but all equally resolved on victimising
poor 'Jack'. They dance with him in the beer-shop – they
drink with him in the bar – they walk with him in the
streets – they go with him to such places as Wilton's
Music Hall . . . The grog gets into Jack's head, the unruly
tongue of woman is loosened – there are quarrels, and
blows, and blood drawn, and heads broken, and cries of
police . . .

Punishments for looting cargoes and attacking and
robbing sailors could be severe. Next to Wapping Old
Stairs, still there today off Wapping High Street, is
Execution Dock, as Walter Besant noted:

This was the place where sailors were hanged and all
criminals sentenced for offences committed on the
water; they were hanged at low tide on the foreshore,
and they were kept hanging until three high tides had
flowed over their bodies . . . Among the many hangings
at this doleful spot is remembered one [in
particular] . . . The prisoner was conveyed to the spot in
a cart beside his own coffin, while the ordinary sat
beside him and exhorted him. He wore the customary
white nightcap and carried a prayer book in one hand,
while a nosegay was stuck in his bosom. He preserved a
stolid indifference to the exhortations; he did not change
colour when the cart arrived, but it was remembered
afterward that he glanced round him quickly. They

carried him to the fatal beam and they hanged him
up . . . [But] no sooner was the man turned off than a
boat's company of sailors, armed with bludgeons,
appeared most unexpectedly, rushed upon the
constables, knocked down the hangman, hustled the
chaplain, overthrew the sheriff's officers, cut down the
man, carried him off, threw him into a boat, and were
away and in midstream, going swiftly down with the
current before the officers understood what was going
on.

There had been gibbets on the Isle of Dogs since at
least the eighteenth century. They are depicted on
Rocque's map (1746), and when the idle apprentice in
Hogarth's depiction is seen being rowed down
Limehouse Reach, it is towards a hanged man on the
Isle that one of his companions points. The seven
windmills lining the bank, which gave Millwall its name,
made an ideal backdrop, symbolic of the slow-grinding
mills of God, and it is said that pirates were hanged
there in chains.

All this does little to recommend life in this part of
the East End into the nineteenth century, and we
should not be surprised to read that:

There is not a single street which is not mean and dirty;
none of the houses are old; none are picturesque in the
least; they are rickety, dirty, shabby . . . there are 'stairs'
to the river and they are rickety; there are warehouses
which contain nothing and are tumbling down; there are

public houses which do not pretend to be bright and
attractive – low-browed, dirty dens, which reek of bad
beer and bad gin. Yet the place, when you linger in
it . . . is full of interest. For it is a quarter entirely
occupied by the hand-to-mouth labourer; the people live
in tenements; it is thought luxury to have two rooms;
there are eight thousand of them, three quarters being
Irish; in the whole parish there is not a single person of
what we call respectability, except two or three
clergymen and half a dozen ladies; there are no good
shops, there are no doctors or lawyers, there is not even
a newsvendor, for nobody in Ratcliff reads a newspaper.

A series of particularly grisly murders at the tail end of
1811 sealed the reputation of the area for ever. The first
attack took place on 7 December, at 29 Ratcliffe
Highway, in the home behind a linen draper's shop, on
the south side of the street, between Cannon Street
Road and Artichoke Hill. The victims were Timothy
Marr, a twenty-four-year-old linen draper and hosier,
who had served the East India Company on the *Dover
Castle* from 1808 to 1811, his wife Celia and their three-
month-old son, Timothy (born on 29 August 1811);
and James Gowan, their shop boy. Margaret Jewell, a
servant of the Marrs, had been sent to purchase oysters,
and escaped harm. The Government offered a reward
of 500 guineas for information leading to the
apprehension of the murderer.

Twelve days later, the second incident, on
19 December, was at the Kings Arms in New Gravel

Lane (now Wapping Lane). The victims of the second murders were John Williamson, a publican who had managed the Kings Arms for fifteen years, Elizabeth, his wife, and Bridget Anna Harrington, a servant.

A certain John Williams, who was supposed to have had a long-standing dispute with Marr, was arrested, but committed suicide by hanging himself in Coldbath Fields Prison. His corpse was dragged through the streets in a cart, which paused by the scene of the murders. Suicide was considered sinful, and justified him being pitched into a hole at the junction of Cable Street and Cannon Street Road at St George in the East, and buried with a stake through the heart. Seventy-five years later his skeleton was discovered during the excavation of a trench by a gas company. The landlord of the Crown and Dolphin public house, at the corner of Cannon Street Road, retained the skull as a souvenir.

The inception of the docks did nothing to improve the level of life for the majority. Much of Wapping was dug up in 1800 to build London Docks. Discharged sailors, often the worse for drink, and slave traders filled Wapping High Street. Among the most notorious pubs were the Red Cow (now the Town of Ramsgate), where convicts awaited deportation to Australia, chained in the cellars. Then there was the sixteenth-century Devil's Tavern, since 1777 the Prospect of Whitby.

The first dock to open was far to the east of Wapping – the West India Dock at the north-west corner of the Isle of Dogs. In 1802 it was given a twenty-one-year monopoly for importing sugar, rum and coffee. Four years later, East India Dock, specialising at first in handling tea from the Far East, opened on a site to the north-east of the Isle of Dogs.

There was always a fair sprinkling of tall ships berthed in the East and West India and the Millwall docks. The smaller shipyards also around Blackwall and Poplar – Green's, Fletcher's and the London Graving Dock – specialised in repairing sailing ships.[8]

From early in the twentieth century the self-styled Squire of East India Dock Road was the landlord of the Railway Tavern, a pub known as Charlie Brown's – 'the haunt of sailor men and dockers and a veritable museum of curiosities gathered from all parts of the world . . . Charlie was a sturdily-built man and a keep-fit fanatic, with a broken nose as evidence of an earlier boxing career or a pub brawl . . . Tales of his activities were legendary . . . Everybody in Poplar knew him. Navvies working on the road stopped swinging their sledgehammers as he rode by, "Wotcher Chawlie" . . .'

He was a figure of respect within the community, even though his hostelry was a centre for all kinds of illegalities, notably contraband and prostitution. It wasn't that he was outside the law exactly, but he was a fulcrum on which, like it or not, life in this community turned. He, a living legend, and his pub occupied a special place in the minds of sailors from Scandinavia, Russia, America, and Asia, and everybody – police included – understood the importance of such a figure to this downtrodden adventurous community. Somehow, they and Charlie Brown found a workable status quo, so that in a way the community was the safer, and certainly the richer, for it.

When he died in 1932 aged 73, his body was laid out in the pub for people to pay their respects, like some regal potentate. One hundred and forty wreaths were carried through the door, and 16,000 people made up the cortege that made its way to Bow cemetery. The East End needed figures like Charlie Brown.

After West and East India docks came, far to the west by the Tower of London, St Katharine's Dock, and the opening of this in 1820 caused the biggest furore, for it was on the site of St Katharine's hospital, a twelfth-century religious institution, which had survived the Dissolution of the Monasteries in the sixteenth century, but not the coming of the docks 200 years later.

It sounds like a case of commerce over religion, but nothing could have been further from the case, for even this holy quarter had succumbed to the immorality of the area. Owing to its immunity to secular law, its warren of alleyways, with intriguing names like Dark Entry, Cat's Hole, Shovel Alley, Rookery, Money Bag Alley, Cherubim Court and Pillory Lane, had become a sanctuary to villains and prostitutes. As Ed Glinert wrote in *East End Chronicles* (Allen Lane, 2005):

When slavery was abolished in 1782 many of those freed came to St Katharine's, and by the beginning of the nineteenth century the neighbourhood was home to more than 11,000 people living in cramped overcrowded houses. It took one month – November 1825 – to wipe out 650 years of history. The residents were evicted without compensation, turned on to the streets to find shelter where they could.

With the expansion of trade the docks grew and so did the labour force, and the grimness of conditions in which people lived. Wages were meagre – five pence an hour – conditions barely humane, work irregular. Spurred on by the success of the East End match girls' strike – workers from Bryant and May – a year earlier, in 1889 dockers demanded an increase in pay of a penny an hour to sixpence – 'the docker's tanner'. They were successful, and their success inspired 'The Red Flag', anthem thereafter of the Labour Party.

The building of the docks behind high walls and with increased security served to curtail the light-fingered habits of the lightermen, but even as wages improved, the pilfering continued until well into the twentieth century, as Wapping-based Lucy Collard recalled:

Everything was picked up from the docks and everything was loaded on and then the tarpaulin would be put over and there were holes along the side of this structure, the ropes would be pulled through to hold the goods on to this structure and they would have two of these big shire horses pulling the goods that came from the various docks.

Then there was Nightingale Lane. It seemed such a
strange name for a place in Wapping. Either side of
Nightingale Lane were these huge high walls which
obviously weren't there to keep the men in but to save
them throwing goods over the wall to somebody that
was waiting the other side. Various goods, like bales of
cotton or whatever, used to come over the wall but then
the owners saw what was going on and they had these
higher walls built.

Punishments for pilferers could still be severe, but
felons were sometimes dealt with on the spot: docker
Bill Abbott recalled a policeman catching a colleague
with 4 lb of figs on his way out of the docks; rather than
arresting him he told him to sit down and eat the lot.

The First World War meant more work for the docks,
and although trade dipped alarmingly on its cessation
in 1918, by 1939 as the world turned again to war, they
had reached their zenith:

In the Port of London the river was choc-a-bloc with
traffic all day long. Every day of the week, every tide.
You don't see one now, not one. It doesn't exist as a
port anymore, only as a waterway. In the old days, if you
fell in the river you were taken to hospital for twenty-
four hours. That's how dangerous the water was. Now
they can catch salmon there.[9]

This period, from the 1920s and 1930s through to the
1970s, constitutes the time span of dockland memories

called on for this book, often triggered by the distinct smells of each wharf or warehouse: tobacco, spices, sugar, tropical fruit . . .

> *Jack Banfield*: Every wharf had a different smell, according to the commodities they used to handle. You grew up with that because we used to walk along the high street backwards and forwards to school. We didn't realise it, but if we were blindfolded and walked along we could tell you where we were by the smell of each wharf that we were alongside.[10]
>
> *Lucy Collard*: The smells of the docks? Mmm, wonderful! In fact I was walking around Wapping last year and it really took me back. Each wharf I went past, I could remember, that was a wine warehouse, that was a tea warehouse, that was coffee, that was the spices.[11]

Childhood memories of boats led to the best seafaring adventure ever written – *Treasure Island*. For Robert Louis Stevenson loved nothing better as a boy than to walk from his Edinburgh home down 'the wide thoroughfare that joins the city of my childhood with the sea' at Leith, where he stood and stared at the great ships, and listened to the song of sailors as they pulled upon their ropes. It was no different for Allan Hunt who, as a boy, looked out over the Thames by East India dock with similar longing:

> I must have spent literally years down there watching the boats. Occasionally one of the banana boats, painted

white and to me huge, would dock in the East India
Docks, the entrance to which was right by the pier. And
then there was the thrill of seeing the Cunard single
funnel Atlantic cargo-liners that did the Surrey
Commercial Docks to Quebec – the names come to
mind now, *Ausonia, Ascania, Aurania*, they always had
two 'Sun' tugs at the bows, and sometimes one at the
stern, to assist them in their negotiation of the river
turns, particularly if it was very windy. 'Sun' was the
name of the premier Towing and Salvage Company. All
the tugs were 'Sun' something. Black funnel, red broad
band with a narrow white band either side of the red
one. There was frantic activity on the river. At the pier
itself there were always barges alongside, and towing
tugs arriving and departing. On the road leading to the
pier, after traversing the Tunnel Gardens, a railway line
ran across. I clearly remember being lifted up onto the
engine one afternoon, with Mother having fits, so she
said afterwards, in case my coat got dirty.

We used to see, in the summer, the paddle-steamers
Crested and *Gold Eagle*, Tower Bridge to Southend and
Margate. When it was low water they used to turn
round at the pier and go stern first for the rest of the
way to the Tower, because there was (so I understood)
insufficient water/room to turn where they docked. Of
course at that time the wharves at Tower Bridge were
choked with ships loading and discharging, and with
rows of barges alongside – no fancy marinas then. I
always yearned to go on the *Gold/Crested Eagle*, but for
some reason we never went.

You should have heard the racket at midnight on
New Year's Eve, each year. All the docks, then packed
with ships, would sound off their sirens, and round
about the factories, all then equipped with steam
hooters, would add to the din. When the wind was from
the south, you'd get a whiff of mingled 'ship smell' –
hot engine room, steam and smoke, wafted over from
the West India Docks, masts and funnels visible over the
roof tops of Lower North Street.

For Jennifer Worth as a young woman, feelings were
equally indelibly impressed on her mind:

I cycled through bright early morning, the sun just rising
over the river, the gates open or opening, men streaming
through the streets, calling to each other; engines
beginning to sound, the cranes to move; lorries turning
in through the huge gates; the sounds of a ship as it
moved. A dockyard is not really a glamorous place, but
to a young girl with only three hours sleep on twenty-
four hours of work, after the quiet thrill of a safe
delivery of a healthy baby, it is intoxicating.[12]

Sally Warboyes' memories are just as nostalgic for a
time that is gone for ever:

The last time I went with Dad to Canary Wharf was not
long after baby Albert came along, when Dad had pulled
a muscle in his back while lifting too heavy a load from
one of the ships. The atmospheric buzz of the Canary

Wharf was magical as were the smiles of red-faced men
who were constantly on the move, unloading towering
ships which arrived from across the ocean and loading
others with cargo outward-bound. Men working long
hours in the docks seemed none the worse for carrying
heavy crates to and fro, their faces shaded from the hot
sun only by the familiar peaked docker's cap.[13]

Talk to the men whose livelihoods depended on the
docks in this same period, however, and you get a different picture. They were organised into various classes of
dock worker – stevedores, cornporters, dealporters,
coopers, riggers, 'gentlemen dockers' (dockers for short-
stay craft), tally men, warehousemen, pilers, baulkers,
blenders, and then, the lowest of the low, but by far the
greatest number were the regular and casual dockers.

The great problem for this last contingent was not
unemployment so much as under-employment. Getting
taken on regularly was very difficult, though father-son
continuity and knowing the ganger could help. One
day thousands of dockers would be needed, the next
only a few, as Stan Rose recalled:

Well, you would line up on the stones and at quarter to
eight the gangers would go out on the stones and
they'd [call you on] – So, right, I would be put up, I
would be called out, or I'd go out and volunteer . . . If
you volunteered you knew the job wasn't much good,
cos all the good jobs are snapped up by the elite like,
you know, so you'd go out and you'd get a job.

'Call On' wasn't the only way to find casual labour however; pubs played a part and failing that the men had literally to fight for their 'tallies'.

> You got an overnight selection, used to meet Harry in the pub and he'd say, 'I'll give you a job tomorrow morning if you'd like to show up at so-and-so ship' and all that sort of thing. That was done. And money exchanged or pints of beer used to change hands, that sort of thing, you know. The system used to work, but it was hard, it wasn't fair, it wasn't at all fair.[14]

Certain pubs were known as places to get work: Charlie Brown's in West India Dock Road, the Abbey Arms (the Plaistow Abbey Arms), the Steps, the Brew Post (near Charlie Brown's) and the Custom House (in the Royal Docks). These dock pubs used to open really early for the dockers coming off shift as well. One of these, the Connaught, between the Victoria and Albert Docks, by the Connaught Bridge, brought back particular memories:

> This was where the people, the dockers, all went in for their drink and many solicited their work by buying the ganger a pint who would give them a job, pick them out, and give him money, and then they would go into the dock and all the men would line up on the stones, as they call it, that's on the kerb edge for hundreds of yards. They'd say, 'Bill and Charlie and . . .' They would pick out who they wanted and of course if it

was one of them that had bought him a pint he would
get a job. And also he would call mates; it wasn't on
ability, it was who you knew and not what you
knew . . .

I went there prepared to do a day's work for a day's
money, but so much happened . . . Many many days two
of them [on your gang] was in the pub [instead of
working], and they'd come back boozed and if you said
anything they'd want to fight you. The few that was
there doing the work would get the same amount of
money at the end of the day. It was a dog eat dog
existence in the dock.[15]

**Sometimes dockers were so desperate they had to fight
for a job.**

It first caught my eye because I saw a chap who I'd been
to school with and his nose was bleeding and his face
was cut and I said to him, 'Where you been?' He said to
me, 'I got that [bleeding face] signing on for four hours'
work.' Well, of course, then I went out to see about it.
The ganger or foreman used to give tallies to his mates
who bought him a pint the night before. He'd have
perhaps thirty to forty tallies [to distribute], according to
the amount of work that was going. And he'd throw
those amongst the men and then they used to fight and
scramble for these tallies. It was bad. That would be in
the morning and it would happen again at one o'clock.
That was for only half a day's work. It might only be half
a day's work, there'd be no work in the afternoon. No

guaranteed day, only what they fought for. And it was real nasty to see it, I mean there was no friends, there was fight for half a day's work.[16]

The worst of it was that the gangers seemed to get pleasure from the power they could exercise over their sometimes desperate men.

After all the registered men had been called, everything became a shambles. Men were calling the foremen by their names. 'Here John', 'Over here Jack', pushing and shoving till it was impossible for the foremen to give the tickets out. Some of the foremen seemed to get pleasure from throwing the tickets on the ground and watching the men scramble and fight to pick a ticket up. Such was the system of calling men on. Is there anything more degrading?[17]

To cut down on the violence, they instituted controlled calling on points:

They was literally caged up, because they used to be called on by a crowd – used to rush the men to take the tally cards off . . . So places like the West India Dock, inside the West India Dock on the right hand side . . . there's a sort of big cage, iron bars all round it. All the casual workers would go in there and the gate used to be shut. And then the men used to be called on from inside that cage.[18]

A docker called Joe Bloomberg also described a 'Black Hole', a 20-by-20-foot room for calling on for the wool boats at the London Dock.

In addition to these indignities, the East End docker in the first half of the twentieth century was at the mercy of politics way beyond his control. Between 1929 and 1934 unemployment rose to more than 75 per cent of the workforce in some areas of Britain. In October 1929, Wall Street crashed and sent tremors throughout the world. Unemployment rose from 2 million to 12 million between 1920 and 1933 in America. By 1931 nearly 6 million were out of work in Germany. Following the Wall Street crash and President Hoover's decision in 1930 to raise tariff barriers, world trade, already shrinking, fell by two-thirds by 1933.

The world was on an unstoppable course towards war.

PART II

THE EAST END WAR

CHAPTER EIGHT

Rise of the working classes

In the East End, in an extraordinary microcosm of what was happening elsewhere in Europe, persecution of the Jewish community immediately preceded the outbreak of war in 1939.

The fact was that the Jews were responsible for the sweatshops and were perceived to have exacerbated housing problems by putting the money they made into property and then 'rackrenting' it. In the sweatshops pay was low and hours long. In many Jewish East End properties there was serious overcrowding.

Jews may have been victims as well as perpetrators, and were certainly tenants and employees as well as landlords and employers, but that didn't endear them to those who would vilify them anyway. There was resentment, and there were tenant revolts as early as 1898, which actually gained the support of the liberal Jewish establishment of the United Synagogue, including Sir Samuel Montagu and the Rothschilds, who perceived the danger of 'the unassimilated alien'.[1]

From the top of Brick Lane, north of Cheshire Street going east, Jews entered something of a no-go area. By 1899 they formed at least 95 per cent of the population south of Cheshire Street and 75 to 95 per cent in Brick Lane and the Boundary Street Estate (the former Nichol Estate between Hackney Road and Bethnal Green Road, north of Old Nichol Street), but less than 25 per cent and often less than 5 per cent in most of Bethnal Green. Among Jewish enclaves in Bethnal Green itself were Blythe and Teesdale streets, where in 1917 there was a fight between more than 2,000 Jews and gentiles. Such isolated enclaves were always vulnerable to attack.

Where the Jews settled there was generally a notable decline in drunkenness and infant mortality – possibly the two were related – but their clean living in amongst the poorest groups of indigenous cockneys only increased resentment.

It wasn't true, anyway, that Jews didn't drink. It was just that drinking was not their priority, whereas it was for many an indigenous cockney. But the non-drinking tag was another way that the Jews could be seen as

East End children, 1905 and 1912, parent generation of many interviewed for this book, when the East End was considered the land of the outcast. In the 1880s a penny pamphlet was published called *The Bitter Cry of Outcast London*, and in 1902 Jack London also described the area as 'outcast London' in his book *The Abyss*. This word 'outcast' incriminated the social group who rejected the East Ender, namely the industrialists and money men up West. (Springboard Education Trust)

Left: 'The East End' meant community and character to those within, and it was a matriarchal community. *'You've got to remember this, that young or old the mother was the top Johnny in the family. What she said was law.'* (Tower Hamlets Library)

Below: *'Father would like nothing better than to be left in peace to enjoy a glass of tipple... Picture a typical pub in Poplar, the regulars all merry and bright on the strong ale they supped in those days.'* (Tower Hamlets Library)

Below: Vendors were part of the theatre of the street. *'There were some Italian people in Brick Lane who made ice-creams. They called the father "Padrone". They used to go out in the summer with the ice-cream barrows and in the winter with hot chestnuts and baked potatoes.'* (Tower Hamlets Library)

Below: The most notorious post-war tenements in the Whitechapel area were in Flower and Dean Street, immediately east of Aldgate Pump. *'This was OUR place. We knew every nook and cranny, every little alleyway...'* (Museum of London)

Above: 'There was always a fair sprinkling of tall ships with rows of barges alongside – no fancy marinas then... We had ships from Africa, meat boats from Argentina, but to me, a young boy, what was interesting was that as you went round different ships and different warehouses you got to know the smell of all the different commodities.' (Fox Photos)

Below: The docks subsisted on casual labour, the daily 'Call On': *'The ganger would pick out who he wanted and of course if it was one of them that had bought him a pint he would get a job.'* (Tower Hamlets Library)

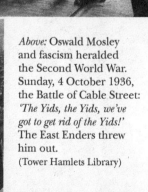

Above: Oswald Mosley and fascism heralded the Second World War. Sunday, 4 October 1936, the Battle of Cable Street: *'The Yids, the Yids, we've got to get rid of the Yids!'* The East Enders threw him out. (Tower Hamlets Library)

Above: The Blitz. 7 September 1940, the first daylight bombing raid, the docks the target: *'The manager cut the film, the lights went up and an announcement was made. "I have to tell you," said the spokesman, "that there is an air raid going on."'* (S & G Press Agency)

Above: Winston Churchill was quick to spot the contribution of East End spirit to the war effort. *'Poverty, hunger, cold, disease, and death have stalked amongst us for generations, and we have just accepted it as normal, so a few bombs couldn't break our spirit... It was an extraordinary time... We were determined not to be beaten.'* (Tower Hamlets Library)

Left: Front-line firefighters, 1940. (Imperial War Museum)

Above: Cockney children were willing targets of religious missions, but generally only when there was something other than spiritual in it for them: *'I suppose it could be said that the Irish and the Jewish stock remained truest to their origins and most proudly proclaimed their roots… We all played together. Whatever our forebears, we were certainly all one thing. We were cockneys.'* (BBC Hulton Picture Library)

Below: Post-war signs of change, advertising, the youth culture of the early 1950s… *'But it wasn't until the mid-sixties that the cockney thing became popular, with Michael Caine and* Alfie *and all that business.'* (Tower Hamlets Library)

Left: Alf Stuart (formerly Schwartz): *'To get a stall on Petticoat Lane you had to be a magician; it's all dropsy, do you know what I mean by dropsy?'*

Left: Shafiq and Pamela Uddin: *'In the beginning it was hard with my parents, well mainly my dad, not my mum. My dad, he didn't come to my wedding. He didn't come because I was marrying an Asian…'*

Below: In 1974 the Jewish synagogue in Brick Lane, which began life 200 years earlier as the Huguenot church L'Eglise Neuve, was turned into a mosque. Embedded in its walls are a quarter of a millennium of East End history.

Above: Andrew Newman and parents, who had a sweatshop off Brick Lane: *'The tailoring workers were a class on their own. They even looked alike... small, round-shouldered men with an eternally weary air.'*

Right: Bernard Kops with Erica, his wife, selling second-hand books off a barrow, around the time he was writing the play that brought him fame – *The Hamlet of Stepney Green.*

Left: 'People always want to see whatever is hidden.' Imposing door of the five-storey No 19 Princelet Street, another time capsule for three centuries of the history of this area. Built for a Huguenot weaver, transformed during the subsequent Jewish occupation, to include a basement-level synagogue at the rear, more recently it inspired Rachel Lichtenstein's book, *Rodinsky's Room.*

Right: 'Brick Lane embraced the whole community because everything you needed was found there...'

Above: 'A disaster in social planning. A community that had knitted itself together over centuries to form the vital, vibrant people known as "the Cockneys" was destroyed within a generation.' (London Advertiser)

Below: The towers of Canary Wharf on the Isle of Dogs from Shadwell Basin. Locals sent in a herd of sheep and a swarm of bees to stop developers opening Canary Wharf as an international financial centre, but today it is one of the East End's largest employers.

different. Eight-year-old Maurice Pelter, wandering the streets of Stepney on his own in 1936, noted:

> The sounds nearby of pub-singing frightened me, even though it was all most cheerful. Pubs were for gentiles: we drank, if we drank, at home privately. It was many years later that I understood that even Jews enjoyed lifting the elbow occasionally in a pub, and more shockingly, owned one or two of them in the Stepney East End of 1936.[2]

Joyce Ayres lived in Chambord Street (close to the Boundary Estate), a narrow cobbled street in what had become the French polishing shop quarter.

> On one side lived the gentiles and the other side, in the bigger houses, lived the Jews. We used to run errands for the Jews and get a penny or a sweet and if there was a Jewish wedding, the bride would sit on cushions in a big chair and all the kids in the street were allowed to file past. We gazed in wonderment at all the fruit and sweets set out in silver dishes.

In 1918, by commissioning Jewish tailors to make up uniforms for British troops in the First World War, and thereby exempting them from military service, the British Government aggravated the situation in an area that had the highest record for voluntary enlistment in London. And when troops returned from war and found the Jews had all the jobs worth having in the East

End, even the best street market sites, they were not best pleased. Indigenous cockney costermongers, who lost their market sites to Jews, and cabinet makers who were in competition with Jewish furniture factories, were among their natural enemies.

Then there was the criminal element, centring on the Boundary Estate, the Old Nichol. One street on the estate contained 'sixty-four people who had been in prison. A warren of alleys and courts, the Nichol was a haven for rival gangs.'[3] Such people could only benefit from a bit of trouble with those who had the wealth they were after, or who, like Arthur Harding, who had plenty of Jewish friends, got stuck in with the fascist groups against the Jews, for love of the action.

> There was that urge of excitement – I couldn't sit at home all the time, and so I used to go down there. To me that part of my life was taking the part of criminal activities. I was born to be involved in something.[4]

In 1927 demarcation lines were drawn in protests against Jews becoming tenants of the new Lenin Estate in Bethnal Green. By the 1930s, the area was a tinder box.

> [The Jews] have spread like a creeping flood from Aldgate, Commercial Road, and Whitechapel; and it is not pleasant to an Englishman to know that his own people have been pushed out of their ancient and historic places, mean though they are, by this

unprepossessing invasion. For they are not pleasing
to the eye, with their predatory noses, and features
which the word 'alien' describes with such peculiar
felicity. One seems to be in a hostile tribal encampment,
and it makes one afraid, not of them personally, but of
the obvious tenacity, the leech-like grip, of a people
who, one feels in one's English bones, flourish best on
the decay of their hosts, like malignant bacilli in the
blood.[5]

Horace Thorogood's views in the rest of his book *East of Aldgate* are not extreme, which makes this paragraph chill with the cold light of truth. Clearly, racism was a fact of life in the East End of the 1930s.

Sam Vincent recalled attacks on Jewish inhabitants, but saw it as part of a wider violence of the East End:

Bethnal Green was a tough neighbourhood and one had
to be tough to survive.[6]

But what was brewing was something more serious than this suggested:

Mum had answered me honestly when as a child I asked
her about the Battle of Cable Street after a Jewish girl of
my age had given me a mouthful, saying that my dad
had been a Blackshirt. This is when the family secret
came out. Mum told me how the Blackshirts marched
through the streets and Dad, being over six foot tall with

broad shoulders, had carried a banner or beat the drums as he followed in Mosley's footsteps on parade.

I asked her if my grandfather knew that his son had taken part in all that and she shrugged it off, saying, 'I've no idea.' She then went on to tell me that it was no more than local gang warfare, with Mosley bringing a bit of fame to our streets, and that it was all over and done with and the ghost buried. She had gone with Dad to the Blackshirt club, though, when a dance or social evening had been arranged.[7]

Maurice Pelter recalled a fascist slogan painted at the entrance to Duckett Street, near Stepney Green:

A double stab of Nazi lightning, S! S!, followed by the imperative initials, standing in abbreviation for a nearly 2000-year-old history of my People – P.J.! P.J.! P.J.! Perish Judah! Perish Judah! Perish Judah! H.E.P.! H.E.P.! It was following me here through the fog like a demonic deathweight on my shoulders. Forgetting chestnuts, pocketed sweets, pennies, adventure, I whirled about me and fled back to the wideness and possibly security of the main thoroughfare [the Mile End Road]. I had almost crossed a line then, a hostile threshold which named itself and separated one man from another.[8]

Philip Bernstein lived in New Road, which connects Whitechapel Road to Commercial Road, and saw nothing of this sort, because he was in the heart of the Jewish East End:

They daren't come there. They operated from Bethnal
Green Road from further up Stepney way, that way,
where there was less Jews. And then forays. They'd run
in and hit a few people and run . . . And you're talking
about 1936 and it took till 1939 . . . for the War to . . .
to start. But you could see something was going to
happen. It was like, like a kettle boiling. You're waiting,
you're waiting for it to come to the boil . . . Oh yes. It
was eventful times.[9]

The fascist leader Oswald Mosley, leader of the British
Union of Fascists, brought the waiting to an end on
Sunday, 4 October 1936, in the Battle of Cable Street.
But before that he and others held regular fascist
meetings and marches, which kept things lively for one
Jewish boy in particular, who asked me to withhold his
name:

In those days it was very very bad the anti-semitism.
When I was 17 I was very friendly with a chappie whose
name . . . let's call him Charlie Potter. And one day we
saw on a shop window, 'Don't buy from the Jews, they
will rob you.' So Charlie, who was a Manchester boy
and a year older than me and game for anything, said to
me, 'We are going to go and really give this man the
works.' So I said, 'Are you sure?' The man had a big
Alsatian dog and used to sleep at the back of the shop –
just him on his own. Anyway he was a furrier, I won't
mention no names because his son has a business down
here [in Westcliff-on-Sea], and he's changed altogether.

But I must tell you this. He said to me, 'I know what we'll do, get a couple of hoods made, put it over us and we'll go and we'll tell him, "You write any more . . . !" We'll frighten him.' So we got in the back way, doped his dog, got through the shop into his bedroom and he was sound asleep. So what we done, we gagged him. We tied him up to his bed, covered his eyes over so he couldn't see us, and we carried his bed out into the middle of the road – the middle of the main road! And left him there tied up! The next day in the paper – 'Anybody knows the whereabouts of the two people that broke into . . . !' No one knew us, because we never spoke and wore hoods.

Monnikendam put the thing in a similar perspective:

We used to go to the meetings with bricks in our pockets. When the Blackshirts were holding a meeting I should think 80 per cent of the young male population went there armed. We never allowed the meetings to proceed. They never lasted long. The police had to intervene. We saw it as our duty. It was a night out. In a way it was a bit of fun. OK, you got a black eye, or a kick here or there. They were our enemies. They really were. They had little support. The East Enders were not anti-Semitic.

Bernard Kops was a boy in the 1930s, when hatred stormed into his world.

'The Yids, the Yids, we've got to get rid of the Yids!'
These were the screams and cries of the Fascists. And
their look of hatred, real hatred, it wasn't put on, I mean
it was real. On a Sunday morning, Mosley would come
and spiel his bile and it was like vomiting with terrible
obscenities. He was saying that one race was better than
another race, that we really shouldn't be in England and
it looked as if the whole country was going to go like
Germany. I would get my Mum's saucepans and we
would all stand on the landing and smash, bang, wallop,
bang, smash, and we drowned out the sound of Mosley.

But it wasn't only racism. In a way the racism was the
surface coating of something deeper going on. Phil
Piratin – who became Communist MP for Mile End
(Stepney) in 1945 – noted that five East London mayors
petitioned the Home Office to have the B.U.F. banned
in 1936.[10] There was a strong left-wing socialist edge to
life in the East End in those days, however hypocritical
it may have been:

We were all broke. Our common enemy were the
Capitalists, and we wanted to be Capitalists![11]

That many Jews belonged to the Communist Party
seems contradictory, but the Jews and the Communists
were making headway together. Hannah was born in
the East End in 1916. Her mother, from Lodz in
Poland, came as an orphan. Her father, from Odessa in
the Ukraine, was a tailor. Her parents met in the

Pavilion – Joseph Hessler's Pavilion Theatre – a Yiddish theatre in Whitechapel.

> He used to take me there when I was young. They used
> to have benefits for members who had tuberculosis or
> other ailments.
>
> Whitechapel at the time was lovely, I didn't want to
> leave it but I did eventually. I joined a political party and
> was very happy and then we come to the time of
> Mosley. I was in my 20s, used to demonstrate every
> Sunday; we used to march with banners. I belonged to
> the Communist Party, which was very active at the time.
>
> I was a shop assistant and I joined the Shop
> Assistants Union in Stepney and that was an extreme
> left-wing branch, so we went to Circle House, I don't
> know if you know it, I haven't been there for years. It's
> off Leman Street [in Little Alie Street, Whitechapel]. That
> was interesting. [People] sitting there in the room playing
> dominoes. It was a big house with several storeys and
> each room was a different union or different
> organisation.
>
> There was a room there where they made tea and
> coffee. You paid, you know, and you sat round tables
> and it was lovely there. Used to have Trade Union
> meetings and we used to discuss the political situation. I
> didn't read *Das Kapital*, but I was one of the ones who
> sold the *Daily Worker* [the Communist newspaper].

Perhaps it was this left-wing threat that put the police on the fascist side in the public imagination. Bernard

Kops had no doubt that there was always a problem between the East Ender and the police, even that the police were 'loaded against us' and saw it as their job to contain the East End:

> Well, take a tradition which wasn't necessarily Jewish, a
> song I remember that we used to sing –
>
> *'Went down the lane to buy a penny whistle*
> *A copper came behind and took away my whistle*
> *I asked him for it back he said he hadn't got it,*
> *Hi, hi curly wig, you've got it in your pocket.'*
>
> Curly wig goes back to the Peelers and the tradition in
> the East End was that the police were there not to keep
> the law going but in fact to stop you getting out, that
> they were there to protect property, not much of which
> was owned by East Enders – it was certainly 'them and
> us'. They didn't come all that often.

This seemed so far from the accepted notion of the friendly East End bobby on his beat that I asked whether Bernard knew the local copper. 'No, no, no, no!' he replied firmly.

Of course the police were always associated with the fascists because they marched with them. Alf Stuart gives us the picture:

> Anti-semitism started coming from Tower Bridge, they
> walked all the way with the police. They were allowed to

walk, with the police walking them. They walked past
my place where I had my business, Gardiner's Corner,
and one of the horses jumped and pushed my cousin
through a plate glass window there (she was a girl).
Anyway, it broke up because the dockers came out, all
the dockers came out and stopped them marching
through, and they broke up.

The dockers were indeed the heroes of the Battle
of Cable Street, for they swung it both in terms of
sheer number and politically, turning what might
have been a victory for Jews into a great working-class
victory against right-wing government. The dockers
were, with the miners, at the forefront of trade
unionism and had tangled with the Government
during the General Strike of 1926. Now, ten years later,
they rose as workers against the fascists and the police.
Indeed, mostly the police, for Mosley didn't get past
Tower Hill.

I thought that this was going to be a purely local affair,
but I was wrong about that. The Communist Party and
the ILP were organising the opposition on vast scales,
although I didn't know about this . . . All the fighting
was between the police and the people for the East
End.[12]

Never was there such unity of all sections of the
working class as was seen on the barricades at Cable
Street.[13]

The Battle of Cable Street was a singular precedent for political revolt for the next thirty years. Right through to the end of the 1960s the police were ranged in battle against left-wing political protesters – students and workers – on the streets of cities all over the Western world.

Cable Street runs parallel to and just north of the old Ratcliff Highway, and is indelibly associated with the docks, not least because it takes the name from its original use as a long straight path for twisting hemp ropes into ships' cables.

People came from all over the country. Newspapers estimated crowds numbering half a million.

Hannah was there, as was her husband, who shared her political motive. He was a member of the people's theatre, the so-called Unity Theatre, which sought to dramatise the struggle of the working classes, and drew its audience partly from the trade unions and organised labour movements. Bernard Kops remembers, 'It was a time for real social drama. You were assured of a really dramatic piece of writing.'

Very often the drama was just as effective on the street, however, as Hannah recalls:

I was in Aldgate. Near Gardiner's Corner. Well there was thousands of people; people came from the provinces. It was packed with people down Commercial Road and Whitechapel, it was amazing.

There used to be marches every week – Embankment, Trafalgar Square . . . – and they were peaceful marches except at the time of Spain.[14] At the time of Spain we all congregated at the Square. They [the fascist Mosleyites] pursued us with police on horse-back.

Politics meant something then. People were very passionate about it. First of all there was mass unemployment, General Strike 1926, and when I left school in 1930, when I was 14, it was hard to get jobs. Mass unemployment. I remember the General Strike, but being a child I didn't realise really . . .

On the day of the battle, Mosley planned to send thousands of marchers dressed in blackshirt uniform through the East End, but there was a rout, as Joe Jacobs, a local Communist party activist, recalled:

By mid-morning the crowds coming to Aldgate were already so big that Gardiner's Corner, a big road junction made up of Whitechapel Road, Whitechapel High Street, Commercial Road, Commercial Street and Leman Street, was blocked and traffic was coming to a standstill. Around midday, the police were beginning to show their hand. There were skirmishes going on all over the place. I was told that down in Cable Street, which is quite a narrow street, it was already impossible to pass. By about one o'clock there was a tram stuck on the rails, right in the middle of the road junction at Gardiner's Corner. Young people were perched on all the lamp posts and any other vantage point, displaying posters and directing the crowd towards the weak spots in the front with the police. The crowds were roaring, 'They shall not pass.'

Housewives threw milk bottles at the marchers from windows and roofs high above the streets, even boiling water was prepared. Recalled Philip Bernstein:

Near Gardiner's Corner, that's where Mosley's Blackshirts were. They had assembled on the other side of Leman Street and the anti-fascists were assembled at Cable Street and all streets that side. Now, we were walking towards Leman Street, me and this other fellow and lots of . . . lots of other people. And suddenly the mounted police started coming towards us on their horses and . . . we should get out the way. There was an old lady in front of us and we could see she's going to fall, so me and this other man, we picked her up and carried her out of the way like, out of the way of the horses. We were there a whole morning till . . . the . . . late afternoon, when it quietened down and it was known that Mosley will not march that day. Because they all had the boiling water on, on the rooftops, and everything ready for him.

Bernard Kops took to the streets with his brother:

I remember my mother was very concerned and worried. A policeman came towards us on a horse and he had a truncheon in his hand, he was going like this and he hit my brother on the head. Someone said to me, 'Give me some marbles,' and said, 'You throw them along the ground and the horses will slip up in the air,' and we did just that.

Such was the size of the crowd the police met that there was no need for strategy, although Jack Miller recalled that some of the men had plans:

There was a special lot of what they call the 'tuckers', those that did boxing and all-in wrestling. They had certain plans, you know, to get through, to attack certain vehicles and all that, or, or let down their tyres or something like that, to get at their cars. I should say it was the mass response really that surprised us all . . . The very density of the crowds made the penetration for the Fascists difficult, so that the police eventually ordered them away.[15]

That Sunday in 1936 was a day to remember. I knew there was going to be trouble in Cable Street for a week before the fight, and, as I was making my deliveries for Feldman, I heard the tailors saying that they were going to stop Mosley and knock hell out of his Blackshirts . . . I used to work overtime Sunday mornings, collecting the boss's debts and my own tips, and I was going the rounds quite easily at first, but by ten o'clock I was beginning to find it more difficult. The crowds were beginning to arrive and Tower Hill and the Minories were filling up with people. Whole armies seemed to be marching through Leman Street, and soon every street in the area was jam-packed . . . The whole of London seemed to be there. And they weren't just Jewish people; at least half the crowd were English, I'm glad to say.

I got back to the workshop about eleven and by then Cable Street was almost full. And then, like a scene from a film, someone called out 'The dockers are coming,' and they swarmed into the street in their hundreds. The whole crowd took up their chant – 'They shall not pass'. Many of the dockers were carrying pickaxes and they used them to prise up the paving stones; some they used to build a barricade and some they broke into pieces to use as missiles. They also had marbles to roll under the feet of policemen's horses and fireworks to scare them. They built other barricades just beyond Backchurch Lane, and they overturned a lorry and piled it high with girders they'd pinched from a nearby builders' yard. Some of them stood on the roofs with bricks, and even vases, to throw at the enemy. The mounted police arrived first, and they were met by a shower of missiles. The woman who owned the fruit shop had neglected to put up her shutters, and the crowd pinched her fruit to throw at the police. She didn't like it much, but it was all in a good cause . . . They'd stood together and defeated the whole of the Metropolitan Police. They had stopped the Fascists in their tracks.[16]

[Afterwards] the poor houses, the mean streets, the ill-conditioned workshops were the same, but the people were changed. Their heads seemed to be held higher, and their shoulders were squarer – and the stories they told! Each one was a 'hero' – many of them were. In the barbershops there was only one topic of conversation for the next fortnight.[17]

CHAPTER NINE

The Blitz

——————

The Second World War was a watershed. It changed everything. It was, as Ken Long put it, 'the end of an era for us all'. For Germany blitzed the East End more harshly than any part of Britain.

The docks were the target of course. Britain is an island, the docks our lifeline, however productive the Land Army inland might prove to be. The German bombers flew in from the east, queuing for their turn to light up their targets with incendiaries, and then disgorged thousands of tons of explosive, obliterating homes and lives, and razing whole areas to the ground, such as Limehouse, before turning round at Tower

Bridge and doing the same again. Night after night. It was a nightmare met with extraordinary fortitude. But in the end it did for the East End. Life was never the same again.

Long before war was declared, there had been plenty of practice, as Frank Lewey recalled:

> Civil defence workers poured in, fleets of ambulances came clanging up at top speed, and nine doctors arrived on the scene within three minutes.
>
> East London had had many practices for this sort of thing, and the Cockneys had had their fun . . . There were many cases like that of the old coster, who, having tired of lying on the pavement waiting for rescue, departed, leaving his label – 'SEVERED JUGULAR VEIN' – bearing the extra pencilled words, 'I ave now bled to def and gorn 'ome.' But, when the real call came, London was ready.[1]

People knew it was on the cards. The barrage balloons in the sky, newspapers one minute full of hope, the next of despair.

> Young as I was I realised that war was soon to come. There was talk at school about evacuation and explanations about how it would take place. Then it happened.[2]

Initially, evacuation was the biggest upset to life, the greatest single movement of population in history, a decision taken only the day before in which ultimately 3,500,000 children would be removed from their homes to avoid the bombing. It was an astonishing feat of organisation, but not perfect.

> Some fortunate children were sent to Canada and
> America but they were certainly NOT from East London,
> us lot were considered too 'lower class' and rough.[3]

Immediately it meant splitting up not only whole communities, but families too, as Sam Vincent remembers.

> On 2nd September we were marshalled at Cranbrook
> Road School with my suitcase with a change of clothes
> and my gas-mask in a box. Because my sisters had left
> school they would not be coming with me, so they, with
> Mum, saw me off at the station. I shall never forget
> Mum saying to me, 'I'll send the comics on, son,' and a
> kind policeman adding, 'That's right, Ma, keep 'em
> happy'. How they felt I don't know.

Initial excitement gave way to sadness and plain weariness.

> We arrived in the late afternoon at Wellington in
> Somerset. We were all given a medical examination and
> then billeted into complete strangers. It was quite an
> experience for a twelve year old, but I soon settled down
> to a totally new world.

For those like Sam Vincent, who had not strayed far from the little complex of streets that was home, this was an altogether new experience.

> There were green fields and country walks and above all, an abundance of apple orchards. For twelve months I enjoyed it but I was always longing for home. I wrote to my parents and my dad came down and took me back to Bethnal Green.[4]

This was of course the great irony of the evacuation. The Blitz didn't begin for a year, by which time many of the children had returned to the East End, and, like Sam, walked slap bang into the middle of the action that their evacuation had been designed to avoid.

In September 1939 children were unaware of where they were being sent, but Bernard Kops could hardly contain his excitement when the train moved out of Liverpool Street. Then he came back down to earth 'with a clunk':

> I looked at my terrible responsibility, my crying, snotty-nosed red-eyed little sister. I had promised to look after her and not be separated from her. 'But where will we be tonight?' she appealed to me. And I shrugged 'Your guess is as good as mine!' – 'But we'll be with strangers.' Rose had never been more than six inches away from my mother and now she was clinging onto me, and the other children were watching.[5]

Their destination turned out to be Denham in Buckinghamshire, a mere 20 miles from London but deemed 'safe'.

Stanley Keyte's reaction to the upheaval was quite different to Bernard's – no excitement, just a terrible sadness as the train drew out of Liverpool Street station. He was sent further afield, to Marsham in Norfolk:

It was a village situated about 10 miles east of Norwich. When we got off the coach, it was probably about 9.30–10.00 at night and we were ushered into a building which turned out to be just one big hall. I later found out, it was a reading room for the locals, more like a class room to look at, in fact that's exactly what it turned out to be later on, our class room. I remember sitting there with the rest of the kids, wondering what was going to happen next, each sitting there with their little labels on and their gas masks. One side of the room was a cluster of people standing near the open door and every now and then a name would be called out and the person from the cluster would go out with the boy or girl . . .

Names were being called out quite frequent by now, and I'm saying to myself, I wonder what [my family] will look like. It got down to three of us, twin sisters and myself. The little girl that had just gone went out with a woman who had a hump on her back using a walking stick, and the thought of being looked after by someone like that was beginning to make me feel a bit depressed.

By now there were just a couple of people standing near the open door, they were just standing there, talking together and they looked as though they might be in charge. Suddenly one of them came over, looked at my label, went back to the other two people, then they beckoned the twins. That just left me. By now I was getting the same feeling that I got in Liverpool Street Station, that feeling of sadness is the only way that I can explain it. Surely, I'm thinking, I'm not going to be left out. Maybe I'm going home, it could have been a mistake. Just at that moment a woman burst through the open door, as I remember she had a grin on her face at the time and she said something and I think it was her way of apologising for being late. She came towards me and said, 'Are you Stanley?' At that moment I knew I was going to a good home.[6]

Stanley had no idea what to expect. None of them had. A few had been to Southend – a trip to the seaside – and some to the hop-picking gardens of Kent, but only ever in summer. This was deep rural England in winter. Mud was something with which no East Ender had ever had to contend, and here were great channels of it, a foot or more deep, rutted by the huge treads of tractors, and slurry from cows that ran in great rivers down the middle of the street. Footwear, which divided 'the haves' from the 'have-nots' at home, had a highly practical significance in the country, as Reginald Baker immediately saw:

Granny Dorling bought me a pair of Wellington boots
because my own shoes had holes in with bits of
cardboard stuffed in to keep out the wet – only it
didn't.[7]

Stanley Keyte was less lucky. The Clarks' farm in
Marsham, equidistant from Norwich in the centre of
Norfolk and Cromer on the north coast, was in effect in
the middle of absolutely nowhere. Here, footwear
assumed a level of importance quite out of proportion
to reality for Stanley. When gradually, in rare letters
from home, he had all sense of security and stability
whittled away as he learned of the break-up of the
marriage of his father and mother, his need for a
watertight pair of boots took on an awesome
significance in his young, vulnerable mind.

The first year I was evacuated I was caught napping. As
we never wore rubber boots in London, all I had was my
school shoes and a pair of slippers and they were for the
summer. That meant that every time I came home from
school I had to go indoors with soaking wet feet. Mrs
Clark lent me a pair of her rubber overshoes but they
were miles too big for me and would only do as a
temporary measure because the mud and the snow
would get down the side of them. Mrs Clark asked me
to write home and tell them that I needed 7s./6d. then
she would get me a pair of the short legged ones. These
were the kind that I really wanted, especially as they
were the kind that all the men wore in the village out

there. What used to appeal to me about them was that they had a short leg with a dull rubber finish and big sturdy heels and soles, that way I could jump up and down in the mud and snow without fear of letting anything in. I didn't like the shiny long legged boots, they were alright for girls. Anyway, instead of writing home myself, Mrs Clark decided to write home for me, she said she had been intending to write home to my mum and dad for some time now and this would be a good opportunity to do so.

I was anxious for the money to arrive and a fortnight went by and I still hadn't received anything. In the morning before I went to school, I would look through the front room window, straight up the lane, for the postman. I wanted to catch him before I went to school because I was getting a little bit anxious by now, also the bad weather was drawing in.

One morning a letter arrived and I could hardly wait to open it up but when I did it contained a letter from Mum and a postal order for 1s./6d., and no mention of the 7s./6d. for the boots. Well, it was some time later that I learnt from Mum that she had not been living at home for a while now. She had been very unhappy at home for several years, but wouldn't leave because of us kids. And she said that now I was being looked after and the three boys were bringing in enough to keep things going, the time had come to make a move.

As Mum was not living at home she obviously didn't know about my request for the 7s./6d.

That morning I went to school feeling very

disappointed. Mrs Clark made me wear her overshoes again and there was lots of mud about in the lane.

After morning school I arrived back home for my dinner, and Mrs Clark said, 'There is a parcel inside for you son, it has just arrived.' It seemed that the postman only delivered large parcels after he had finished his morning delivery. I opened up the parcel, it was a shoe box wrapped up in brown paper and inside was a pair of shoes. Well, if I was disappointed before I was certainly disappointed now. The shoes, although they seemed in good condition, were second hand and had been re-soled and heeled. I was never going to get over those shoes. They were a brown casual type with a side buckle, and where they had been repaired the soles were twice the normal thickness, this made them higher at the front than they should be. The edges of the soles were glossy where they had been heavily waxed and I could tell by the uppers that they had been well used.

Inside the shoe box was a letter from Dad, which read something about me needing money for boots, 'So I have got you some good stout shoes which should keep the rain out.'

Mrs Clark must have noticed my disappointment, although I didn't say anything to her at the time. The following Saturday, [she] bought me some boots from her own money, but I shall never forget those shoes.

Britain declared war with Germany on Sunday 3 September 1939 at 11.15 a.m., but it was 7 September

1940 before the first daylight bombing raid occurred. This date and June 1944, when the first V-1 rocket, or doodlebug, hit the railway bridge on Bow, between Victoria Park and Mile End tube station (there is a blue plaque on the bridge now), are the most memorable dates of the war to East Enders. The doodlebugs were flying bombs and really scary – you had time to count to ten between the noise of its engine stopping and the explosion.

There had been night bombing of London in August 1940, and the RAF had replied with several attacks on Berlin. Germany was now about to wreak a terrible revenge. The first bombs that fell that day on docklands could be heard clearly miles away in Brixton, the roar of the planes, the coughing of the guns, the anticipation, and then the dull explosions and vibrations on the ground. The fear was that the whole of London would be flattened, and that then the invasion would begin.

The Seventh of September was one of those beautiful early autumn days which feel like spring, and can make even London streets seem fresh and gay. A new soccer season had begun and the big match in the East End that afternoon was between West Ham and Tottenham.

> There was hardly a wisp of cloud in the pale blue sky. At 4.43p.m. the sirens wailed, and the population trooped to the shelters.[8]

Being a Saturday afternoon, many East End children, who had by now returned from their strange excursions in rural England, were at the cinema. Jim O'Sullivan was at the Regal, Hackney.

> Shortly after my return home, the sirens sounded, their moans swiftly being drowned out by the roar of aircraft. Instead of racing for shelter, everyone seemed to be gazing up at a great armada of bombers and escorting fighters flying serenely towards London's massive complex of docks where more than a quarter of the nation's imports were discharged. Neither random anti-aircraft fire nor our much vaunted barrage balloons perturbed them, not even that errant balloon based in nearby Meath Gardens which had earlier caused great amusement when it broke free from its moorings. For a few minutes everyone seemed mesmerised by the display above, but as the bombs dropped we all scurried for cover when the sound of distant explosions brought us back to reality. Dad hustled us and two of our neighbours, Mr and Mrs Dingle, into the cellar, to wait for the all clear.[9]

Charles Chisnall was sitting in the Troxy when heavy explosions and gunfire were heard and alarm spread through the building.

> The manager cut the film, the lights went up and an announcement was made. 'I have to tell you,' said the spokesman, 'that there is an air raid going on. You may

leave if you so wish, but this building is of strong construction and I think it would be safer to stay where you are until the 'All Clear' . . .[10]

Anne Griffiths remembered she was watching a Bette Davis film with her sister when a similar announcement appeared on the screen. Her sister took two seconds to make up her mind that she wasn't staying – 'Tell me what happens,' she shouted as she dashed out of the stalls and made for the door.

I said, 'Yes, all right,' and sat there. I was watching the film and every so often there was a big loud crash, bang and still I sat there. I was thinking I must see the end of it, I must see the end of it. And I . . . I was looking sideways, there was no-one either side of me at all and I thought, Oh plenty of people behind. And the time was going on and I was getting to a lovely part of the film, so nice, and I looked around and there was me and another two people in there, and I thought, 'Oh good God I'd best go home now.' But I still stayed for five minutes. Then a great big loud resounding crash came and I jumped up and at that time I . . . I had to go home. As I came across Green Street, going to my street Neville Road, shrapnel was falling and everything – pieces of brickwork and masonry was all falling all around me and I was doing a little run and then going into a doorway and running again until I finally got into my house, and down the air raid shelter. My sister was sitting there with my mum and my sister said to me, 'What happened?' I

said, 'I nearly got killed, that's what happened'. And I
never did see the end of the film until after the war.[11]

Ivy Alexander and her friend, Irene, who lived some
way further east, in West Ham, had been cycling in
Epping Forest when the air raid siren started. Ivy wrote
about her experience in her diary:

> From the Forest we could see hundreds of planes
> crossing to London. We thought they were British, but
> apparently they were Jerries. Many air battles were going
> on and there was plenty of gunfire. We saw five planes
> brought down and saw several airmen bale out. Rene
> and I chased off on our bikes to try to find them, but
> soldiers were on the scene before us. Shrapnel was
> falling everywhere, so we decided to go home and the
> 'All Clear' sounded when we reached Wanstead at 6
> p.m. As we approached London we could see huge
> black smoke clouds and thought we were in for a storm.
> We later discovered it was smoke from the many fires
> started by bombs.[12]

Unbeknown to Ivy, the Germans had dropped time
bombs all the way along the route they took home,
primed to go off when people emerged from their
bunker shelters after the All Clear. They discovered this
when they arrived at Ivy's house and a warden told
them that one such device had actually landed in Ivy's
front garden.

The shelters that many used during the bombing

raids – or Anderson shelters as they were called, not after the then Home Secretary Sir John Anderson but after David Anderson, one of the civil engineers who approved the design – were purpose built and available six months before war was declared. By September 1940 over 2.3 million of them had been distributed countrywide. Measuring 1.8 by 1.4 metres and 2 metres long, and made out of corrugated iron, they cost £7 to buy, but were free to families earning less than £250 a year. One problem with them was that they flooded easily. Another was that you needed to have a garden site in which to erect it, and many in the East End did not have gardens.

So it was that people flocked to the Underground instead. The Government hadn't thought of that. Thousands upon thousands pushed their way into the stations, demanding to be let down to shelter. Among them Bernard Kops and his family made their way to Liverpool Street station:

> At first the authorities wouldn't hear of it and they called out the soldiers to bar the way . . . I stood there with my father and mother and brothers and sisters thinking that there would be panic and we would all be crushed to death.

The alternative for the Kops family had been 'a ground-floor flat crowded with hysterical women, crying babies and great crashes in the sky and the whole earth shaking'.

The people would not give up and would not disperse,
would not take no for an answer. A great yell went up
and the gates were opened and my mother threw her
hands together and clutched them towards the
sky . . . 'It's a great victory for the working class,' a man
shouted, 'One of our big victories!'

Bernard made the most of it, riding up and down the
escalators, and travelling a station or two to visit other
encampments:

I bagged any space I could along the platform. The family
followed and we pitched our 'tent' (of scarves), then we
unravelled and unwound and relaxed. And out came the
sandwiches and the forced good humour . . . Our spirits
would rise for a while, we were alive for another night,
we would see another dawn . . . Here was a new life, a
whole network, a whole city under the world.[13]

Otherwise, people hid in cellars and crypts of churches.

The crypts of churches provided shelter for hundreds of
people, and whole communities lived day and night in
the churches. More than one baby was born in All Saints
[Poplar] crypt, as I learnt from the Sisters. The
overcrowding was terrible. Each person had just enough
room to lie down, and no more.[14]

On the first daylight raid Harry Willmott, a young lad
living in Bow Common, was found wandering the

streets while everyone else was below ground or in shelters – a thrill all of its own:

My parents, my twin sister and baby brother born in 1939 all went to the cow barn shelter at the Whitethorn Street end of Tidey Street. I stayed behind and stood at the street door, I told my parents that if nothing happened I would go on to the barber's for a haircut. As I stood there I had a feeling that I was the only one alive, there was a deathly hush everywhere, there was no sign of any other human being, there was no sound of a dog barking even. Suddenly I heard faint explosions in the distance, these got louder as the bombers drew nearer, and then an enormous explosion a very short distance away was followed by some more . . . I ran at speed to the cow barn shelter and got there just in time as the bombs came down. I remember looking up and seeing several bombers and hearing the sound of machine guns as our fighters attacked them. In the shelter my father and I lay across my mother, sister and baby brother to protect them from shrapnel or flying debris.

Suddenly there was a terrific explosion and the whole shelter shook as if in an earthquake, all the lights went out and a strong smell of oil and paraffin permeated the shelter. I knew then that Merriots oil shop on the corner of Tidey Street and Bow Common Lane had gone.

In the shelter a lot of women and children were screaming and some were trying to remember half forgotten prayers, a lady who was elderly lay next to me on the floor quite still, the shock of the explosion had

killed her. When the All Clear went, we emerged dazed
from the shelter and gazed on a scene I shall never
forget. We seemed to be surrounded by a ring of fire.[15]

The war had finally come to our doorsteps. The
London Docks were set on fire, with huge balls of smoke
rising into the clear sky. As night fell the smoke took on
a red glow from the flames reflected on the silver-
sheened barrage balloons which acted as beacons.
Confirming our worst fears, the Germans returned
guided by the fire and illuminated balloons.[16]

And then the reality of the horror hit home.

Whole streets had been destroyed. All through Sunday
and Monday East Enders drifted miserably westwards,
looking for shelters; most of them had no baggage; they
had lost everything; some carried pathetic and clumsy
bundles of their remaining belongings; some pushed
battered perambulators stacked with salvaged, broken
treasures. They had nowhere to rest, nowhere to wash.
In the West End attempts were made even to exclude
them from some shelters. On a 38 bus in Piccadilly a
wretched-looking woman with two children got in and
sat down next to me; they still had blast dust in their
hair and their tattered clothing; they were utterly
miserable, and the lady opposite moved her seat and
said loudly that people like that should not be allowed
on buses. Fortunately the conductor announced with
promptitude that some ladies could take taxis.[17]

Phil Piratin and other Communists took a group from Stepney to the West End to shelter. They went to the Savoy's shelter where they were initially met with a poor reception but the waiters took their side and served them. A Stepneyite commented, 'Shelters? Why we'd love to *live* in such palaces.'[18]

Meanwhile, the children of the East End found themselves a new playground. Michael Moorcock celebrates in his fiction the modern transition from the cockney-Jewish East End that he knew as a child, but his root culture is never far from the surface.

> I must admit I have a fondness for ruins. I loved the bombsites the way most kids did, because they offered freedom and adventure. We liked nothing better than a bombed house, particularly if it was still roughly intact. We learned to walk from beam to beam, from joist to joist, avoiding the treacherous boards and plaster; we learned to test walls; we learned what to push to destruction, to make the rest of a house more or less safe. We could tell which roofs were likely to fall on us, which would hold, as we ascended swaying staircases into airy space, heading for attics no adult dared attain and discovering storehouses of weatherbeaten treasures. We once pushed a piano from a top storey all the way to the bottom of the brick-strewn garden, crushing hollyhocks and roses and raising a huge cloud of dust which gave us away so that we had to climb carefully back to the ground and run for it . . .'[19]

What struck one was the immediacy of what was going on, that you might walk upstairs, as Lawrie Alexander did, and find that war had broken out in the bedroom and was burning a hole in your bed:

Lawrie came rushing in and said I had left the light on upstairs and not drawn the blackout curtains. He hurried upstairs to discover that it was an incendiary bomb that had come through the bedroom roof and landed right in the middle of the bed, and burned right through the new bedspread which my mother had secreted away, for a special occasion no doubt. Catastrophe!

We had been warned about incendiary bombs. These usually preceded high explosives and were used to guide the bombers on to their target. We had been told to keep a bucket of sand ready, to smother the bomb I believe, and a bucket of water. We all swung into action. Mr Holding, Sam Rowe from number two, and Lawrie were to man the stirrup pump and pass buckets of water, whilst I was at the kitchen tap filling the buckets . . . The sand didn't seem to be required, so I tipped that out and filled the bucket with water. Very soon I heard a shout from Mr Holding, 'Sod it! There's sand in the water and it's clogging up the stirrup pump!' He was a very mild mannered man and that was the strongest expletive I had ever heard him utter . . . They finished up climbing the stairs and throwing buckets, bowls and saucepans of water on the fire, abandoning the stirrup pump in disgust.[20]

Later that night the planes came back, and the street was bombed. Then the writer Ivy Alexander's mother returned, found out about the bedspread, and all of a sudden the old reality returned to their lives: 'What's that bedspread doing out? . . . It's ruined. If you hadn't got it out it would have been saved.'

When tragedy reached beyond individuals to the level of a whole community, it seemed to crystallise people's feelings of utter helplessness behind the tireless and courageous efforts to keep things going. One such instance was at South Hallsville School in Canning Town (east of Blackwall), on 10 September 1940. The school was being used as a centre for bombed-out families awaiting re-housing, and suffered a direct hit. Everyone inside was killed. The story has it that a bus which had been sent to pick them up from Canning Town had gone to Camden Town instead; local people believed that the official death toll of 73 was far too low.

Then there were tragedies made worse by the feeling that they had been avoidable, an unnecessary consequence of the war. The horrific Bethnal Green Tube Disaster of 3 March 1943 was one of these: 173 people (84 women, 27 men and 62 children) died of suffocation after a crowd surged down the stairs of the tube station and a woman tripped and fell, probably scared by a rocket from the new battery in nearby Victoria Park. This disaster is supposed to have accounted for a third of all deaths in Bethnal Green in the war years.

The sheer commitment of people to the East End community in the war years was staggering. People would go to work as usual and then come home and stay up most of the night working as Air Raid Wardens, 'or members of decontamination squads, ambulance men, relief fire men, helping to put incendiaries out, or dig out anyone trapped, and trying to clear up any mess in one's own house, damaged by "blast". Very little sleep was had, and any grub had to be got when you could get it.'[21]

Frank Lewey was Mayor of Stepney during the worst days of the Blitz and paid tribute to all the different people who contributed to the effort, noting in particular unsung heroes, like the water engineers who went into craters to fix the pipes so that the water supply could be maintained: vital for fire-fighting as well as for everyday life.

Then there were the cockney cabbies, like Charles Poulsen.

You went into work on the morning of September 5 and found that out of every twenty cabs in the garage, fifteen had been taken over by the Government, commandeered. About a year before the war started a Home Office official visited our Union branches and made an appeal to the members that in case of hostilities beginning they shouldn't volunteer for the armed forces because their intimate knowledge of London would be of major importance in the defence of the capital. And therefore they said don't join the army or navy, join civil defence, the fire service, something concerned with London where you'll be invaluable. If you get a shout, a call from one part of the City to a desolate unknown back street in another, only a person like a cabman can do it.

Cabs that were requisitioned were used as fire engines – for pulling trailer pumps.

The whole of the Government's Blitz policy was based on a very large number of small units which could be manhandled or dragged or taken anywhere through streets. It paid off. The cabs were requisitioned by the Government to carry six men, which was the crew, and tow a trailer pump, usually a Dennis trailer pump, a very good one on two wheels, ladders on the roof and all the other gear that you need for fire fighting accommodated somewhere on the cab. It made a very, very heavy load for the cabs, which weren't designed for it, but they were all we had you see and we had to use them.

I drove a fire engine most of the time, which was what most taxi drivers were doing. The bloodiest one was what was called the Bank incident, you know about 290 or 300 I'm not sure fatalities there and literally hundreds of injured . . . We'd just come in from about 24 hours' continual fire fighting, we were soaked to the skin, frozen and hungry. And we had to go out, so my crew, of which I was driver, my six men under the charge of a large chap we called a leading, leading fireman, were the first ones on the scene there, it was our job to climb in under over the dead and the wounded on our bellies dragging lengths of hose and foam to deal with the burning gas main before we could start on the rescue operation. Things like that, they weren't all like that I'm glad to say.[22]

The spirit, camaraderie and patriotism were exemplary.

We were secretly rather proud of having had a greater tonnage of bombs dropped on us than any city in the world had then had.[23]

In 1944 Clement Attlee, leader of the Labour Party and soon to be Prime Minister, wrote:

In my long and intimate acquaintance with the Borough of Stepney I have always known from hundreds of examples how much courage dwelt in the hearts of those who lived in its dingy streets. The hard circumstances of life have been faced with fortitude, kindliness and humour.

It was therefore no surprise to me that, when Hitler chose our Borough as the centre of his target for the Blitz on London, he found there an unconquerable spirit. Wherever I went in those grim days I never found anything but cheerfulness and an utter determination that Hitler should not beat Stepney.[24]

An idea current among East Enders during the war was that Hitler had targeted a poor district for the bombing in order to provoke an uprising against the British Government.

> As for the Cockneys who were to lead the English
> Revolution on Hitler's behalf . . . they went jostling and
> laughing and jeering into the forefront of battle.
> Grannies and costers, Jews and Arabs, Indians and
> Negroes, tailors and trouser-basters, consumptives and
> fit, Chinamen and Vicars, and schoolkids and gasmen;
> and they fought the bombs and they fought fire, and
> they fought panic and disease and sleeplessness, and
> they used burning incendiary bombs as hand-torches by
> which to do rescue work – and presently the Luftwaffe
> reeled back, and the crisis of the war was passed.[25]

Mayor Lewey recalled a bus driver who, as he pulled up in Aldgate going east, would shout:

> Any more for London's fav'rit 'ealth resort? Marvellous
> fireworks? 'Otter than the Riviera! 'Otter than 'Ell fire![26]

East Enders were used to suffering. But here was suffering with a measure of exhilaration, enshrined in the knowledge that the East End had been sought out and engaged in war by Hitler, and was winning:

> Poverty, hunger, cold, disease, and death have stalked
> amongst us for generations, and we have just accepted
> it as normal, so a few bombs couldn't break our spirit.
>   We were used to overcrowding, so the shelters didn't

seem too bad. The loss of house or rooms was no worse than eviction, and most people didn't have much furniture to lose, anyway. A family would just move in with neighbours who still had a roof over their heads.

It was an extraordinary time . . . We were determined not to be beaten. Two fingers up to Hitler was the attitude. I remember one old woman we pulled out of the rubble. She wasn't hurt. She gripped my arm, and said, 'That bugger Hitler. E's killed me old man, good riddance, e's killed me kids, more's the pity. E's bombed me 'ouse, so I got nowhere 'a live, bu' 'e ain't got me. And I've got sixpence in me pocket an' vat pub on' corner, Master's Arms, ain't been bombed, so let's go an' 'ave a drink an' a good laugh an' a sing-song.'[27]

Behind this extraordinary spirit in the face of adversity was a pride too in being British, and the Royal Family detected this and responded in kind. They decided not to leave the capital during the Blitz, and when Buckingham Palace received the first of nine direct hits, Queen Elizabeth, mother of our current queen, famously remarked:

I am glad the Palace has been bombed – it makes me feel that I can look the East End in the face again.

It was almost as if she was acknowledging all the wrongs dealt the outcast East End through the ages, and asking its forgiveness. And then of course famously she came in person to visit families and pick over the rubble of the war. People rose to that; the East End psyche thrilled to it. It was then that the royal walkabout was born. As Queen Mother, Elizabeth Bowes-Lyon, a woman who came from the north-east on the Tyne, another great working-class area, remained the most popular royal right up to her death.

Patriotism marked the end of the war too. VE Day, 8 May 1945, saw a fly-past of RAF bombers, showing red, white and blue lights. For the first time, the people of the East End could look up to the skies and cheer, instead of running for cover.

Three days later the *East London Advertiser* recorded a royal visit:

> Their Majesties the King and Queen remembered east London's rocket blows during the two days of VE celebration and, accompanied by Princess Elizabeth and Princess Margaret Rose, visited scenes of incidents at Poplar and Stepney. At Hughes Mansions, the crowd broke the cordon and surged round them, singing.

The special focus of the Royal Family's visit were the V-1 and V-2 rocket attacks, in particular the Hughes Mansions Flying Bomb strike, which had taken 134 lives just six weeks earlier. The King and Queen made their point and then went on an extended tour of the whole of east London.

With that, the party spirit really began to flow.

At the outset there seemed uncertainty among people about what they should do. Then flags appeared and soon the decorations began to grow, until the much-blitzed town was ablaze with colour.

Ships in the docks were bedecked with flags. Rockets fired from them starred the sky. Lights flashed V-signs from the ships and hooters sounded the mystic V-signal so often heard on the radio.[28]

PART III

POST-WAR BLUES

———

CHAPTER TEN

Broken but
not beat

Clem Attlee's post-war Labour Government promised the new welfare state: a National Insurance system that meant pensions for all, free medical care, family allowances and means-tested national assistance. But could the Government afford to deliver?

The war came to an end, soldiers were reunited with their families, but money and day-to-day goods remained in short supply. Rationing continued until long after the war ended. Queues were commonplace even for essentials. While nobody went hungry, supplies were pretty basic. Bread rationing was introduced in July 1946 and lasted for two years; potatoes were rationed in 1946–7; a major fuel shortage due to declining productivity, inadequate transport and the winter of 1947, which saw snow drifts reaching first floor window level, closed factories and left houses without electricity for five hours a day.

Britain went cap in hand to America, trading on the sacrifice made for world peace in the war. America, who felt they had won the war, was not impressed. The deal we came away with was not enough and tied Britain to America as a poor relation. Then America awoke to the wisdom of a speech by Churchill about the danger of Stalin, whose power was spreading into Eastern Europe, and billions of dollars came in to Britain to ensure that we would be on the right side, many Americans viewing with concern the rise of socialism in Britain as tantamount to communism. This money underwrote the welfare state and the fabulous fifties, which saw the start of television, ventures into space, and the affluent society – Tory Prime Minister Harold Macmillan's era, when apparently we never had it so good.

Relieved of poverty, the decade was one of major rebellion when the young came to the fore, as never before in history, and challenged existing attitudes to sex, class, authority and 'good taste'. It was the time of Elvis Presley, Marilyn Monroe, James Dean, and the Angry Young Men (Amis, Braine, Osbourne, etc). But first, London came alive with the Festival of Britain, intended to redefine Britain after the war, a microcosm exhibition on the south bank of the Thames and in satellite exhibitions throughout the country. There was the architectural novelty of the Skylon and the Dome of Discovery, the modernity of a John Piper mural, and the response of London theatre, with Olivier and Leigh's *Antony and Cleopatra*, Shaw's *Caesar and Cleopatra*, and Alec Guinness's *Hamlet*. Most of all, there was, as novelist and journalist Keith Waterhouse wrote, a sense that 'something was going on, something had started, something had happened, or was about to happen'.

These new artistic energies were felt in the East End in the opening, in 1953, of Joan Littlewood's Theatre Workshop at the Theatre Royal in Stratford, which gained international fame with seminal productions like Bertolt Brecht's *Mother Courage* (1955), and the East End inspired *Fings Ain't Wot They Used To Be*, which ran from 1959 to 1962, Shelagh Delaney's *A Taste of Honey* (1958), and *Oh! What a Lovely War* (1963).

But nothing could undo the devastation that war had brought to the ordinary East Ender, particularly in the dockland area, or hide the fact that nothing would ever be the same again.

I remember when the war did end it was terrible, we had snow and all them that come back from the Middle East were given tickets to get coal for the fires, because there was no work, my Frankie was out of work for a year when he first come back from the army.

They [the returning soldiers] got a de-mob suit, and I'll never forget my Fred was looking for his suit and my mum said you'd better go down the pawn shop,

> because they had pawned his bleeding suit! You laugh
> about it now, but it wasn't funny.
>
> I know my husband was out of work for 18
> months.[1]

'It was like a bomb site after the war,' recalled Andrew Newman. That is exactly what it was. The scene was of rubble and more rubble, people even got possessive about whose rubble belonged to whom. The Blitz bombed Limehouse flat. It never recovered.

Politicians expended a great deal of shoe leather during the war convincing the populace that the welfare state would rebuild their devastated community. Phil Piratin, Stepney's Communist MP from 1945, pointed out that in reality there wasn't anything like as much money for redevelopment as was needed, or indeed promised. The area needed new schools and health centres as well as housing, but it didn't happen. And Piratin was perplexed in particular that money could be found for a refit of Clarence House, the London home of Queen Elizabeth the Queen Mother from 1953, while East Enders were left to live among the rubble, or be uprooted and cast out of the area altogether.

The planners showed no respect to communities at all. Next door to Limehouse, Ratcliff was planned out of existence altogether. The Commercial Road, the London and Blackwall Railway, the digging of the Rotherhithe Tunnel, and the programme of slum clearance saw it off the map. Today, the only reminder of the

East End 'village' of Ratcliff is Free Trade Wharf, which you approach from The Highway via a huge gateway, bearing lions and the coat of arms of the East India Company. Pass through the gate, originally built in 1796, and reflect that you are walking on what was once one of the most infamous quarters of London – but is now buried under foot and quite forgotten.

The slow and generally badly conceived policy of re-housing, and the inability of Government to meet the promises of a wonderful new era in which the values of the East End would shine forth, made for a poor and depressing sequel to the sacrifice of war.

Among Government solutions were new flats in high-rise blocks – the cities of the air that began to spring up all around – and there was a general drift away to new housing estates further east, a move that had already got itself a bad press in the programme of slum clearance before the war.

John Blake describes how he and his wife were moved from Poplar to Dagenham in Essex, after the Ford Motor Works began operations there in 1931 (the works would eventually cover an area of 600 acres on the Thames Bank). Many felt pushed into following suit, almost as if there was a Government conspiracy afoot, and resisted.

> It was not until the big council estate at Dagenham [Essex] began to take shape that officialdom started snooping around, and trying to persuade people to move out.[2]

Before long, John Blake moved back, because his wife was lonely in the new estate, while he was away working all day. That would never have been the case in the East End they knew. Now, however, Poplar had been razed to the ground in the Blitz. This time they had no choice but to move out again.[3]

Lucy Collard moved to Highgate with her husband, and hated it at first, encountering people who looked down on the East End and thought its inhabitants were beyond the pale.[4]

Arthur Harding's family moved to Leyton in Essex and his children soon had their rough corners ironed out. They became 'a wee bit selecter', as he put it. 'They'd forgotten all about Bethnal Green, and even today they don't want to know anything about it. They changed.'

The feeling was that it wasn't simply the bricks and mortar that were lost to these people, but a manner of life, values, a sense of community. A whole unconscious philosophy of life was disappearing.

They lost, or suppressed, their East End identity, while others we will meet in this book stayed and wore their East End identity with pride in the late 1950s and 1960s, and exported it to the world.

The re-housing programme took many years to effect, with large families in greatest need at the back of the queue, because the Housing Act limited the number of children who could be assigned to a room.

The post-war prefab (prefabricated bungalow) was intended as a temporary solution, but many of them stood for years after the war. The policy was adopted all over the country, and they were counted as acceptable if new mod cons came with them:

> We were moved from our tenement buildings into a prefab in Bishops Way, Cambridge Heath, and life was never the same. I remember when we first moved in, the prefabs were fitted with a fridge. This was a miracle. We had never had an inside toilet before or even a kitchen, but now we had a fridge. My sister and I would invite all our old friends from the street and make them line up. Then we would let them peer through the window to look at the fridge. We couldn't let them in because we had new lino on the floor. Overnight we had become 'posh'![5]

A prefab with modern plumbing was, on the face of it, preferable to Chandra Vansadia's terraced house in West Ham. Even in the early 1960s she still had to go to the Plaistow baths to get a weekly wash, while her mother was reduced to bathing in the garden because, no matter how cold it was, she wanted to wash daily.[6]

Sally Worboyes' family was re-housed in a flat in the new Bancroft council estate, just beyond Stepney Green station. The newness of the flat and 'novelty' of light switches, built-in wardrobes, fitted shelves, all thought-out for convenience, and of course a bath, fed by hot water through taps, enhanced her mother's self-esteem because it appeared to lift the family up a class. The

Worboyes covered their stone floors with dark red lino, and filled the balcony window boxes with colourful flowers.

With the modern lifestyle came a material focus to life, and a strange sort of preciousness, as Daniel Farson observed:

> The etiquette was rigid, and various objects of the East End home became familiar: the toilet-roll cover in the form of a ballerina; blue rinse inside the toilet bowl; furniture consisting of a three-piece suite in colourful Dralon; a telephone table with spring ashtray; a massive radiogram in polished veneer, with a record-holder with yellow cords containing LPs by Perry Como, Frankie Lane and Jimmy Young – and a rubber plant.
>
> And of course there was the obligatory bar in the corner, with a round, metallic-blue ice-bucket on the counter, bottles of Snowball behind, and various signs and insignia on the wall. Other decorations included the Green Lady and a bull-fighting poster bought on the Costa Brava with the name of the toreador replaced by that of the East Ender.
>
> Oh yes! a fireplace with flaming artificial logs, and tongs which chimed.[7]

But the high-rise developments were also a social menace. The planners hadn't understood that they were not simply building buildings, they were constructing communities, or, as it turned out, they were decon-structing them and leaving a vacuum in their place.

Families in tower blocks no longer connected as they had in the East End terraced streets, or even in tenement blocks, where there were courtyards and balconies looking onto them, and open staircases and inner-facing landings, which invited and occasioned interaction between tenants. In a high rise there was nowhere for women to enjoy a good natter of a fine evening, or for the occupants of eight houses or more to sit and stand around and quite simply commune.

The whole basis of life in the East End – what made it special – had been ignored and lost.

> The communal life of the tenements, with all its fraternity and friendship, all its enmity and fighting, was replaced by locked doors and heads turned away. It was a disaster in social planning. A community that had knitted itself together over centuries to form the vital, vibrant people known as 'the Cockneys' was destroyed within a generation.[8]

Efforts were made to counter these problems. Stan Rose was moved from his Victorian terraced street into a tower block in Plaistow in Essex. He missed the old sense of community, but in time a tenants association was formed, and trips were organised to the seaside, and generally occupants began to look out for each other.[9]

However, in 1968 Government optimism over high-rise blocks was dealt a serious blow for another reason, when their safety was called into question. One day at dawn an entire corner of a new high rise called Ronan Point came crashing down. Two women and a man were killed. Serious doubts were expressed about the safety of the system-built building and families insisted on being re-housed. 'I wouldn't live there rent-free,' said one tenant who was offered temporary accommodation with her neighbours.

CHAPTER ELEVEN

Changing faces

———

Meanwhile, in Stepney, and in the original heart of the East End, Whitechapel, where whole streets had been earmarked for demolition, orders were not serviced for twenty years. Here people might indulge a preference to camp out in their blitzed kitchen, if only to remain East Enders. But increasingly it was not an area that held much allure. For the Jews, whose culture had made the area what it was, were going, and there was a dangerous vacuum left.

After the war, many thousands of Jews moved to north and west London. The Jewish experience had been for a long time, 'You come here, you struggle, and then you move on. That's how it works; that's how it will always work.'[1] But, as Philip Bernstein and Anna Tzelniker comment, the Jewish community started to disintegrate post-war for the same reasons as everyone else's – bomb damage. Philip and Anna elected to stay and were involved in Yiddish theatre, but that also declined, partly because people moved away, but also because the younger generation didn't speak Yiddish any more.[2]

So, here was another culture being lost to the area.

In 1956, Bernard Kops was writing the play that would bring him fame – *The Hamlet of Stepney Green*, inspired by watching John Osborne's *Look Back in Anger*, not because Bernard was fired by the supposed working-class realism of Osborne's play, but because he was not. In his opinion *Look Back in Anger* was nothing like the real thing; he was not impressed – 'I can do better than that,' he told himself. He wanted to put the record straight by writing about the Jewish experience in the East End, and he took his Jewish *Hamlet* first to Joan Littlewood.

The Kops family had been bombed out of their tenement building in Stepney and moved to Bethnal Green. 'We moved into the last remaining dwelling house called Queens Buildings in Gossett Street,' in the area of the Old Nichol estate, 'where the Blackshirts still kind of tried their obscenities'.

Incredibly, while servicemen were still reeling from the sights they had witnessed of Hitler's concentration camps, Mosley, who had been interned during the war, but was released in 1943 on health grounds, began inciting East Enders and others to renewed action against the Jews, renaming his movement the British League of Ex-Servicemen and Women. People were incredulous –

> We couldn't believe it, these bastards were on the street again giving the Fascist salute![3]

Jewish ex-servicemen formed The 43 Group, forty-three being the number of men who turned up to the first meeting, and retaliated. Fierce battle was joined with the fascists in Walthamstow, Victoria Park, Shoreditch, Hackney, Kilburn, Maida Vale, Tottenham, and elsewhere. The Group disbanded in April 1950, but there were still skirmishes in areas like Bethnal Green after this.

As Bernard walked through Brick Lane with his wife Erica, he was aware that the days he was writing about had already passed. Wandering down Old Montague Street, he and Erica saw the old Jewish school being dismantled, and that the all-night vapour baths in Brick Lane and little kosher restaurant in Wentworth Street had closed. So they walked into Whitechapel and breakfasted instead at Bloom's, an icon of the Jewish East End for many years, and for the next forty years Britain's most famous kosher restaurant.

Maurice Bloom, a refugee to Britain from Lithuania in 1912, and an expert in meat pickling, opened a little restaurant at 58 Brick Lane in 1920. On 1 January 1921,

a son Sidney was born. In 1951 Maurice died, and
Sidney opened the Bloom's that everyone remembers
in Whitechapel Road. It closed in 1996, and his
grandson now has a similar business in Golders Green.

The Whitechapel restaurant was one with which Alf
Stuart was especially familiar, as by this time he had left
selling combs and was in business opposite Bloom's, at
Gardiner's Corner:

> I had the whole corner, a big place, wholesale textiles –
> the Textile Clearance Company Ltd, well known. I was a
> clearance house for Courtaulds, and became very
> friendly with Frank (later Lord) Kearton, the Courtaulds
> chairman of the 1960s. We became pals. I done very
> very big business from nothing. Sidney Bloom had the
> place in Whitechapel Road next to Albert's, a well known
> shirt firm – he was there for years. In the East End years
> ago were loads of kosher restaurants, salt beef bars.
> There was Blooms, Felv's, Strongwaters, Barnett's in the
> Lane, and another one in Commercial Road. But Sidney
> Bloom built up a very, very good business. I went to his
> son's wedding.

The restaurant was frequented by celebrities. On
one occasion when Cliff Richard came, such a large
crowd gathered outside that the plate glass window
gave way. Feeding the famous, while good for publicity,
did seem to have its drawbacks for Bloom. When he
sent Frank Sinatra a take-out on silver dishes (the
singer was staying at the Savoy), the dishes mysteriously

disappeared. Bloom didn't only cater for the famous, however. Indeed, as Daniel Farson recalled, Bloom's was 'the one restaurant in London where rich and poor all eat together, remembering their past or speculating on each other's future'.[4] Rich and poor mucking in together is rare today, but Charlie Chaplin, a personal friend of Bloom, was so taken with the idea that when he was invited to jump the queue for a table, he refused to do so. Stories about Bloom's proliferate, and it fell to fellow Jew Ivor Spencer to tell the most famous:

> A Jewish man was being served there one Sunday by a Chinese waiter. Very good waiter, very efficient. And when he went out he said, 'Sid, lovely lunch. I enjoyed it. Beautiful salt beef. I am intrigued. Very good waiter. Chinese waiter. He speaks perfect Yiddish. I was very surprised.' Sid said, 'Don't tell him, he thinks he's learning English.'

Sidney Bloom, Alf Stuart, Ivor Spencer, Bernard Kops were just four of thousands of Jews who still inhabited the East End, but as Bernard intuited, their day was already over.

> 300,000 Jews had once crammed themselves into Whitechapel. By 1958 only about 6,000 remained . . . the place was dying.

The Jews moved out and the Maltese moved in. Rooms in dangerously dilapidated properties were let out and men, particularly Maltese immigrants, began a lucrative trade in prostitution:

> I walked down Cable Street, Graces Alley, Dock Street, Sanders Street, Backhouse Lane and Leman Street, and the atmosphere was menacing. Girls hung around in doorways, and men walked up and down the streets, often in groups, or hung around the doors of cafés smoking or chewing tobacco and spitting.[5]

The Maltese were filling part of the vacuum left by the Jews, but there were others. Jennifer Worth paints a depressing picture of a West Indian immigrant begging for a room, and within hours of securing one, filling the room with twenty or twenty-five of his compatriots.

Ordinary East End families could not afford the kind of rent that twenty men to a room could, and unscrupulous landlords forced them out, while those who managed to meet the landlord's rent requirements suddenly found themselves in a neighbourhood of transient immigrants living in appallingly overcrowded conditions.

Then one day a new restaurant opened up to do business next to the White Hart pub in Whitechapel Road, in the same parade as Bloom's. It was unlike anything that had traded there before. It called itself Wimpy Bar.

The concept was new. The first Wimpy Bar in

England had opened three years earlier within the Lyons Corner House in Coventry Street off Piccadilly in the West End, a dedicated fast-food section within the more traditional Corner House restaurant. The name 'Wimpy' came from a hamburger-eating character in the popular American cartoon series *Popeye*, and the whole formica venture spoke loudly of modern America. But this Whitechapel branch was run on a franchise basis by a Jewish family called Silver, who built up quite a culinary empire in Britain over the following years. Yet more interesting, yet more of a novelty, was that Silver's manager had seen fit to employ an Asian front of house.

He had spotted that the population in the neighbourhood of Whitechapel was in more of a state of flux than usual, and this new employee, the first Asian ever to be on such visible display in Whitechapel, was there to bring the new crowd in. In 1956, while the Jews were moving out en masse, the floodgates had opened to an unprecedented programme of immigration from the Indian sub-continent. Andrew Newman first spotted the change in his father's sweatshop. Suddenly they couldn't get Jewish workers, so they had to take on black 'soapers' instead.

> I remember as a kid going up to the factory and seeing a black man working, it was very unusual, and when they first came into the factory, they were called soapers. In the inside of the garment they used to put tailors 'soap' to stiffen the front of the garment – now they put

interlining – and that was their job. Then they were
brought in to be under-pressers to do the ironing, and
then used Hoffman presses, and then they were taught
how to use the sewing machines. The Jews taught them,
because the Jewish people weren't coming in to the
business and they had to find someone to work those
machines.

Besides 'soapers' these immigrants – all male, almost all
from Bangladesh, and sharing crowded quarters in the
neighbouring terraces – were also at first known as
'Ali's', and few of them spoke English, which was why
the tailoring job suited them.

Eventually they didn't like being called Ali, they liked to
be called by their real name which was obvious, and I
found that they were very hard working people who did
command respect and I felt that you should give respect
where it's due and not talk down to them, they were the
same as everybody else. That was sort of the end of the
era of Jewish workshops or factories, it was going into
the hands of the Asian community, it was sort of going
round in a circle.

How this came to be is a fascinating story, the consequence of British greed, and guilt. Britain had had
a field day in India for centuries. The British East
India Company was given its first Royal Charter in
1600 to market indigenous Indian industry worldwide,
and might have brought tremendous prosperity to the

impoverished sub-continent, had it not profited unduly not only from marketing Indian goods, but also by extracting land revenues from the Indian landowners, and trapping elephants, tigers and rhinos, selling skins and horn and keeping the money it made for itself and the British individuals who ran it.[6]

> Bengal[7] was regarded by the British public in the light of a vast warehouse, in which a number of adventurous Englishmen carried on business with great profit and on an enormous scale. That a numerous native population existed they were aware, but this they considered an accidental circumstance.

In time dissatisfied with its remit as a mere commercial trading venture, the company came virtually to rule India with its own army, right up to 1857, when the Indian Rebellion – instigated initially by a mutiny of sepoys (local recruits to the British East India Company army) – led ultimately to its dissolution. The situation was tidied up politically in 1858, when effective rule was transferred from the East India Company to Queen Victoria, who was proclaimed Empress of India eighteen years later.

What this meant was that from 1858 until India's independence from the British in 1947, the period of the British Raj, *all citizens of India were British*. Good from a British point of view because they could be called up to fight under the British flag, which they did in two world wars. Good from the Indian point of view if you happened to be high-caste, in which case the British would teach you how to play cricket. There were no other advantages, although most Indians lived under the illusion that the mother country awaited their presence with brotherly good feeling.

The first Asian settlers came to Britain in the 1920s from Assam, which is now Sylhet in north-eastern Bangladesh. Said one:

> We were born under British rule, and we were citizens of this country. I didn't come here as an immigrant . . . I have been here since 1926. I was a merchant seaman. I came here because I was asked to come, it was the mother country.

But Indians were evident in the East End long before that. More than a hundred years earlier, Bengali people were used on East India Company boats virtually as slave labour.

To get work on a British merchant ship you had to find your way to Calcutta, where serangs (foremen) found you a place at an extortionate cost of three months' wages. Likely, you would be given the job of fireman in the mistaken belief that an Indian could withstand the massively high temperatures better than a white man. If so, you would work four-hour shifts, then eight hours off, round the clock. Lascars, as the Indian seamen came to be called,[8] were increasingly in demand. Conditions in which they lived at sea were horrendous. Diseases (distemper, scurvy, beri-beri, etc) were common, as was death. In 1804 a ship's surgeon wrote that the lascars were –

> A class of men whose labours have been employed, to a greater extent than ever before, for the advantage of the British nation and of the Honourable East India Company.

Many were discarded or jumped ship in London. By 1815 there were as many as 1,100 lascars in the East End at any one time and they were allocated a barracks at Gravesend, which replicated the appalling conditions they had endured on ship, their exploitation culminating in 1832 in the Lascar Act, which did little to help. Thereafter they were housed instead in the notorious lodging houses of Cable Street and Ratcliff Highway, where they'd be robbed and cheated out of their pitiful wages and left destitute to beg on the streets, or turn to crime. Some were 'herded like cattle' into cellars without bedding or 'confined in boxes by the head lascar'.[9]

Nevertheless, the legends persisted that migration was possible and that there was money to be made by coming to Britain. There are many reasons given for the emigration from Sylhet – the wanderlust inherent in the people of the area, the dire state of farming, but Haji Kona Miah maintained that they went for the money, 'that was the most important thing'.

As time went by, the barest of infrastructures began to be built so that it was possible, just possible, to make a life in Britain. Asians berthing at the docks came with the addresses of a handful of settled migrants and found their way to their homes, meeting, eating and exchanging views. Some, like Shah Abdul Majid Qureshi, were tempted to stay, but thought better of it:

> I saw that those who had escaped [from the ships] were living here and there, they had no jobs, some are in bad conditions, some do bad things you see and I didn't feel like staying, and I went back to the ship.[10]

By the 1930s the Asian community had begun to build to a few hundred, and in 1943 Ayub Ali, who arrived in 1938 and showed himself a leader, formed the Indian Seamen's Welfare League with Shah Abdul Majid Qureshi, who had arrived two years earlier.

But for those who planned to jump ship and stay, jobs were scarce and only the most streetwise survived. One Soab Ali had a harmless little gambling scam. He would buy a chocolate bar for a penny ha'penny, slip into a pub and surreptitiously sell drinkers tickets numbered 1 to 6 for a penny each. Whoever's number came up got the chocolate bar cheap and Soab Ali made four pence ha'penny. There was also a good trade in Indian perfumes concocted in their lodging houses and sold to ladies at the seaside. Abdul Malik made a business out of the clothing coupons given to Indian seamen arriving at the docks.

> I used to buy the coupons from them for ten shillings
> and sold them for five pounds. Well, ten shillings was a
> lot of money for them – they could buy three or four
> suits in Pakistan with that. That was in 48 or 49.[11]

Then of course there were the Jewish sweatshops, like
Alf Newman's in Whitechapel, and the boiler rooms of
big hotels, where the fallacy of the Asian's impervious-
ness to high temperatures could be traded once more.
Or, it was off to the cotton mills and factories of the
North.

Gradually, the East End got quite a reputation
among young Asians, so that a seaman called Sona
Miah actually jumped ship in Glasgow but took the
effort to travel all the way down to an address he had in
New Road in Whitechapel. Most of the Asians settled in
this area, but it was a precarious business:

> I had one or two addresses, but they were wrongly
> written, they were not correct, and when I showed them
> to anyone, they didn't know.[12]

This was Shah Abdul Majid Qureshi, who jumped ship
to find a place in the 1940s and became totally lost,
until suddenly he heard the sound of a man speaking
in Sylhet dialect:

> I was so very glad, I held him, embraced him. I said, 'By
> good luck, at last I have found someone who can help
> me.' He said, 'You have come from the boat?' I said,

'Yes.' He said, 'Come with me, I will give you shelter, I live in Mr Munshi's house.'[13]

Mr Munshi's lodging house was one of a handful of places for which immigrant Asians made. Another was a café at 76 Commercial Street run by Ayub Ali, who had settled there in the 1920s and had a house also at 13 Sandys Row, close to Liverpool Street station. These were places to go to ground for a period long enough for the shipping line to give up looking for you. When it came to registering their presence legally at India House on the Strand, there was no need for a British passport, for they were already British citizens. There was no question of repatriation.

Nawab Ali arrived in England on 28 August 1939, his ship docking at Cardiff. He jumped ship that night, climbing over the dock wall and making for the house of a friend, who hid him for a few days, before taking him to London, to a house on the east side of Commercial Road, full of sailors.

After three weeks he got a job in an Egyptian coffee shop in Cannon Street Road.

Five weeks later he found his way to India House and by chance met two girls, one of whom he knew from Calcutta. He was closely questioned by an official but told that he would receive his papers in due course (there would be enormous complications over this, at one stage the official branding him a spy). Outside, the girls greeted him. One had bought him a tie, and he walked with them to the Savoy Hotel, where the girls were working. They left him with the gateman, who gave him a cup of tea and spoke to him. Nawab barely understood, but answered 'Yes' and 'No' as he thought sounded appropriate. Then the girls returned and told him they had arranged for him to work in the Savoy kitchens.

That's how migration was effected. But it was never easy. After some unspecified trouble, Nawab was turfed out of his place and had to sleep on the street – 'down some steps in a doorway in Settles Street' – where a Jewish shopkeeper gave him some soup. Later, in a café, he bumped into the brother of a friend of his from India, who took him to a place where he was living, actually sharing a 'three-quarter bed' with another man. The English wife of the Indian owner took pity on him, pressed his clothes and gave him a room of his own. Each morning he would walk miles and miles to the Savoy, where he was cleaning the kitchen. Later he would work in a factory in Coventry, brave a significant amount of racist provocation in that city, and save enough to buy cafés and restaurants of his own in East London and elsewhere. During the war he fought in the British Navy and during rationing made money on the black market.[14]

Back home, as the first true migrants were settling in the East End, India was working towards independence from Britain. In 1931, Mahatma Gandhi, who played a pivotal role in this and was frequently imprisoned by the British for organising acts of civil disobedience, had visited London for the Round Table Conference, which looked at changing the constitution of British-governed India. Two sisters living in Bromley-by-Bow in the East End, Doris and Muriel Lester, offered him a place to stay. Having dedicated their lives to the poor of the East End, and to women's rights, Doris and Muriel took in Gandhi at Kingsley Hall, the HQ of their project, off Bruce Road, E3. There is a plaque there to this day, and the little room in which he stayed has been preserved.

When war came in 1939, politically astute Gandhi demanded independence as the price for support-ing Britain. Meanwhile, contact between Asian immi-grants and the British Government developed. In the 1940s English MPs met regularly with Indian political workers at Shah Abdul Najid Qureshi's restaurant, called the Indian Centre, in Charlotte Place, off Charlotte Street.

In 1947 independence was won for India, but to Gandhi's horror the country was partitioned into two sovereign states, India and Pakistan, and the latter, itself sub-divided as West and East Pakistan, later became Pakistan and Bangladesh, with India geographically between them, a political separation that marked a religious distinction between Hindu (India) and Muslim (Pakistan and Bangladesh).

Shah Abdul Najid Qureshi described the distinction this way: 'Hindu people were the cultured society – the student community . . . people who were studying law and philosophy and medicine and all that.' But the more fundamental difference was Shafiq Uddin's:

'Only Hindu has classes or castes, which dictate social position according to what you do. There is no class distinction in Islam. Islam forbids that. If you are a Muslim you can sit at the same table as anyone; not if you are Hindu.'

Gandhi realised the danger of the separation, and immediately it resulted in Hindu-Muslim riots. Gandhi fasted until the Hindu rioters in Delhi swore themselves to non-violence, but on 30 January 1948, on his way to pray, he was assassinated by a Hindu infuriated by his success in bringing the two religions together.

In Whitechapel, meanwhile, Nawab Ali took a lease on a place in Umberstone Street in Aldgate, and opened it as the Commonwealth Club, after India became a Republic within the British Commonwealth in 1950 – no alcohol, but gambling (cards) and Indian food. He also opened the first halal butcher in Britain at 42 Hessel Street, which had been for so long the home of Jewry in Stepney. Then he took a lease on a place in nearby Hanbury Street and opened an Advice Bureau for incoming Asians, planning to combine it with another gambling club, but Peter Shore, a member of the Labour Party from 1948 and later MP for Stepney, Poplar and Bethnal Green, said that wouldn't do.

The flow of Asian immigrants was as yet quite small however. Then, in 1956, the door opened wider. Having prised the greedy fingers of the British from this jewel in the Crown, the sub-continent now looked to their erstwhile masters for reparation. There was a debt to repay.

After hundreds of years of interference, exploitation and domination, the British had left India in terrible poverty, the like of which no Englishman could even imagine. 'Sometimes I think when I got married I was disfigured by being poor,' said one.[15] Reparation came in the form of passports.

First, they were granted to relatives or dependants of 'distressed seamen', men left in such poverty as a result of working for the British that giving them a passport to possible wealth in Britain was the only way out. Then pressure was brought and others were given passports too, and the massive immigration of Asians into England from the 1950s began. Travel agencies opened in Sylhet in north-eastern Bangladesh and in Dhaka, the capital, and in London a reciprocal agency was set up – Orient Travels, first at Sandys Row, E1, then at 96 Brick Lane.

1956 was dubbed the year of the passports. The few hundred migrants in Whitechapel and Stepney were eventually joined by thousands upon thousands, and the character of the area changed completely. By the early 1970s many Bengalis followed a similar path to progress that the Jewish immigrants had taken before them. They moved from working for other people to working for themselves. Banglatown began with material shops, clothes shops and an Asian corner shop in Brick Lane. They opened their businesses and worked hard.

In 1974 the Jewish synagogue in Brick Lane, which had begun life as a Huguenot church, was turned into a Mosque. And, as ever in the East End,

Everybody got along well with each other, there was a real community feeling amongst the local people.

CHAPTER TWELVE

Love and respect

A t this point Shafiq Uddin was studying for his
A levels at Mongolchondy High School, Tajpure,
which is in Sylhet in the region of Osmani Nagor
(Blagonj) – 'Yes, English exams, like GCSE with
English. I was in ninth year of taking GCSE, or tenth.'
Shafiq's family were farming people, 'mainly dry
land farming', as opposed to rice. Already his thoughts
were full of England. He used to meet English people
in a tea garden owned by a British company in
Sylhet.

Tea was the big industry in Sylhet. We used to

talk . . . also sometimes at school. The secondary school
where I studied was founded by one of the
Commissioners who had worked for the British. He built
the school on his estate, and he would come in to
school and tell us about the United Kingdom.

A friend of Shafiq's father had gone to England in the
late 1940s after the war. He would send photographs
home to his family, which Shafiq saw. At that time, his
idea of England was 'a sort of a dream'.

I thought that everywhere you would see light shining,
colours everywhere. I thought of like Buckingham Palace,
Tower of London, St Paul's and Westminster, all those.
Really in my mind was a picture of one of the nicest
places, where everything is perfect, nothing will be
wrong. That's how I felt before I came.

Shafiq had been expected to continue his studies in
Bangladesh and take a degree. So, when he was thinking about coming over to London, his expectations of
what he would achieve here were greater.

Greater expectations of getting a good education,
maybe doing things well. But mostly I was thinking it
could be the best sort of life.

His father's friend tried to convince him otherwise,
telling him that it was very cold in London, that he
didn't think he would like it, that it was better to finish

his studies in Bangladesh. But when Shafiq turned 18
he made his decision to quit school –

> It was the final exam for GCSE, and I didn't take it! I
> came on February 15, 1958. It was winter time. There
> was five to six inches of snow everywhere.

Unlike the first Asian migrants, but like most others in
the late 1950s, Shafiq travelled by plane to Britain,
arriving at Heathrow Airport. His father's friend was by
then living in Sheffield, but a couple of other friends
from the same area had arrived in England six months
earlier and were living in Peter Street, off Wardour
Street in Soho.

> So, I took a taxi to Peter Street, it must have been
> around 4 o' clock in the afternoon and it was all dark,
> you couldn't see anything. It was like you couldn't tell
> the difference between day or night, it was just really
> dark, and so cold. I came in trousers, a jacket and shirt. I
> did not realise it would be so cold.
>
> When I arrived and knocked at the door, a white
> woman came out and asked me, 'Have you paid the
> fare?' So, because it was hard for me to speak, I wrote
> on a piece of paper, 'Yes, I have paid 10 shillings.' She
> said, 'Too much! Too much!' The taxi driver who brought
> me had said 7 shillings or something.
>
> I was surprised to see a white lady there. She said
> she was Italian. Then her husband came out and said to

me, 'Don't worry, your cousin let us stay.' I went in and
it was so cold.

Clearly Shafiq was apprehensive. He had arrived in the
middle of Soho to find people he didn't know living in
a house where he had expected to find only his 'cousin'
living. He had seven or eight pounds in his pocket, 'a
lot of money for those times', but –

I felt weird in my mind. It was being alone. It was very
hard to cope. You don't know where you are, what sort
of situation you were in, what was expected, what was
right or wrong. I was really shocked, I was shaking. So
this woman put me near the heater, a coal heater. So
that is how I came here.

Shafiq stayed there six or seven weeks and found it
impossible to get a job. So, he travelled to Sheffield and
stayed with his father's friend, who had a job in a
factory. This man saved him. Shafiq calls him 'Uncle',
though he was no relation.

He was very nice to me, like he paid for everything and
he said, 'Look, you stay here, and you look around.' He
was always telling me not to worry, we look after each
other. I still remember, and I repaid him with thanks all
my life, until he passed away.

But I couldn't get a job in Sheffield either, and after
ten or twelve weeks I said to him, 'Uncle, look, I have no

chance to get work in the factories. I come to them as a student. I have never worked in my life.'

So, I wrote to my friend in the West End, and said, 'What can I do?' And he said, 'Come and work in a restaurant. That's an easy option.' So I returned to London, and now one of the guys I met from back home was living just off Brick Lane in Heneage Street. It's still there. An Irish woman called Miriam was also in the house. She was married to one of our Asian guys who owned the house. They offered me a place to stay. I didn't want to sleep with anyone, so I said I want a small room. She said. 'OK. Give me whatever you can afford, because you are a nice boy.'

I stayed there and looked for a job. I would travel from here to the City where there were a couple of agents. From Aldgate I used to get a ticket for 4d., but I couldn't get any job. Then suddenly one day I was sitting in a room in the house in Heneage Street, and an older Asian guy, who lived downstairs, said to me, 'Excuse me, you are very young boy, but there is a job somewhere. Do you want a job?' So I said, I am looking for one.

This man, although he was Bengali, spoke very good English and arranged for Shafiq to meet a drinking friend of his, an Englishman, in the White Hart on Whitechapel Road.

He said put your smart clothes on and everything. Somebody else said to me, 'Don't believe him, he is always drunk.' But I went. I thought I have nothing to

lose. And as we walked, next to the pub there was this
Wimpy. And the guy says to me, 'That's the place, the
Wimpy Bar.' And I said to myself you must be joking,
how could I work there, really, really smart place!

So I went to the pub with him and a very smart,
young, tall English guy – came in and said, 'Do you want
a pint, and one for your friend?' He was called Clive
Linley. My friend had been talking to him, told him that
he had this young Asian boy. Now Linley wanted to
attract Asians into the new Wimpy. He, or Mr Silver, had
seen that it was an Asian area and perhaps Asians
hadn't wanted to go in.

So, it was agreed. Shafiq would start work there that
evening, beginning with washing up, but within a
couple of weeks he was front of house, on display –
the first Asian to get a job in a Wimpy Bar. With
his confidence restored, Shafiq shone. Before long he
rose to Manager of the Bar, and pursued a successful
career with the Silver family that spanned forty years.
The regular clientele of the Wimpy took to him
immediately:

In the evening you would see thirty, forty, fifty Mods
lining the pavement outside the Wimpy, with their
scooters, and they did help me with my English.

He became a feature of the Whitechapel Wimpy. 'They
used to say to me, "Hello Mr Wimpy. Hello Wimpy
man!" And soon Shafiq started to attract the interest of

female customers too. The Asians arrived without women, young men all living together, sometimes ten, twenty to a house, a bachelor existence. English girls were described by many as interested, curious, they asked a lot of questions. There was no sense that they looked down on them.

I think every girl used to try and chat Sheffie up. You would walk in the Wimpy Bar. You'd go up to the counter and he was just standing there next to the till and it was just amazing, his hair! I had never seen anybody with hair like that, it was beautiful. He was stunning. He looked really lovely with that lovely mop of hair on his head, very very thick hair, lovely, gorgeous! He did give me the eye as well, and I gave him the eye, you know I made myself noticed. He asked me, he actually asked me, 'Would you like to come out with me?' I said, 'I'm not sure.' I said I'll think about it you know, and then I said, 'Yes, I will.'

Pamela was still at school when she first set eyes on Shafiq. Hers was a typical cockney family. They lived in a five-storey tenement called Bullen House in Collingwood Street, between Whitechapel Road and Cambridge Heath Road.

We were on the second floor. There must have been about 200 flats in a court. I still go there now to see the old Jewish lady, Mary, Mum's neighbour, bless her heart. I remember her from a baby. She was on the same balcony as me and Mummy, and her sister Dora. She died and her mum died. Mum used to work for her, clean for her sister and all that. Mary is 93 now. She knows you and doesn't know you. She has my mum's home help, Cathy. So Cathy phones me up and tells me how she's getting on, and I go to see her whenever I can. There are about a handful now that were there years ago.

As children we all played together, in and out of each other's flats. We used to play around together in the park and the grounds. We used to save up and go on beanos together, in the coach to Southend, Brighton, Margate, and all that. We had fun. Crazy times. It was lovely. Didn't have much, but . . .

Pamela's father, a night watchman, was not happy that she was seeing an Asian.

The father was the most important person in our family. The father was the bread winner. Mother was important, but my dad was like a sergeant major. Sometimes when we was naughty I remember he would lock us in the bedroom. We weren't hit or anything, but punished by stopping pocket money and stopped going out. We was disciplined.

Still less was her father happy when two years later Pamela announced she intended to marry Shafiq.

In the beginning it was hard with my parents, well
mainly my dad, not my mum. My dad, he didn't come to
my wedding. He didn't come because I was marrying an
Asian, but at the end of the day I was fine, just to be
there with Sheffie, to marry him. A lot of my girlfriends,
they, oh my girlfriends . . . When they knew I was going
out with my husband and they knew he was Asian and
all that, they disowned me, didn't want to know me,
didn't want to know me at all, a lot of them they were
against it.

**If Pamela had gone out with a Jewish boy would they
have felt the same way?**

Well, I don't think . . . I think it was the colour that made
the difference. A lot of my girlfriends I was brought up
with . . . I knew them for years and years and years, and
as soon as they knew I'm with an Asian, they didn't
want to know me! But me I got on with all the Asians.
But then a couple of my girlfriends they met Asians after
I met my husband, and they got on like a house on fire.

**Shafiq described Pamela's cockney community as
'closed – it was a closed community, then.' But Pamela
saw the East End as having 'no barriers', and trotted out
the culture of trust that we have heard from other East
Enders –**

You would go out all day long, keep the key on a piece
of string in the letter box. Mum would leave the key in

the letter box on a bit of string, come home from
school, put my hand in, get the key, unlock the door.
You could leave the door open all day and nobody
would go in and rob you.

So, if there were no barriers, why did they not trust
Shafiq? Were the doors left unlocked because there
wasn't much to steal in those days, no televisions, etc,
rather than that everyone trusted each other so?
Pamela conceded:

There wasn't much around, televisions, washing
machines and things like that. Everything was done by
hand. Mum had an old mangle. She had it on the
balcony . . .

Shafiq saw the culture first hand with a good deal of
objectivity:

I remember that the only thing that did go missing was
the money from the gas meters. They used to be penny
meters. They would break in to the meter, get about a
pound, and blame a black person, if there was one
around.

But he also accepted that his own society at home in
Bangladesh was just as closed. It was unheard of for
most Asians to consider a mixed marriage, or even
marriage where the husband made his own choice of
wife.

> Our people did not like the idea of it. The majority
> would say, 'I am not going to co-operate if you are
> going to marry an English woman.' Back home they
> used to think, Well, oh well, he has gone. Do you
> understand what I mean?

Shafiq had particular trouble with an aunt and with his
father over the intended marriage. It was simply not the
Muslim way. He would have been expected to allow his
parents back home to find a wife for him. But it did not
deter him.

Pamela made the critical concession. When Shafiq
asked her, she agreed to convert to Islam, and then they
got married in a register office.

> I did not force her. Most Asian men did not marry
> English girls, they lived with them. But I did not want
> people to think, 'Oh, just a woman living with him.' I
> wanted people to know that she was my wife, and we
> are not allowed to marry a non-Muslim. So I spoke to
> her and she said, 'I don't mind.'

Shafiq's winning way was the respect he showed
Pamela.

> I found, by going with my husband, that he had more
> respect for me than English boys showed. I liked that. He
> treated me well, good manners. A lot of the English
> boys they was just rough and ready, you know drinking,
> smoking, it was just . . . You know, it was the start of

mods and rockers and all that. But with my husband it was like he had respect for me, he treated me well. Why did I convert to Islam? I respected him. He asked me, I respected the way he asked me. Also, I wanted my children to be brought up like him.

Pamela and Shafiq have six children. She sent them to her old school, Stewart Headlam Primary in Tapp Street. But they were brought up in the Muslim faith. So, there was continuity with her side and with his. It was 50:50, mutual respect. And when I was told that Shafiq's code of respect was not individual to him, but traditional – 'where I come from we show respect' – it was easy to see why Pamela wanted them to be brought up within the same code.

Mutual respect facilitated their marriage. For Shafiq it meant that, 'I celebrate in Christmas, and I used to do my own religious way.' It enabled him to resolve the conflict within Pamela's family over their marriage: 'We had a problem with her dad, but he became eventually a very close friend to me. He explained he had had a bit of a problem, some relation with some black people, and he used to think, is Shafiq like this? But then after he met me a few times, he was a changed man with me, he knew what sort of person I was.' In the end, this code of mutual respect made the question as to whether Shafiq has become more cockney or Pamela more Muslim immaterial. It was always 50:50.

Children of mixed race may encounter problems, but the Uddin children are imbued with this code of respect, because Shafiq has won their respect and valued it, and they have wanted his, and in every case they have been shown it, genuinely, when they have earned it, and it has served them well.

> My oldest son, when he was young, became involved with music, as a pop musician. A couple of boys and him, they went to America a few times, had long hair and everything, and I never used to halt him. I used to teach him like our other kids. He knew he had to do what he wanted to do, but he had to respect my ways. Suddenly, fourth time in America and one night he just came home, short hair and everything. I was shocked. He said I wanted music and it helped me to find it, and I said it's up to you what you want. He became himself and educated himself and he is now better than me. I could not educate him because I haven't got the experience.

Mutual respect takes the sting out of conflict, and may even resolve it. Success also lies along this path, and the riches of diversity, as Pamela showed me:

> The eldest child, Monwar, is married to an Iranian girl, part Iranian, part Gujarati. He has three children, two girls and one boy. Sufia is married to an English gentleman. He is in the army. They have one baby boy. Fatima married an Englishman, who has his own printing company in Old Street. Mina married a half Bengali, half English, and they have their own property business.

Anwar is a professional footballer, with Dagenham and
Redbridge at the moment. Then I have my baby Dean.
Dean is 24. He is a designer and works for my son-in-law
in the printing company.

Shafiq, who still lives with Pamela in Stepney today, can
look back over half a century with satisfaction to an
experiment that worked well at every level:

I own a house now, and a house and some land in
Bangladesh. We have six children. They all own their
own houses, except my young one. None of them is
unemployed. All have been in work since leaving
school.

The East End was the pot in which the Uddins brewed
their special recipe. Could anywhere have been found
more conducive to it?
Says Shafiq:

Now we are thinking we might move out, but I cannot,
because I love the East End and I always think I am
going to miss something.

It is hard to believe that in the 1970s this attitude was
met with forceful opposition by the British National
Party and the National Front.

They used to call us 'Paki', they would swear at us. They
wanted us to leave the country: this was a white country

and it should only have white people in it. They did not
want black people. I used to think that we cannot live in
this situation, we will have to go back home because it is
really hard living here. I found it extremely sad.

**When Pamela went down to the markets on a Sunday
morning, she read the abuse on the walls.**

Oh tell me, Brick Lane, all those marches,
demonstrations and everything. I remember the end of
Mosley, and then came the National Front. Oh, terrible.
Terrifying. We used to go down to the market all the
time, Brick Lane market, didn't we? Sometimes you were
frightened to walk down there. I was always worried for
Sheffi being in the Wimpy Bar that time when all that
trouble was there. A lot of violence we saw. Oh my
good God, I was coming one day from home with my
three babies in the pram to meet him from the Wimpy
Bar. I was just crossing over the road, and then in
Osborn Street the British Party and the National Front
was running down a lot of Asians. They started fighting.
It was just terrifying.

They did not beat people up lightly, they beat people
up really badly. Four or five people would beat one
person up, then it would be hard to defend yourself or
hit back. The police were always there, some on horses.
One time a policeman hit that Asian man for no reason.
It weren't his fault, you know? The police were hitting
the Asians and they should have been hitting the white
men. I went over one time and I said to this policeman,

'It weren't his fault!' I just run over there and I pulled
him off and his hat come off, and they got hold of me
and they said, 'I arrest you!' And I said, 'You can arrest
me if you want to.' It was terrible it really was. I was
shaking, terrified. It was wrong though, it wasn't those
Asian boys' fault, it was the white boys' fault.

**The Wimpy Bar was on the front line, as it were, and
Shafiq used to have a lot of problems –**

Some of them used to come in and I used to serve them.
Even then I used to say, 'Look, your business you are
doing, my business I am doing.' But I was scared, and
my staff was really scared. We had a notice: 'Manager,
Mr Uddin'. So, I used to say, 'Everything OK, service all
right?' – 'Yes, thank you very much.' I wanted to be
nice. I wanted them to feel that they were degrading
themselves. If he does cause me problems, doesn't
matter what colour he is, you kick him out.

One became a friend in the end. He was Maltese,
and I would say to him, 'Look, I know your family, where
you are from, etc. So, what do you do this for?' He used
to come with his other friends and I used to serve them
at the Wimpy. I used to say, 'I serve you because you are
a customer. I get money, and I am shamed that you are
not shamed to come to my shop and have me serve you.
I personally serve you with my staff.' So, we come to
talk. Once, he was telling me what happened in the
attack, and I said, 'Listen, put your head down and look
at me before you attack me.' And then we became

friends, and he admitted to me that these people [the
NF], 'They help me, they give me money.' Eventually, I go
to his family and then he stopped.

I was not scared. I used to have myself exercise with
the self-defence so I knew one or two moves.

But the Asians took so much violence from the National
Front that eventually they organised weekend sit-downs
in Brick Lane, where right-wing agitators gathered.

The NF used to have their meeting past the brewery, up
the top end of Brick Lane, the Bethnal Green end. They
stood there and the Asians on the other side. The
National Front had a warehouse like, where they would
meet, not in Brick Lane, but on the other side, on
Bethnal Green Road, where they used to make all the
pamphlets – there was like a warehouse.

It was the same boundary line beyond which the Jews
had not dared to walk earlier.

Up to the other end you would not go alone, especially
an older man. You wouldn't go beyond the end of Brick
Lane. You wouldn't walk down there. You would see the
boys, skinheads, big bother boots on, tattoos all over
their bodies. They were young. The older ones were
telling them how to do it.

So, the Asians, in the end, we decided that our
youngsters should fight. They should defend themselves.
So they did fight. Eventually they started to hit back.

It is commonly supposed that out of this came a fervent desire among the Bengali community to stake a claim on the area of Brick Lane as Bangla Town.

Said Pamela: 'It's not Brick Lane no more, it's Bangla Town. The signs are there, "Bangla Town".'

But Shafiq Uddin cannot see that as the way forward. 'I'm not happy about that. Never.'

Pamela agreed: 'They should have kept it Brick Lane.'

Shafiq: 'Changing it into Bangladesh is not my idea. It was not the idea.'

The idea was about mutuality and respect. That was the lesson learned.

PART IV

FAMILY
BUSINESS

CHAPTER THIRTEEN

Violence and respect

———

At the top end of Brick Lane, the Bethnal Green end, where the boundary line first separated the Jews from their persecutors, and then the Bengalis from theirs, life was dominated by criminal gangs and powerful indigenous cockney families, many of whom had lived in the area for generations. It was an area that had known villainy for hundreds of years. Charles Dickens created the legend of Oliver Twist here, or was it the legend that created him?

> It was a chill, damp, windy night, when the Jew,
> buttoning his great-coat tight against his shrivelled body,

and pulling the collar up over his ears so as completely to obscure the low part of his face, emerged from his den. He paused on the step as the door was locked and chained behind him, and having listened while the boys made all secure, and until their retreating footsteps were no longer audible, slunk down the street as quickly as he could.

The house to which Oliver had been conveyed was in the neighbourhood of Whitechapel. The Jew stopped for an instant at the corner of the street; and, glancing suspiciously round, crossed the road, and struck off in the direction of Spitalfields.

The mud lay thick upon the stones, and a black mist hung over the streets; the rain fell sluggishly down, and everything felt cold and clammy to the touch. It seemed just the night when it befitted such a being as the Jew to be abroad. As he glided stealthily along, creeping beneath the shelter of the walls and doorways, the hideous old man seemed like some loathsome reptile, engendered in the slime and darkness through which he moved: crawling forth, by night, in search of some rich offal for a meal.

He kept on his course, through many winding and narrow ways, until he reached Bethnal Green; then, turning suddenly off to the left, he soon became involved in a maze of mean and dirty streets which abound in that close and densely-populated quarter.

The Jew was evidently too familiar with the ground he traversed to be at all bewildered, either by the darkness of the night, or the intricacies of the way. He

> hurried through several alleys and streets and at length
> turned into one, lighted only by a single lamp at the
> farther end. At a door of a house in this street, he
> knocked; having exchanged a few muttered words with
> the person who opened it, he walked upstairs.
>
> A dog growled as he touched the handle of a room-
> door; and a man's voice demanded who was there.
>
> 'Only me, Bill; only me, my dear,' said the Jew,
> looking in.

Scuttling vermin-like along the dark, dank corridors that separated the squalid slum-dwellings of the old East End, Fagin seemed to embody Dickens's Kafkaesque vision of the metropolis which has haunted his readers since the novel first made its appearance in 1838.

Fagin's walk took him from the warren of little streets off Whitechapel (which we explored earlier) in the direction of Spitalfields, perhaps up Leman Street and Brick Lane, 'until he reached Bethnal Green'. Then he turned 'suddenly off to the left' into the 'maze of mean and dirty streets', which is the Old Nichol, the Boundary Estate, the heart of the criminal East End, off limits even to the police.[1]

Bill Sykes, who hangs in the book, lived in the area of the Old Nichol. So did the notorious gangster Arthur Harding a few generations later. Had Fagin turned right when he came to Bethnal Green, he would have found himself in the area of Vallance Road where, a generation or so after Harding, the Kray twins lived.

Arthur Morrison's novel *A Child of the Jago* (1892)

(his name for the Old Nichol) has several local family-based gangs within the estate. Arthur Harding was a local gang-leader in the early years of the twentieth century. The stories about him controlling the street markets, intimidating business rivals and vicious street-crimes chime perfectly with Morrison's fictional portrayal of the *Jago*.

Harding's greatest rival was a man called Isaac 'Ikey' Bogard, otherwise known as 'Darky the Coon', on account of his tightly curled black hair. Bogard had a gang of ex-boxers. Guns were used. In a show-down between the two gangs, each about a dozen strong, on 23 December 1911, in the Bluecoat Boy pub in Bishopsgate, Harding's gang attempted to kill Bogard. In the event, Harding was convicted only for causing an affray, the chief witness, the publican, having beaten a hasty retreat out of London. Nevertheless, at the trial, Mr Justice Avory lamented 'that a portion of London should be infested by criminal ruffians armed with revolvers . . . If the existing law is not strong enough to put a stop to it, some remedial legislation is necessary.'

Avory had a point, for a year earlier the East End had witnessed a full-on armed battle between burglars and police. On 16 December 1910, Harris's Jewellery Shop in Houndsditch was robbed by armed men. A policeman had been alerted to the raid by a strange hissing noise: it turned out to be the first time an acetylene torch was used in a crime. The gang shot the policeman and escaped to Sidney Street in Stepney, where, on 3 January, there was a shoot-out with the police and military. Two gang members were killed and a third, Peter Piatkov, nicknamed 'Peter the Painter', miraculously escaped. The episode became known as the Siege of Sidney Street:

> I was one of the crowd who saw this famous fiasco. I remember the soldiers lying prone in the roadway, taking pot-shots, the battery of artillery in the road outside Smiths Paint factory on the corner, and Winston Churchill bobbing in and out of that gateway. The guns (artillery) were silver unlimbered.[2]

Guns, often looted from the Irish police, continued to be a feature of East End crime for many years, as did Arthur Harding. Bogard, who survived Harding's attack on him, became a First World War hero, and eventually went straight.

In the East End, the gang mentality was bred in the bone. If anyone from one family started on another, revenge would be taken and respect restored. Even as a child, you recognised it as a condition of the world in which you lived.

> Many many years ago, I was only seven or eight, I think, but I always remember it . . . One evening, about 6 or 7pm, a gang of Maltese was outside, throwing bricks and everything and my Uncle Alfie went out there and knocked the living daylights out of them, and a little boy run up to the Butcher's [the Jolly Butcher in Brick Lane]

and got the family and they came down and made
amends for Uncle Alfie.

This was one of Tony Burns's earliest memories in
Bethnal Green. Four generations of the Burns family
were brought up in Bacon Street, but Tony was actually
born in Bridgend in Wales in 1940, his mother Megan's
home town, shortly after his father, Harry, was called
up.

My mum died while I was there. I came back into
London after the war. I was about six. By that time we'd
received a note to say that my dad was killed in Dunkirk.
So, I never had a mother or father.

This confused me, as I knew Tony's father Harry was a
force in his life for decades after the war.

Yeah, he was. He turned up. He turned up when the
war was over. He stayed dead for the rest of the war. He
stayed in the pub. He read the letter – reported missing,
Dunkirk. We knew.

After the war, Harry met and married Violet. The Burns
family was a very big family in the East End at the time,
and if you started on one of them you knew you would
get a visit from the others. And of course if in the
process you got the better of the aggressors, you were
the villain, you were the bad, bad boy. Said Tony –

It's a pain in the backside sometimes when the second or third generation causes a bit of trouble but then you have to look after them.

We had a big family. We had a massive family. Four brothers. Teddy, Charlie, Alfie and Harry, and they all had children. Three of them lived in Bacon Street and one of them lived in Fuller Street. So that carried a lot of weight. At the top of Brick Lane after the war, it was debris, you know? 'That's my debris. No, don't touch that debris, that's the Burns's debris!'

At the top of Brick Lane you had the Burys [another big family]. Over here, in Vallance Road [just a stone's throw away] were the Krays. At the end of Roman Road you had another big family. So, everybody respected each other. What I tell people today . . . For instance, someone would come and see you, 'Tony, my son has got in trouble with drugs. He owes these people £10,000. If he don't come up with this £10,000 in a month or a week or something like that, er they are going to hurt him.' You go and see someone and you have a talk with them and you say, 'Look, do us a favour and I'll owe you,' you know? And you make sure the kid don't get hurt . . . and he'll pay his debt over a period of time.

That's how it worked, that was the culture in which Tony was brought up.

You could always go and see someone. Today, you can't. That's the difference. I don't want to be rude, but it's the

Eastern Europeans, they don't understand. They can't
even talk English. And they've got no respect for
anybody. They don't give a monkey's about favours and
things like that.

The Burns family did not themselves live on the wrong
side of the law. The only time Tony was tempted to get
into trouble was when a brother was set upon. Equally,
the Burns family would never sit down in Brick Lane to
protest about the BNP, as Shafiq and his friends were
doing in the 1960s. If challenged by someone, they
would get stuck in. Respect is required to be shown,
and will be reasserted by force, if necessary. As Shafiq
admitted, the Bengalis came to a similar conclusion in
the end, meeting the racist disrespect and violence with
violence.

At ten, Tony embarked upon a career as an amateur
boxer. On account of his place of birth he boxed for
Wales twenty-two times, sixteen of them as captain of
the national team, and was Welsh National Champion.
He didn't turn professional because his mother and his
wife didn't want him to. The promoter, Micky Duff, was
a personal friend, so it would have been easy.

I knew what was going on with the kids when they
turned pro and I wasn't a big fan. I don't need money
now anyway. So I did the Repton instead.

The Repton is located in a converted bath house on
Cheshire Street, around the corner from Bacon Street, at

the top of Brick Lane. The club was originally established in the nineteenth century by the famous Derbyshire public school, as part of its remit as a charitable organisation.[3] Until well into the 1960s the main aim was to dispense funds from a trust in response to appeals from the East End. There would be the money-raising dinners at which the Repton Club boxers would take on others. Also on the charity agenda was an offer from Repton School of two places for two East End children. Harry and his brother Charlie were directly involved with the school, helping to organise the trust activities.

Since Tony became senior coach for the club in 1967, the Repton has won 200 titles. Last year Tony was presented with the ABA Lifetime Coaching and Development award. His boxers have included fighters such as light heavyweight Courtenay Fry and Audley Harrison, the heavyweight who won Olympic gold in the 2000 Olympic Games. His fighters have won, on average, near enough five national awards every year he has been in charge, at ABA senior, ABA junior, NABC and schoolboy levels.

Also in the gym I had a kid named Maurice Hope.[4] I had Maurice as a little boy. He won National Schools Champion with us, and in them days – I know it sounds ridiculous – but he was about the only black kid up there.

I've been to seven Olympics, three Worlds . . . I've been everywhere. I would say we have at least 200 kids here. We are the biggest and strongest and oldest club in the country. This was the Repton School thing, they formed us to show the rest of the country they were sponsoring young kids in London, 1890 or so. Now they have pulled away from us. We have connections at the committee level, but financially none. You can't take a couple of kids out of the East End and put them in a public school. It's like putting them in prison.

My son just asked me now. What time is it Saturday and Sunday. I said about ten o'clock Saturday and about four o'clock Sunday. That's for eight-year-olds – seven, eight, nine, ten. Cos you've got to get them early in this sport, or they'll go to football. They are not allowed to box until they are eleven, but you let them play box. Last night there was nothing under thirteen, fourteen. They were all schoolboy champions. We'll get maybe fifty kids playing and their mums and dads. They get in the ring and go on the pads, and then once every month or so they'll do a bit of sparring and they'll box with a kid from Newham. There's no decisions, no medical, no nothing, and they just love it. And we just hope we can keep them.

And every so often you are watching and you see one who just might make it as a champion?

Oh no, I don't have to watch. They just walk through the door. You can see . . .

Boxing is a great sport for fitness, I say, but what else are you giving them?

I would say 75 per cent of the families that come here want a bit of respect from their children. This is one of the places where a kid will get into the ring and see a snotty-nosed kid, and all of a sudden the snotty-nosed kid will bash the life out of him.

I am a big fan in the business of respect . . .

Ali. I was with him one day in a hotel, and he had all these people running about, and all of a sudden a fellow came in, they wanted him to open a Mosque in Saudi Arabia. He said, 'How much?'

'Two million.'

'Saudi Arabia. I don't like flying.'

'It's only seven or eight hours.'

'I don't like flying.'

All of a sudden there was a noise at the door. I am trying to look over to see what's happening. There was a fellow trying to get in to see Ali, and the minders . . . Ali says, 'Hold up, hold up, what do you want?'

The fellow says, 'I have got a school around the corner and I want you to come and see the kids.'

Ali says, 'What time do you want me there tomorrow . . . ?'

Respect, it's all about respect.

Boxing ensured that you were fit and could look after yourself. I asked Tony about his connection with the Krays, another family that demanded respect. Ronnie and Reggie were born on 24 October 1933. Ronnie died in a mental hospital and Reggie in prison, in 1995 and 2000 respectively. Elder brother Charlie saw the light of day seven years earlier, and died five months before Reggie. The family – with father Charles and mother Violet – lived in Stene Street in Hoxton until 1939, then at 178 Vallance Road, named after William Vallance, an infamous clerk of Whitechapel Workhouse.

I knew Tony Burns to have been a visitor to Ronnie in Broadmoor and Reggie at various prisons since the 1960s, but had no idea that he inherited his worldly goods.

> Ronnie left me everything he owned – his jewellery, his money, everything, even his false teeth! My Mark took his teeth out, didn't he . . . and his glasses. They are brilliant, his glasses. I have still got the stuff now, in cases, in store. There are loads of letters in there, hundreds of letters. Pictures of Judy Garland . . . Oh, and Ronnie's teeth! I've got his medical card of when he was in Broadmoor . . . Yeah, as I say, he left me everything. Ten years ago this was, and I put it in store. And I was Reggie's best man at his wedding.

Fighting ran in the Kray family. Grandad 'Cannonball' Lee was a bare knuckle fighter, who fought for a few shillings in Victoria Park on Sunday mornings.

> When I was a kid they was in the club, and they came along to the Repton when I took over the senior coaching there, they was always involved with the club and I looked upon them as good friends in them days.

But Tony never boxed the twins.

They were older than me, but they always used to come
and watch me box, always used to be at the York Hall
and have bets and things like that. I'll always remember
one-armed Lou. He wanted to bet on the other fella.
Ronnie says, 'I'll have Burnsey and if he fucking gets
beat I'll break your other arm.'

They weren't big in boxing. Ronnie was unbeaten,
and Reggie lost one. That was out of eight bouts. And
he didn't get on with Micky Duff. Micky told them – ten
out of ten to Micky, he said, 'I've got a bigger army than
you.' Because, you see, the Krays, they wanted to get in
the fight promotions business.

Were you not shocked when the Krays started murdering people? I asked.

What they done later, obviously they regretted
theirselves, you know. It may sound ridiculous, but it was
just the accepted thing in them days.

They were boxing in the Web, that building next to
us [next to the Repton], the youth club and the gym
used to be at the top of the stairs. Everyone boxed
everywhere, the Northampton, the Repton, St George's,
you know. So you went to any gym really. And I always
remember one day someone coming up to me and
saying, 'Ronnie and Reggie bashed a fucking kosser up
in Cambridge Heath Road.' I said, 'You are joking!' That
was a shock. Because you never touched a policeman.

Bethnal Green and Commercial Street, the police was always in the pub the weekend with the old man. All on the piss together, the lot of them. The old man's mates were the police. I thought we always respected the police.

That meant to me, you know, they are in trouble now. All of a sudden, everyone was terrified of them. I don't think they meant to do it, but after that they was really er . . .

As kids on the streets of Whitechapel and Bethnal Green, the twins were involved in gang warfare like Arthur Harding and almost everybody else. They were first arrested at 16, charged with GBH[5] for an attack on a rival gang outside a dance hall in Mare Street, Hackney. The judge said, 'Don't go around thinking you are the Sabini brothers.' The Sabinis were well-known gangsters of the day, who had control of the race tracks of southern England, and who locked horns with Arthur Harding's mob. 'Mad' Frankie Fraser, another mobster from the 1940s on – twenty-six convictions, forty-two years inside – served his apprenticeship as a ten-year-old bucket boy for Darbo Sabini.

Both the Sabinis and Fraser became involved with the Krays. Fraser, older than the twins and a drinking buddy of their father before they got started, amazed the Underworld by joining Charlie and Eddie Richardson's South London gang, whose success in servicing West End clubs with one-armed bandits in the 1960s brought them into conflict with the Krays, and at length, in 1966, to a shoot-out at Mr Smith's club in Rushey Green, Catford. Dickie Hart, a member of the Krays, was shot dead. Frankie Fraser was shot in the hip. Eddie Richardson, who had a scrap metal yard in Greenwich, took a bullet in his backside as he dived for cover behind a sofa.

The twins learned a lot from the Sabini brothers and from another gangster who was big during the 1930s, 1940s and 1950s, Jack 'Spot' Comer, born Jacob Comacho on 12 April 1912.

The Jewish Comacho family came to the East End from Lódz in Poland, in 1903. Jack and his young friends, including Morris Goldstein (Moisha Blueball) and Bernard Schack (Sonny the Yank), formed a gang and used to fight the local Irish Catholic gangs. Spot was naturally tough and a born leader. He started out, as many did, as a bookie's runner, before becoming involved in a protection racket in Petticoat Lane. His nickname came from a black mole on his left cheek.

At one stage, in partnership with a man called Billy Hill, Spot ran just about the whole of London, which meant running the gambling, betting and protection rackets, at a time when gambling and off-course betting were illegal.

Early in their careers, the Krays met Spot and Hill in the Vienna Rooms, off Edgware Road, and would sit for hours listening and learning. The twins then worked for Spot, for a while providing protection for bookmakers.

Martin Leonard remembers Jack Spot well and was anxious that I shouldn't glamorise him.

I knew Jack Spot very well. He used to come into my place. He used to go to Triber's the tailor, order three suits, and never paid them a penny . . . 'I'll give you the money,' he promised, but he never paid them a penny. He wasn't such a marvellous fellow Jack Spot. What did he do? Well, you see, in the fights – the boxing – you'd bet in a betting block, and they used to have a runner, one fellow who took the bets. Jack Spot's mob was there. No one dealt with him direct, his runner would take the bets. And I can remember one fight when Roy Ankrah, the Ghanaian, came over and fought the fellow that was undefeated. I had heard about Roy Ankrah, and they were betting 2 to 1 on the English boy, Ronnie Clayton, to beat him. But I took the odds because I had heard about Ankrah. A few people did as well. And this Roy Ankrah beat the English boy and became Commonwealth (British Empire) featherweight champion, and the runner came over and said to us, 'Where's the money?' And we said, 'What are you talking about? We bet. You gave us 2 to 1, and we won the bet.' But everybody was scared of Jack Spot and we had to shell out the money. He was a con man. You know how he ended up? Working in Cadbury Hall, packing sandwiches and things. That's how he ended up!

In 1995 Spot died a pauper's death at Nazareth House,

Isleworth, of 'cerebro-vascular accident and immobility'. He was 83.

Within this muscular East End culture racial tensions occupied a unique place. In the gym, all races came together. Tony Burns has known white boxers mix happily with black in the Repton and yet saw the same white boxers 'march up and down Roman Road with the Blackshirts'. This didn't surprise him. It is a culture of apartheid that speaks volumes about the inward-looking nature of the communities (cockney and other communities) in which many are brought up.

Tony has a telling story about his father, Harry:

I remember we were in Shoreditch Town Hall. We were in the Blue Room and Ronnie and Reggie walked in – 'Hello Mr Burns.' 'Hello Ron, Hello Reg.' 'Tony, you have done well.' 'Thanks Ron. Reg.' My father, Harry, looked up: 'Ron, who's the big spade?' And the twins said, 'Mr Burns, that's Sonny Liston. Y'know, the heavyweight champion of the world.' 'I don't give a fuck who he is. Get him outahere!' No one laughed. They just thought, Oh, we've upset the old man, y'know? And Ronnie said, 'We'll piss off.' Y'know? I've never known any different.

Today, I've got maybe twenty, thirty kids here who are Asians, Muslims. I torment the life out of them.

Tony sees the situation as it is, not as he might like it to be. He is aware of the tensions and deliberately de-fuses them with humour. Do you have Eastern Europeans? I ask.

Yes, I torment the life out of them, too. Because I don't want to hide nothing. For instance, the Pakistani will come down and the Indian will come down and the Bangladeshi will come down, and they are at war in their native lands. Down here there is no more of that, but I always put India and Pakistan and Bangladesh in, in that order. I don't believe in hiding things. I'd rather joke about things.

Historically, boxers and gangsters played their part in the race problems. There was a veritable army of boxers in the East End at this time, men like Jack Martin, who lived around Backchurch Lane and Commercial Road and made a pitiful living from the sport, but who could use his fists.

My name is Jack Martin. Now, you say it backwards, Nitram, that was my boxing name.

I was a professional boxer, I've got all me photos. I boxed at Blackfriars Rink. I boxed Jack Solomon's shows. How old do you think I am? I'm 92. Jack Solomon had the corner fish stall in Hessle Street market and he always smoked cigars. He is as tall as you and always smokes cigars. He went to Devonshire Hall and he asked me, 'Jack you want a few fights?' The money was no good, I got about £2 for six rounds – horrible money.

The Blackshirts would come in. Yeah, yeah, the Blackshirts, the Mosley crew. Well, two chaps – two boxers who could fight, Georgie Peck and Jack Hicks, and me – three of us, we could fight with our hands,

and we done well with them. Yeah, in the street. The
police nicked one of us. Well, Georgie Peck got taken in,
but they let him go.

These men fought valiantly alongside Jewish gangster
Jack Spot against the fascists in the 1936 battle of Cable
Street, and Andrew Newman knew people close to the
Krays who were involved in the fighting on the same
side:

I always remember somebody who worked for my
father, his name was Jumbo – must be a nickname.
Leman was his surname. He saw a man walking along
Whitechapel Road with a little tiepin swastika and he
went over to him and says, 'What's this?' Bang!! He
introduced my father to Charlie Kray, who wanted to get
into the fashion business because he knew there was
money to be made, knew there was a lot of cash
floating about. My father was thinking about it, but
people said you must be mad getting involved with
them, so he just left it.

On the other hand, Arthur Harding marched with the
Blackshirts against the Jews. He admitted it, talking
about 'that urge of excitement' that got him out on the
streets.

I did give them a hand after the war, when they were
holding their meetings in Dalston, at Ridley Road
Market . . .

The Mosleyites made him into something of a hero, calling him 'uncle'. In Bethnal Green they met at the Salmon and Ball.

Last time I saw Mosley I had a drink with him in the Bethnal Green Road.[6]

Besides running betting scams at the races and at boxing matches, East End criminal gangs were heavily into illegal gambling, or 'spieling' as it was known, in casino-style clubs, which had their beginnings on the street.

In the Nichol, Harding's appetite for this was whet early on in a game called 'pieman', played by children with two halfpennies spun in the air and a special wooden device to ensure that the thrower could not manipulate the result. From organising this, Harding went on to run adult gambling games outside the Crown and Anchor, and had to pay off-duty policemen to turn a blind eye. It was said that police were not averse to turning up to collect a pay-off when not actually on duty in the area. Spielers proliferated around the Commercial Road and Whitechapel, and were a vital source of insider information for the police, which was partly why they were prepared to 'play the game' with these hoods.

Betting and gambling were endemic to the East End, as they were to many a poor neighbourhood, where Lady Luck is always welcome. Jews were as greedy for her favours as Gentiles, but she was at her most colourful as a seductress among the Chinese, who arrived in the East End from the start of the nineteenth century. British shipping companies first employed Chinese sailors during the Napoleonic wars to replace the British sailors who had been called up to the navy. They soon discovered that they were cheaper, didn't get drunk and were easier to command.

Like the Bengalis, the Chinese settled in the East End after jumping ship, or simply because their merchant-seaman contract had come to an end. They lived in dockland and developed their own ghetto, which included lodging houses, shops, restaurants, opium dens, gambling dens, and clubs and pubs.

By 1890 there were two settled communities, one in Poplar around Pennyfields, Amony Place and Ming Street (between the present Westferry and Poplar DLR stations), the other around Gill Street and Limehouse Causeway.

The communities became more and more settled and some of the Chinese married English women – indeed the Chinese had a reputation among English women for making better husbands, kinder and less violent than Englishmen, though marriage presented difficulties, as an English girl marrying a Chinese man actually lost her British citizenship, and if he left her, she would almost certainly be reduced to the workhouse.

Leslie and Connie Ho grew up in Limehouse. Said Connie: 'In Limehouse Causeway the children were mainly from families with Cantonese fathers. Pennyfields was mainly Shanghai and other districts of China.' Said Leslie:

> We were low profile. We used to do what everybody else did. Our street used to fight the next street with sticks. We called it the gang warfare. We weren't very good at it. The Anglo-Saxon is a bit fiercer than you think, and we used to charge them with these sticks and when they made for us we would run away and the little ones at the back used to be beaten up.

By 1911, the whole area had been dubbed Chinatown. Said Donald Barlin, son of a Chinese father and English mother:

> The facilities . . . Well, they were fairly basic because the East End of London at that time was by modern standard fairly well run-down . . .
>
> Pennyfields is a road which branches off the West India Dock Road, and I suspect that Pennyfields at that time was called as such because the front room of every house...the so-called front room, was a gambling house. And if you walk along Pennyfields any time of the day or night perhaps, all one could hear was a crash of Mahjong pieces being thrown to the table, with the exclamation 'Aiya!' . . . Pennyfields was always a well-known area for its small Chinese restaurants, and also for its gambling houses.

It was not just a case of Mahjong. Pennyfields was home

to Fan-Tan and Pak-a-pu gambling and to the reputedly sinister opium dens. In Fan-Tan a random cupful of haricot beans is placed in a basin and turned upside down on the table. Players must forecast how many beans remain after they have been divided into groups of four. Sounds simple. It is, and deeply addictive when money is involved.

But Pak-a-pu (originally Baige piao, third century BC) was the more popular among East Enders. It was played on a sheet marked with Chinese characters. You would be dealt a piece of paper about 6 inches square, along the top and bottom of which would be marked forty Chinese characters. You would then be allowed to pick ten characters along the top and ten along the bottom for 6d. a line. A prayer would then be said by a Chinese priest, parts of which locked into the characters that were visible and you won according to how correctly the characters you picked were officially marked. In that sense, it is not a little like a magical form of Bingo! You won more money according to the number of officially marked characters correctly forecast. You could win £80, a great deal of money in those days, if you got them all correct.

As far as crime goes in the East End or Limehouse or Chinatown, it was very very minimal. There were of course a few opium sellers and a lady who was very close to us in fact did sell opium. And every now and again the police would come to find out who was selling opium and then there would be a ticking off. Opium

would be confiscated and police would turn a blind eye
to anything else that might have occurred.

The opium problem in the Chinese ghetto was Britain's
fault, another appalling example of Victorian greed
involving the British East India Company, which had
created a monopoly on opium trading in Bengal,
thwarting a ban China had placed on opium imports.
By 1838 the British company was exporting 1,400 tons
a year into China. Then Britain's triumph over China in
the so-called Opium Wars – two of them, between 1839
and 1860 – effectively forced the Chinese government
to tolerate the British opium trade. The result saw
millions of Chinese opium addicts, and China became
a leading international supplier of the drug.

Famously, Dr Watson visited an opium den in the
East End in Arthur Conan Doyle's story, *The Man with
the Twisted Lip* (1891). He found it at the Bar Gold in
Upper Swandam Lane, 'a vile alley lurking behind the
high wharves which line the north side of the river to
the east of London Bridge . . .'

> Between a slop-shop and a gin-shop, approached by a
> steep flight of steps leading down to a black gap like the
> mouth of a cave, I found the den of which I was in
> search. Ordering my cab to wait, I passed down the
> steps, worn hollow in the centre by the ceaseless tread
> of drunken feet; and by the light of a flickering oil-lamp
> above the door I found the latch and made my way into
> a long, low room, thick and heavy with the brown

opium smoke, and terraced with wooden berths, like the
forecastle of an emigrant ship.

To his surprise he found Sherlock Holmes there. By the
late nineteenth century, a night out in the opium dens
of the East End was fairly common practice among the
more adventurous from up West, as James Greenwood
recorded:

The person who would enjoy the inexpressible treat
attendant on the smoking of a genuine and
unadulterated pipe of opium must make a pilgrimage for
it. 'There are two ways of arriving at the opium-master's
house,' a friend told me. 'One is to make for High
Street, Shadwell, and keep along till you spy a tavern,
the sign of which is the 'Hoop and Grapes;' next to it is
another tavern, the 'Gunboat,' and opposite is another,
the 'Golden Eagle;' while within range of a pea-shooter
are three other taverns, the 'Home of Friendship,' the
'Lord Lovat,' and the 'Baltic' – and the last-mentioned is
at the corner of the very street. Or you may go another
way, down Cable Street, till you arrive at a not particular
inviting-looking thoroughfare, on a corner of which is
inscribed 'To Rehoboth Chapel.' From the end of this
street you make out a dingy-looking little public house,
called the 'Coal Whipper's Arms.' The opium master's
house is just handy – up a court.' [i.e. it was in among
the hell holes between Cable Street and The
Highway.] . . .
    There was no one at home but the opium-master's

wife; but as she is English, I experienced no difficulty in making known to her my desire.

'I 'spect it won't be long before he's back,' said she; 'will you call again in a little while, or will you come up?'

'I will stay till he comes in, if you have no objection,' said I; whereupon she shut the outer door, and toiled slowly, like a person who is very ill, up the narrow filthy little staircase. I followed her . . . The filthy little house seemed full of some subtle sickening essence lurking on the stairs and under the stairs, and ascending in invisible vapours through the many chinks and holes in the rotten woodwork. It seemed likewise to lie on the handrail in the form of a fine dust, that instantly melted to some loathsome moisture the moment the hand was laid on it . . . Arrived at a landing, the opium-master's wife pushed open a door. 'Come in and take a cheer, sir,' she said, politely.

The room, at a rough guess, may have been eleven feet long and nine wide. An awfully dilapidated little den, the much-begrimed ceiling patched with rain leakage, and broken here and there, so that the laths were visible; the walls black with smoke and grease; the shattered upper panes of the foul little window plastered with brown paper. There was a bedstead in the room – a bedstead so large that there was left but a yard or so of space between it and the fire-place – a 'four-poster,' amply hung about with some kind of flimsy material, the original colour of which it is impossible to guess. But the bedding was more remarkable than the bedstead; for the bed was 'made' the wrong way – across the length of the bedstead instead of its width, with a long bolster; and it was covered, instead of a counterpane, with a huge breadth of fine Chinese matting. A table and three chairs, if I remember rightly, constituted the remainder of the furniture in the opium-master's smoking-saloon, with a few gaudy prints on the walls, and the mantelshelf crowded with ornaments, evidently of Oriental origin . . . The woman placed a saucepan with water in it on the fire, and then proceeded to fix on the mouth of it a sort of little sieve, the finely-woven meshes of which hung into the water. Then she shredded some cake opium, as sailors shred Cavendish for smoking, placed it on the sieve, and put on the brew to simmer . . .

[Opium] should be cooked – stewed in the manner that I have described; then the essence filters through the sieve, and falls to the bottom of the pot in the form of thinnish treacle, while what remains in the sieve is of no more account than common tea-leaves . . .

After a while the sound of ascending footsteps was heard on the stairs . . . I had pictured to myself an individual of commanding aspect, richly costumed as a mandarin; but here came a shabby, shambling, middle-aged Chinaman into whose apparel, if I mistake not, vulgar corduroy entered, and who wore his pigtail over a sort of stableman's smock. He had on Chinese boots, however, and a Chinese cap, which, on seeing me, he removed, bowing with great cordiality and politeness, as gracefully as his lame leg would permit. He looked at his wife inquiringly, and uttered the word 'Smoke?' and, on her nodding affirmatively, he again bowed and rubbed his dirty hands, and turned with what I knew from its tone to be a whisper of apology to his two friends.

It was plain that he was explaining to them that probably I had been waiting some time, and it would be no more than courteous to let me have my pipe at once. But they were of no mind to be put off. They were dirty, savage-looking villains, evidently fresh from ship-board, and sorely itching for an 'opium drunk'. They wore knives at their waistbands, and their very pigtails seemed to stiffen in anger as they scowled on me. I hastened at once to declare that I was not in the least hurry, and would give up my turn quite cheerfully . . . This little difficulty smoothed, the two dirty Chinamen, restored to good-humour, flung off their caps and leaped upon the bed with the agility and eagerness of cats bent on stealing fish from a dresser. They curled down on the mat counterpane, about three feet apart, and mowed and grinned at each other as they wriggled into a perfectly comfortable position, with their heads on the bolster.

Then, with much gravity, the opium-master commenced operations. Out of a cupboard he produced his tools – the two pipes, a sort of a tinder-box of the old-fashioned pattern, a slender iron bodkin fixed in a little handle, and a small brass lamp. The pipes were not a bit like ordinary tobacco pipes. Let the reader imagine a sixteen inch length of dark-coloured bamboo, as thick as a man's forefinger, hollow, and open at one end. There was no 'mouth-piece,' except the wide, open bore: while, at the closed end, an inch or so from the extremity, was a screw hole. Into this was screwed the tiny bowl, made, I think, of iron, and shaped like a pigeon's egg. The opium-master lit the little brass lamp, and stepping up on the bed, squatted tailorwise between his customers, with his tools ready at hand. The thing like a tinder box contained the opium, but it was not, even after the stewing it had undergone, as yet ready for smoking; it had to be frizzled. It seemed to be about the consistency of treacle, and dipping in the tip of the bodkin, he twaddled it round till he had secured a piece as large as a common grey pea. This he held in the flame of the lamp till it was done to his liking.

Then he clapped the precious morsel into the pipe that one of the Chinamen was already greedily sucking, and, to all appearance, the ugly fellow was at once translated from earth to heaven. As the woman had previously informed me, the smoke that was drawn up through the stem was not blown out from the mouth – it was swallowed or otherwise disposed of by internal machinery. Nothing but what seemed to be the thinnest possible thread of purple vapour escaped from the pipe-bowl; and as the awful-looking being on the bed rapturously sucked and sucked, the thread became thinner, his face lit up with a strange light, and his pig-like eyes closed till but two mere streaks parted the lids – two streaks that glowed as though his eyes had turned to opals. While he was thus tasting felicity, the other villain was served, and presently there was a pretty pair. I never should have supposed the human countenance capable of wearing an expression so sensuous, so bestial and revolting. Faintly and more faintly still they sucked, till a gurgling sound in the pipe-stems announced that the opium in the bowl was spent; then the pipes fell from their lips, and they lay still as dead men. I couldn't bear to look at them. I felt as though I were assisting at some sacrifice with a strong flavour of brimstone about it; and felt quite relieved when I turned my eyes towards the fireplace, to observe the woman engaged in nothing more supernatural than gutting a haddock for her husband's supper . . .

Now the opium-master was at my service. I would have given more money than I had about me to have postponed my initiation . . . but the demon on the bed was politely beckoning me . . . The dose was toasted, and I took the great clumsy pipe-stem between my jaws, and sucked as I had observed the Chinamen suck. I swallowed what I sucked, or desperately endeavoured to do so, and the result was precisely what might have been expected. Without doubt I was stupefied, or I never should have ventured on another pull. That did it! Before I ventured on my perilous expedition I had a vivid recollection of what came of smoking my first cigar; but that dismal remembrance is now quite eclipsed by one a hundred times more dreadful. 'Sispince, please!' said the still polite opium-master, extending his hand; but I hastily pressed on his acceptance the whole of the half-crown I had brought for the purpose, and was glad enough to find myself once more breathing the free and delicious air of Shadwell.

People were fascinated by the Orient, mystified and not a little apprehensive. So much so that authors, songwriters and film makers conspired to catch the public imagination with wholly fabricated stories about what went on in the East End's Chinatown. In fact, it was a community of no more than a hundred families, basically law abiding and well integrated. Only the opium caused occasional problems with the police. Yet the 1913 publication of the first in a series of novels about the evil genius Dr Fu Manchu, by Sax Rohmer, kick-started a near-hysterical interest in London's Limehouse, turning it from a few drab streets of shops and restaurants into the most infamous patch of land in Britain – which supposedly harboured cunning 'Chinamen' who lured white women into their opium dens.

> Imagine a person, tall, lean and feline, high-shouldered, with a brow like Shakespeare and a face like Satan, a close-shaven skull, and long, magnetic eyes of the true cat-green. Invest him with all the cruel cunning of an entire Eastern race, accumulated in one giant intellect, with all the resources of science past and present, with all the resources, if you will, of a wealthy government – which, however, already has denied all knowledge of his existence. Imagine that awful being, and you have a mental picture of Dr Fu-Manchu, the yellow peril incarnate in one man.[7]

Then came D. W. Griffiths' film in 1919, *Broken Blossoms*, about Chinatown, and spinning off that came the hit song *Limehouse Blues*, with Gertrude Lawrence singing, 'In Limehouse, where yellow Chinkies love to play . . .'

The Fu Manchu stories became Hollywood films and a popular radio series during the 1930s. Newspapers, such as the *Daily Express* and *Daily Mail*, blackened the reputation of the Chinese as responsible for the drugs industry and white slave trade. 'Young girls hypnotised by yellow men – what our representatives saw in Pennyfields . . . this plague spot of the metropolis.'

The trial of Limehouse restaurateur 'Brilliant Chang' in 1924 was greeted by the press as a battle won in the war against the London drugs trade. But the jailing and deportation of the man known to his mother as Chan Nan said more about hysteria and xenophobia.

So commercial a proposition did Chinatown become that Thomas Cooke ran bus tours there. The coach trip from Charing Cross to Limehouse cost half a crown, but only 4d. on the bus. When the coach came through, children would shout out, 'Throw out your mouldies,' and the tourists used to throw out their halfpennies and pennies for the kids to scramble after.

After Limehouse was bombed out of existence in the Second World War, and the planners moved in, the Chinese population more or less disappeared from the area, but an appetite for gambling survived, and inevitably the Krays became involved in satisfying it in their own way.

Emma Bennett was in her late twenties when the war came to an end. She had left school at 14 and taken her first job at 6d. a week with Davies's Feather Mills.

I made cushion covers, eider downs and all that. You worked at a sewing machine. Round here years ago was all dress factories, the Jews came in and it was all dress factories. They brought a trade to London didn't they? They brought the trade in. They were either tailorists or you used to see them in the windows making boots and shoes all along here.

Then one day a Jewish lady living next door to Emma changed her life.

She was a Yiddisher woman, I thought she was a money lender. She took to me, I don't know why. She had a club in Stepney, a club in Stamford Hill, and we used to go and collect the money. Then when I come home one night, my Frank said, 'Where you been?' And I said, 'With the woman next door.' And he said, 'Now, you want to be careful.' I said, 'Why?' And he said, 'I don't want you to go there no more. She's collecting for the Krays.' And I said, 'Never!' And he said, 'I'm telling you, she's collecting money for the Kray twins.'

And that's how I got the job at the Krays' club in Black Lion Yard. My husband was out of work. So, I thought to myself, I'll get a job off her. When I went to her she said, 'It's only a little job of a morning, cleaning at the betting shop.' She says to me, 'There's a spieler upstairs and you might do all right.' Well I did do all right for me. I got good wages and I used to get a lot of clothes from her, and I stayed there until they shut it down. Well, the police shut it down at the finish.

I enjoyed it. Upstairs, we would have Lita Rosa [*How Much is that Doggie in the Window?*] was a big hit at the time] and Tony Bennett – he was up there, I've seen a lot of celebrities up there performing. And you know what a spieler is? A gambling club. I used to clean in there. They knocked a big hole in the wall, they would look through the hole, see the coppers coming from Leman Street, and then they would all be gone before the coppers could get them.

Then, when they turned it into a betting club, I used to go and get all the papers, pin them all round the wall and that, and there used to be a copper . . . I'll never forget him, old Dobbs. The governor of the club, Jewish man he was, he used to say to Dobbs, 'Now, if she is in there on her own . . .' I used to get there at 7 a.m. and Dobbs used to knock, and he used to say, 'It's only me, don't open the door. I'm on my way round,' and he used to have his lantern and he used to shine his light all the way up the wall and go round – the policeman, old Jack Dobbs.

I also used to go round to Vallance Road, that's where Violet Kray lived with the twins' father, Charlie Kray. I used to have to go round there every Monday morning before we would be allowed to open the betting shop, to pick up a lot of money – £30 a week

old Violet Kray used to give me, and I used to take it
back to the club.

I seen many a good day there.

I met Emma in a group of elderly people in Toynbee
Hall. At 91 going on 92, she was still incredibly tough
and strong, with clear memories and this particular one
that Violet Kray was anything but the sweet little woman
who had taught her three boys to be gentlemen, which
is the Kray legend.

The woman of the house in the East End, nine times
out of ten, set the tone. Violet Kray was, said Emma –

A little woman like me, but vicious, vicious. Charlie Kray
[her husband] was a pussy cat, but her, she was a cow
she was, she really was bad.

Following their arrest for GBH at 16, the twins were
soon in trouble again. They'd been standing outside a
café in Bethnal Green Road with some friends, when a
policeman told them to move on and he pushed
Ronnie in the back. Ronnie didn't let anyone push him
around. He hit the policeman and they all ran off.

Very likely this was Pellicci's café, still there today.
Tony Lambrianou, an associate of the Krays, confirmed
that Pellicci's 'was one of the places that the twins used
to hold their afternoon meets . . . Neville, the guv'nor,
often jokes about the number of people Ronnie
knocked through the window.'

Mr Pellicci has only good memories:

> They were children when I started serving them. They
> were very respectful, charming. If my mother was behind
> the counter and someone swore they would ask them to
> show some respect.

After the incident with the policeman, when the police tried to arrest Ronnie, Reggie got involved. Sudden violence. No rhyme or reason. They were both arrested and charged with assault.

Later the twins bought a snooker club in Bethnal Green, and called it the Regal. Some foolish Maltese tried to collect protection money from them and ended up with a bayonet through his hand. There followed various arrests for GBH and possession of a firearm, but while Ronnie was serving a three-year sentence for beating up a man called Terry Martin outside a pub in Stepney, Reggie began to build up their ownership of nightclubs. First came The Double R in Bow. Thereafter, many clubs were 'rescued' from bankruptcy after mysteriously being burned out – some thirty clubs and bars, so it was said, made up the Krays' empire at its height.

The rise of the Krays was attended by astonishing respect from their fellow cockney East Enders. There was fear certainly, but the twins made sure that they had plenty of ordinary traders and local community leaders happy to speak well of them. Said Alf Stuart:

> I knew the Kray boys. They used to come into my
> business at Gardiner's Corner, and they were as good as
> gold with me, they never interfered with anything, they

opened a club in Bow. They said, 'I want you to come as
my guest in Bow.' And I went there one night, had a
drink there and they were as good as gold to me, and
that was that.

Daniel Farson, not a cockney, but who had a pub in
Limehouse, was invited to the opening of a club of
theirs called the Kentucky in the Mile End Road.
'Everyone was immaculately dressed, the men in dark-
blue suits, dark ties and white shirts, the women with
elaborately structured hairstyles . . . Billy Daniels
appeared on the makeshift stage and gyrated his
energetic version of *That Old Black Magic*.'

Farson describes how the local mayor and vicar were
also invited and the twins were described in speeches as
local businessmen. This was typical. The Krays were 'of
the locality', respectable, or at least worthy of your
respect. Mostly, they were very well behaved, and when
Farson lurched around drunkenly they ticked him off,
because there were ladies present.[8]

And if anyone failed to show them respect, then very
likely they would be taken outside and taught a very
painful lesson. Farson watched an unfortunate suffer a
roughing up after he made the mistake of chatting up
Reggie Kray's girlfriend.

When honour was satisfied, they shook hands, wiped off
the blood, put on their jackets and resumed their
drinking at the bar. This was Gentlemen Jim stuff and I
was enthralled . . .[9]

There was a rightness about the Krays, good manners. This was the unusual aspect of their mob rule. They embodied an East End tradition that had never been written down, but was as real as Robin Hood's. Wrote Iain Sinclair of the Krays

> No other strata of society has such a sense of
> tradition . . . The East End had its reputation to uphold:
> sentiment backed by strict discipline.[10]

Inevitably, 'demanding money with menaces' was soon added to the list of offences of which the twins stood accused, and Reggie spent time in Wandsworth prison, where he met Jack 'the Hat' McVitie and 'Mad Axeman' Frank Mitchell, whose names would soon find their place in the cast list of the Kray drama.

The twins had big plans which took them outside their manor – a seaside development in Nigeria, where a large amount of money mysteriously disappeared. The deal brought them close to members of Parliament, the homosexual Lord Boothby in particular. When they were arrested for demanding money with menaces in 1965, Boothby spoke up for them in the Lords. Were the twins getting beyond themselves?

Ambition was growing, certainly, and how it irked them that the Richardsons from South London had a highly profitable and legitimate foothold in the West End through their one-armed bandit business. The Krays wanted control. The Richardsons were not going to step aside. So, in March '66, things came to a head at

Mr Smith's Club, as I have described. Dickie Hart, an associate of the Krays, was shot dead. Richardson gangmember Frankie Fraser was arrested, but later released. The following night, Ronnie Kray walked into The Blind Beggar on Whitechapel Road and shot another Richardson associate, George Cornell, in the head. It has been suggested, but never proven, that Cornell was in fact Hart's executioner at Mr Smith's and had managed to escape before the police arrived. Later that same year the Krays broke Frank Mitchell from prison and were charged with his murder. Then Jack 'The Hat' McVitie was killed by Reggie.

It could not be allowed to continue. On 8 May 1968 the twins were arrested. Found guilty of the murder of Cornell and McVitie, they were sentenced to life imprisonment with a recommendation to serve at least thirty years.

But the people of the East End could not forget the legendary aspects, and Ronnie's funeral in 1995 was a memorable opportunity for mass sentiment to flow. Reggie was allowed out of prison to see his twin brother in the chapel of rest, three days before the funeral. It must have been while Ronnie was laid out at W. English's funeral parlour at 464 Bethnal Green Road that someone stuck their finger in his mouth and hoiked out his false teeth, adding them to the effects that came under Tony Burns's care.

On the day of the funeral thousands lined Bethnal Green Road to pay their respects to Ronnie and to get a glimpse of Reggie. The hearse was pulled by six black horses. The pallbearers were drawn from family and the London Underworld. Brother Charlie Kray was among them, and Frankie Fraser would have been, only he turned out to be too short, which would have made the coffin lop-sided, so instead he walked in the cortege with Reggie.

Thirteen years on, you can pay to go on a tour of The Blind Beggar and other East End haunts of the Krays with Frankie Fraser. There have been many books and films, all part of a 'performance cockney' movement exporting to the world.

The emergence of the East End into wider society, the repeal of its original 'outcast' identity, began with the exposure of its suffering and courage on newsreels of the Second World War, when the character of its people triumphed over the Blitz. The welfare state was then their reward, and it was fitting that in the decade following, the export of the working-class cockney tradition made such a massive impact.

When tailor's son David Bailey came out of Stepney with his camera in the late 1950s, he was a novelty in the London publishing scene:

> In fact, there was everything wrong with me in a way, because I wasn't queer, I wasn't upper middle class, and . . . I remember when I first went to *Vogue*, I was very young, about 20, I think. Some of the editors used to pat me on the head and say, 'Isn't he cute the way he speaks!' I thought, I'll show you, dear, how cute he is.

Did you play up your cockney background?

I didn't, in fact. Remember, the cockney thing wasn't popular then. This was pre-rent-a-cockney. It wasn't until the mid-sixties that the cockney thing became popular, with Michael Caine and *Alfie* [1966] and all that business. But I didn't play on [where I came from]. I just liked taking pictures, to be honest.

Nevertheless, Bailey's East End working-class confidence and cheekiness was what was needed to break the hold the toffs had on photography at that time.

Most photographers before I came along were kind of upper middle class.

People forget that the visual thing happened before the music in the sixties.

The music at that time was Adam Faith and Cliff Richard. *What Do You Want?* and the other one was *Living Doll* by Cliff Richard.

In this context, Bailey's association with the model Jean 'The Shrimp' Shrimpton was defining of what was to come.

Vogue gave me a contract [and] I took a few risks then. In fact, the first risk I ever took was using Shrimpton. I'd been at *Vogue* for about a year or so, maybe longer and

I saw this girl and I thought she was wonderful. She was actually doing a Kellogg's picture with someone called Duffy [Brian Duffy, another photographer from the East End], he was a photographer at *Vogue* at the time. I said, 'Introduce me, I like her.' Then I said, 'I want to use this girl,' and they said I couldn't because I was sleeping with her. But in fact I wasn't sleeping with her then. It was a 14-page lead, and they said, 'If you screw it up we are giving this job to somebody else.' There weren't as many pages in *Vogue* then, so a 14-page lead was quite a thing. As it happened it went well, and after this things kind of snowballed and Jean and I worked together every day for about three years.

And broke out a new style?

I don't know. I just liked Jean's legs. I never really cared much about fashion. I only ever took pictures of frocks because girls were in them . . . I think partly the mini skirt was Jean's legs, because I used to pull the skirt up higher and higher every time I took a picture and *Vogue* used to air brush it down. And the more they airbrushed it down the more I pulled it up. And it became suddenly acceptable that you could wear a skirt up to your knickers.

This period coincided with a revolution in all sorts of artistic areas in which other cockney boys were also influential. It was the beginning of the swinging sixties, East End-led.

Yes, and we were all friends, which was nice. There was Terry Donovan, he was a friend, and Mick Jagger was a friend. Terence Stamp was a friend. And Jean of course. And this little group had no idea that this was the scene of swinging London, or whatever. I hate that phrase. But in a way we were doing it without knowing. To us, it was just . . . we were naive kids in a way. We were all friends.

I knew Terry from the East End days vaguely. We weren't friends, but I knew who he was. He was one of the people that was around in Stepney and places like that. Then we were both in love with the same girl when we were fifteen. That was in the early fifties and then I didn't meet Terry again until the sixties.

Terence Donovan, the only son of a cockney lorry driver, was brought up in the Mile End Road. The bomb-damaged industrial landscape of the East End became the revolutionary backdrop of his photography. Terence Stamp also hailed from Stepney, and rose to fame in such films as *The Collector* and *Far from the Madding Crowd* in the mid-1960s, before being offered the part of Alfie in the 1966 film, which had everyone speaking with an East End accent for a decade, wherever they came from. But he turned it down, allowing Michael Caine, who emerged from south of the Thames, in Southwark, to get his chance.

And then I met Mick because he was going out with Jean's sister. So in a way it was all very incestuous. And then later, Jean went out with Stamp. It was just a very small group.

By 1965 Jagger and the Stones were causing riots wherever they played in Britain and America. In 1967, Bailey married French actress Catherine Deneuve, star of Roman Polanski's seminal sixties flick *Repulsion*, with Mick Jagger as his best man. The 1960s were supposed to be about permissiveness, but Bailey saw it as very much a working-class revolution.

> Permissive? It wasn't permissive. It was only permissive because the workers were allowed to do it. I mean, the aristocracy had been at it for years, since the word go! It was suddenly that the permissiveness was open to the working classes.

Working-class authenticity was where these East End boys fitted in. When the *Sunday Times* wanted to profile the Krays, Bailey was the natural choice for photographer. It was the perfect match, but his return to take the photographs in an East End pub went unrecognised in his own land.

> I'd been with the Kray twins for about three weeks, with [the writer] Francis Wyndham. We were in a pub. All the women were in one bar and all the men in the other bar, just like . . . rather like *The Cossacks*. Ever read Tolstoy's *Cossacks?* And I was taking the pictures and somebody said, 'Who do you think you are . . . David Bailey?'[11]

PART V

WORKING CLASS HEROES

———

CHAPTER FOURTEEN

Solidarity

━━━━━━━

Gerard Donnachie moved with his family to Wapping in 1962. The Donnachies lived just south of the old Ratcliff Highway in front of the Pumping House in Wapping Wall, by Shadwell Basin, the last of the Wapping docks to be built, and the only one to remain to this day.

Gerard's dad was the engineer in the Pumping House, which provided hydraulic power for cranes and lifting bridges throughout London. To get back from school Gerard would walk from the Highway down Glamis Road and across a steel bridge, which rose to allow ships to enter Shadwell Basin from the Thames.

The daily challenge to a young boy was to get over the bridge before bells started ringing and red lights flashing, announcing that it was about to be raised. Miss it and there'd be a fifteen-minute wait, just yards from home. He also recalled seeing the Dockers' Union leader Jack Dash 'calling out the dockers on strike from a balcony on a block of flats. Then the docks moved in the late 1960s and we had years of barren wilderness.'

Essentially, Gerard Donnachie saw it all – the docks still busy in the early sixties, two decades of union agitation, leading to their closure in 1981, and the movement of business down river to Tilbury – the end of an era almost 200 years old.

Jack Dash was a highly vocal militant trade unionist during a period when labour relations in the docks were at their worst. His extremism has been blamed for the closure of the docks, but if he hadn't been there, someone else like him would have stood in his place. For over a hundred years labour relations had brought the dockers into a political conflict that could never end profitably for either side.

The first great dockers' strike occurred, as I have said, in 1889, when 'the docker's tanner' was won – an increase in wages of a penny an hour to 6d. They won because they convinced workers from other industries – rope-making, printing, chemicals, biscuit-making – to join them. By the third week, 130,000 men were striking.

Fearful of the strike escalating further, the Lord Mayor of London set up a committee to solve the dispute, and brought in Cardinal Manning, Roman Catholic Primate of England, to appeal to the predominantly Irish Catholic workforce. Agreement was reached to the dockers' benefit.

Worker solidarity across industry was the key to their success, and characterised the conflict as political. The concept of worker solidarity ranged the workers not only against the dock owners, but also against the Government, and suggested that the workers had the power to bring the whole country to a halt. Their committee secretary was Karl Marx's daughter Eleanor, who processed triumphantly along Commercial Road to Hyde Park with them, singing their new song, 'The Red Flag'.

The concept of worker power then gained further credibility in the run-up to the Russian Revolution under Lenin in 1917. By then, the dock owners had formed the Shipping Federation, dedicated to stamping out strike action and unionism for ever, implying that they posed a threat to the established order.

But East Enders showed where their support lay. In 1912 a strike over the 'Call On' occasioned rallies on Tower Hill. Great suffering for the strikers ensued, but the East End community came to the rescue, with, for example, the Prices Bakery stopping their pony van in the middle of Louder Street and disgorging loaves of bread onto the pavement for strikers' families to help themselves.

In 1919, national Dockers' Union organiser Ernest Bevin led a campaign to secure wages of 16s. a day for a

44-hour week. Two years later the Transport and General Workers' Union was formed, with Bevin at the helm, consolidating the efforts of thirty different unions, and further strengthening the workers' hand across industry.

In 1925, after a dispute between miners and mineowners over a reduction in wages, the General Council of the Trades Union Congress (TUC) threatened widespread worker support in other industries. The Government responded apparently benignly by making available a subsidy to restore wage levels for a period of nine months, during which time a Royal Commission would investigate the problems of the mining industry.

When the report was published, however, it recommended a reduction in wages. Around the same time, mineowners projected further adjustments to wages and hours. And it was this inflammatory situation that led to the General Strike of 1926.

The TUC brought the East End dockers out on strike in sympathy with the miners, along with railwaymen, transport workers, printers, builders, iron and steel workers – some three million men – engineers and shipyard workers to follow, if their terms were still not met.

The strike was called on 1 May. Six days later the chairman of the Royal Commission, whose report on the mining industry had caused all the problems, got in a huddle with the TUC and together they hammered out a set of proposals – a National Wages Board with an independent chairman, a minimum wage, etc. The proposals were accepted by the TUC negotiating committee, who then called off the General Strike.

The men went back to work, and only then were the proposals rejected by the employers' Miners' Federation, and by the Government, who even introduced a Bill into the House of Commons that permitted the mineowners to announce new terms of employment based on an eight-hour working day, which had earlier been reduced to seven.

The miners had been cheated, sold down the river. They held out on strike on their own from April until December, when hardship forced them to drift back to work.

In 1927 the Government passed the Trade Disputes and Trade Union Act, which made coming out on strike in sympathy with another industry illegal. The General Strike had been an unmitigated disaster.

It later emerged just how duplicitous Stanley Baldwin's Government had been – even the wages subsidy granted in 1925 had been designed simply to give them time to prepare to smash the unions. The Government justified its strategy on the basis of the threat worker power posed to national security. It was inconceivable to a government bereft of conscience in the matter of worker-exploitation during a hundred years of industrial revolution, that the British middle classes would not support them in a deception designed to retain the status quo. This despite the fact that, as Henry Hamilton Fyfe, editor of the *Daily Herald*, wrote in his autobiography, *My Seven Selves* (1935):

There was not a single member of the General Council
of the Trades Union Congress who would not have
shrunk with horror from the idea of overturning the
established order – if it had occurred to him. I am certain
there was no one to whom it did occur. They decided on
the strike in desperation. They had promised support to
the miners, and they did not know what else to do.

Wrote Herbert Morrison in his autobiography (1960):

Suffice it to say that in Hackney, as in every working-
class area, there was great sympathy for the miners, who
had been treated abominably, and there was a universal
and reasonably justified feeling that the mine owners
were a wicked lot.

The utter disrespect of Government and mineowners
for the workers gave young people a cause and
encouraged left-wing political extremism. As Jennie
Lee, a miner's daughter and student at Edinburgh
University at the time, declared:

Until the June examinations were over I was chained to
my books, but I worked with a darkness around me.
What was happening in the coalfield? How were they
managing? Once I was free to go home to Lochgelly my
spirits rose. When you are in the thick of a fight there is
a certain exhilaration that keeps you going.

Stanley Baldwin promised that there would be no
victimisation when the miners went back to work.

> That was one more piece of deliberate deception. My
> father was not reinstated – for four months he trudged
> from pit to pit, turned away everywhere. Uncle Michael
> was also victimised, and so sadly he came to the
> decision that the only thing to do was to go off to
> America.

The worse the deception and exploitation and humiliation of the working man, the more he would turn to Socialism, and the more easily he would deliver his future up to political extremism, even anarchy. The Government had read the workers wrong and encouraged them along a path that would be their undoing. Either that, or it deliberately encouraged a challenge to its authority, so to overcome it. This was the political background to industrial action in the second half of the twentieth century that destroyed the East End dock industry, wiped it off the face of the London map.

Following the Second World War the docks were soon fully operational and business good. Docklands was teeming with labour in the 1950s, and by the early 1960s, 'the total volume of goods handled by the Port of London broke new records.'[1]

The dockers' trade union had picked itself up after the defeat in 1926 and now set about improving worker conditions. In 1947 the National Dock Labour Scheme (NDLS) started a Register in order to 'de-casualise' work. The NDLS became responsible for the proper registration, allocation, payment, training and medical care of dock workers.

Yet, labour relations remained bad throughout these decades. Major strikes over wages and working arrangements threatened to bring the port to a standstill. The evil of the 'Call On', the way it had been administered since time immemorial, and the economic difficulty of worker under-employment, might seem a just cause, although Bill Abbott, a docker, regarded de-casualisation as 'the biggest mistake'.

Doing away with casual work and paying a docker a fixed wage removed the one thing that fired him up to get work and to work hard so that he would be picked for a gang the next day too. In any case, it was all too late, for the industry was changing. Progress was all about a reduction of labour, about mechanisation, containerisation, and deep-water berths, where whole lorry-loads could be craned off at a sweep and with a tiny proportion of the man-power that had previously been required. Saddling dock companies with an employment policy that ignored this was counter-productive for everyone.

The militancy of union activists like Jack Dash, who was anarchic of industry, was the last straw.

Yes, I've been accused of shutting the docks, but in fact none of the docks closed until after I had left the industry. It was changes in trade that made them close.

Dash denied it, but the militancy of the dockers during the 1960s made it impossible to meet the changes that faced the industry. The Government had lit the fuse of extremism among the workers; the militant unionists had brought it to the point of explosion, instead of concentrating on adapting the industry to the future.

In Rotterdam and elsewhere, containerisation, and roll-on, roll-off ferries, on which lorries could cross the Channel without even unloading, were the future, and a whole new employment strategy was needed.

The NDLS staggered on, but was eventually abolished in 1989, by which time the idea of full-time labour in the docks was, in Employment Secretary Norman Fowler's words, 'a total anachronism'. Casual labour was reintroduced, but by then the East End had lost its docks.

In 1981 the 200-year-old battle between employers and dockers over how to run the docks, hire the men and devolve the work, ended with neither side winning, for that year the last of London's docks closed. Business moved down river to Tilbury. And Jack Dash had become rhyming slang: 'I need a Jack Dash (slash).'

CHAPTER FIFTEEN

Outcasts
no longer

The Isle of Dogs, once home to the East and West
India and the Millwall docks, was possibly so named
because it once served as kennel grounds for the royal
hunting dogs from the palace of Greenwich. As early as
July, 1905, *The Strand* magazine wrote:

> Years ago this desolate spot was farm land. It might yet
> be secured and made into a green playground for the
> children, who at present have only the roads and the
> miniature mountains of rubbish that have gradually risen
> at the end of side streets closed in by factory walls. If
> this central desert could be secured and 'humanised' and

turned into a healthy playground, it would be a grand
thing for the Millwall that is – and grander still for the
Millwall that is to be.

A century later, a playground for children it is not, nor
was it exactly 'humanised' after the docks closed.
Instead, the decision to move all dock activity to
Tilbury, and Margaret Thatcher's deregulation of
financial markets and relaxation of planning controls,
signalled the OK to the City to expand into the void.

The idea for Canary Wharf kicked off in 1984 during
a lunch between Michael von Clemm, chairman of
Credit Suisse First Boston Bank and also chairman of
Roux Restaurants, and executives of the London
Docklands Development Corporation (the LDDC), set
up by the Government to use State money to encourage
private investment in the now vacant docklands. They
dined on a barge alongside Shed 31 at Canary Wharf.

The LDDC had heard that the Roux Brothers
(famous restaurateurs and chefs) were looking for a
space for the large-scale preparation of pre-cooked
meals. The idea grew. Clemm's American property
adviser Travelstead suggested moving the London HQ
of First Boston – the whole operation – to the Isle of
Dogs. This led to discussions with the LDDC and
Margaret Thatcher's Government about a new financial
services district of ten million square feet, located at the
old West India Docks, with an extension of the Jubilee
line of the Underground leading to it.

Not until 1988, however, did the first phase of

building get going. First, the plug was pulled on the scheme owing to lack of funds. Then, when Canadian developers Olympia and York took it up, a downturn in the property market caused the company to crash and left the site looking like a ghost town. However, the project was eventually revived, with some of the same personnel involved. It opened in 2002 and now covers some 15,000,000 square feet, containing within it the UK's three tallest buildings: One Canada Square at 771ft, and 8 Canada Square and the Citigroup Centre both at 654ft.

Throughout the building, local residents made their hostility to the project felt, infiltrating the ground-breaking ceremony for Canary Wharf and sending in a herd of sheep and a swarm of bees amongst the dignitaries and government ministers in attendance. There was even a lawsuit, which reached the House of Lords. But in the end the project was completed and the Wharf now employs thousands of Isle of Dogs inhabitants, with 25 per cent of the total 90,000 workforce from neighbouring boroughs – in employment terms, a fine replacement for the docks.

Tenant companies include banks, law firms and news media, and the 2012 Olympic Games organisers also operate from here. There is a shopping centre, and bars and restaurants. Take the Docklands Light Railway through it, and there is a Star Wars sense of post-Armageddon, but this is an island and there are plans to contain the development within this one part of the East End, as a kind of financial ghetto, which is

certainly in line with the East End's historical development as a series of ghettoes. Meanwhile, the Museum of
Docklands, which holds many of the archive materials
used for this book, stands like a custodian of the past,
overlooking West India Quays, ensuring that the
modern buildings will never eclipse what went before.

Of course there have been other developments, and
the Gherkin, which seems sometimes to double
unnervingly as bullet or shell, is visible from almost
everywhere to remind us of the recent encroachment
of the modern world. The fact is that the dock warehouses, which once were so busy with dock business,
make beautiful and efficient spaces for living and
working, and have done for more than a quarter of a
century now. Two years before the Roux Brothers were
courted for Canary Wharf, Terence Conran teamed up
with financial consultant Roger Seelig and builder Lord
McAlpine to buy Butler's Wharf, a string of warehouses
on the south bank of the Thames (Shad Thames) at
Tower Bridge, opposite where Conran's father started
Conran & Co (an importer of gum copal) more than
fifty years earlier. As for the developers of Canary
Wharf, this turned out to be one of the costliest mistakes of Conran's career. Eight years later his Docklands property company went into receivership.
However, again like those interested in Canary Wharf,
Conran returned. To celebrate his sixtieth birthday he
opened Le Pont de la Tour, followed by Blueprint Café,
La Cantina, and the Butler's Wharf Chophouse, and
today everywhere you look, there is Conran, Conran,

Conran. A two-minute stroll towards the front-door buzzer of Conrad Holdings will take you past a Conran coffee kiosk, a Conran wine merchant, a Conran bakery, a Conran food store and four separate Conran eateries. The Design Museum, which Conran set up and continues to be his baby, is also here, though there are rumours of a move.

It is easy to fall in love with this area of the Thames for all sorts of reasons, one of which is that you can sense that it has been a colourful place of trading for many hundreds of years, and there is continuity in all this.

But is there community?

The East End, so close to the centre of London, is now 'prime real estate', and with developments on the Isle of Dogs and further north and east for the Olympic Games in 2012, it is changing and it is bound to change. But what it was once – its real claim on our attention – is that it was a special community.

Among the modern communities settling in the East End is the artist community, which is a good sign. Samuel Augustus Barnett, the vicar of St Jude's Whitechapel who initiated Toynbee Hall and insisted that a generation of politicians who would launch Socialism in this country come and be and live in the East End, and let it go to work on them, also saw fit to found the Whitechapel Gallery, originally The East End Art Gallery, in 1901. Barnett understood that art and community were inseparable, the one feeding the other and vice versa, a means of expression for a community and an inspiration for it.

Art is political in that sense, which is why in the 1930s, when the people of Stepney wanted to let the freedom fighters in the Spanish Civil War know that they were with them in their battle against fascism, they hired the Whitechapel Gallery to exhibit Picasso's *Guernica*.

There are dozens of art galleries in the East End today, from Flowers East at 82 Kingsland Road to a host of little galleries on Vyner Street by Cambridge Heath Road, at the western tip of the newly restored Victoria Park.

But this is so obviously a place for artists to settle, a place of diversity, colour, change, ideas. Its newest immigrants are not the Bengalis, but artists such as designer Marianna Kennedy, book-binder Charles Gledhil, and artist Tracey Emin, living in an area where once the artistic tradition was upheld by the Huguenots, with their beautiful gold and silver-threaded silks and intricate floral designs.

We are back in Brick Lane, but not the southern end among the four dozen Bengali restaurants, and the Jamme Masjid Mosque (the old Huguenot L'Eglise Neuve), rather, north of Hanbury Street, in the area of the Trueman Brewery, among trendy shops, pubs, cafés, clubs, boutiques and galleries. And further north, off Sclater Street, so close to the Burns family sites in Bacon Street, Cheshire Street and the old East End, as to make one wonder at the presence of Shoreditch House, a celebrity private members' club, with bars, bowling alley, gym, 16-metre pool, sauna and steam room, games room, dining room, cowshed . . .

The Lounge Lover is also, famously, nearby, scooped

out of a former meat packing factory in Whitby Street by three antiques dealers, who have Les Trois Garcons down the road, at No 1 Club Row. Here, you are as likely to bump into Sienna Miller or Madonna – she celebrated her 48th birthday at Lounge Lover – while at Les Trois Garcons, favoured customers are Liz Hurley, Donatella Versace, Nicole Kidman, Jade Jagger and Yoko Ono. And in autumn 2008, at 2–4 Boundary Street, Sir Terence Conran opens an exclusive hotel right in the black heart of the Old Nichol estate.

This is the same Old Nichol that was once 'as foul a neighbourhood as can be discovered in the civilised world (savage life has nothing to compare to it), and amongst a population depressed almost to the last stage of human endurance'.

And this is the same Club Row where 'birds in cages once sang, dogs could be purchased from a shilling upwards, also cats and monkeys – 'You could buy almost anything down the Row . . . Sunday morning always meant a walk down the Row, or the Lane. There was Club Row, Sclater Street and Brick Lane, through to Wentworth Street and Petticoat Lane . . . and although we had no money to spend, we got one hell of a kick from window shopping.'[2]

It is impossible to live round here and not be aware of the distinctly different cultures that exist cheek by jowl and *never* mix, which, as we have seen, has always been the case in the East End.

Ed Husain was brought up in Stepney in the 1980s and worshipped with his father at the Brick Lane Mosque, before pledging his allegiance to the East London Mosque in Whitechapel Road, a transition which he has described as one from conservative spiritual Islam to political ethical Islam.[3] He told Rebecca Taylor,

> There was no alternative; either I became involved in Islam or I joined a gang. There were simply no other outlets for young Muslims . . . We believed in Islam's political superiority over the West; the creation of a true Islamic society and the importance of removing disbelievers – or the 'kuffar'.[4]

His views make disturbing reading, though he has drawn back from them now, the whole picture well delineated in his book, *The Islamist* (Penguin, 2007).

It is interesting that lots of East Enders mention that religion was never a divisive force here until now, that the various nationalities were aware of each other's cultures and respected them, even sharing each other's festivals. This is the 50:50 respect that Shafiq Uddin mentioned, and is a fundamental tenet of the old East End.

There is something special in the East End, in the variety of the communities that have established themselves here over the years, and in the ability of these to play it 50:50, to show mutual respect, rather than seek to remove another community because it was different, a 'kuffar'. It is only when a community failed in that respect that violence erupted (as in the Mosley riots) and they were soon seen off. As the Reverend Samuel Barnett might have said, the East Ender has shown himself adept at embracing the values that arise naturally from community, and escaping the 'isms' that threaten to asphyxiate life – Marxism, capitalism, fundamentalism. Has it something to do with a continuing awareness of the past, of what-has-been, in the East End?

The old East End community was not an antidote for loneliness, it was a series of extended 'families', many of which never met, but from which arose the values by which everyone lived. The values grew out of the local community and were not thrust upon it, although there was always an awareness of the greater East End community, in which everyone was rooted. There was a shared feeling of belonging and a deep sense of loyalty, fraternity, 'active citizenship', interest in your fellow man and a requirement of respect. The alternative was the 'locked doors and heads turned away' attitude of the West End.

There were village communities in other parts of London, but the East End was special because of the docks and the constant potential for new immigrant communities settling, and its rejection by greater London historically, which gave it its insular sense, and episodes such as the Blitz and the Mosley riots, which showed the world East Enders at their best exercising their values.

There are things of value, and then there are values, the things we live by, and a balance between them is what the East End got right in the past.

Today, young Muslims face pressures that Shafiq never faced. If the Muslim religion forbids alcohol there does not seem to be the same avoidance of drugs, and with drugs come street crime and prostitution to pay for them.

> It took just five minutes wandering down the backstreets of Brick Lane in East London before three Bangladeshi teenagers loitering outside a council block offered this reporter 'skunk'.[5]

The artist Sanchita Islam, who lives in Brick Lane, told *Time Out* in November 2006:

> The main customers for the prostitutes around here – mostly white crack addicts – are Bengali men. They're probably having unprotected sex with them and with their wives, and those women won't go to a clinic to get themselves checked out. There are Bengali girls having anal sex to protect their virginity and at the same time they're trying to maintain the façade of having close-knit families.

That phrase, 'the façade of having close-knit families', is compelling. These are second or third generation immigrants of the Sylheti immigrants of the sixties and seventies, born within the sound of Bow bells.

Remember H. V. Morton's description of the beautiful young second or third generation Jewish girls in 1940, with 'the eyes of Ruth among the alien corn' and the 'larynx of Bill Sykes'? These Bengali kids are cockneys, but according to one of them, only 'maintaining the façade'.

There are some 70,000 Muslims currently in Tower Hamlets. Their values are encoded in their religion. But in the wider community the East End has its own values, which are largely in tune with them. There are several references to the idea that Brick Lane and other areas of the East End were replacement villages for Sylheti immigrants. The Indian immigrant Prafulla Mohanti 'felt at home' in the East End because of its Indian shops and sense of community; his own experiences of growing up poor in an Indian village helped him to understand the communities he moved into in East London. For him, the East End is honest and friendly, while the West End is a completely different world.[6]

The community concept of the East End is as intuitively natural to immigrants from Sylheti as it was to the immigrant Jews before them, in the face of their appalling persecution, and as it was to the indigenous cockneys, as the Reverend Samuel Barnett noted.

Barnett wanted to wake the world up to the cockney East Ender's sense of community, because he saw how important a concept it was to the wider world. The rising politicians, academics, journalists and church-men, whom he invited, came and saw, and drew on what they found in order to map our social and political future. Likewise, today, the East End is still a microcosm, with this ready-made solution in the values its history reveals to us.

Perhaps that is why one artist tried to mummify and preserve the East End's history symbolically. On 25 October 1993, after two years of planning and preparation, Rachel Whiteread completed her in-situ 'cast' of a Victorian terraced house, symbolic of the old East End, at 193 Grove Road in Bow, a road in which every other house had been knocked down. She called the sculpture, *House*, the work attracted huge media attention and tens of thousands of visitors. What were they looking for? They probably didn't know, but they came.

My first outing in the research for this book was to walk the area covered by the Thameside villages – St Katharine's Dock, Wapping, Shadwell, Ratcliff, Limehouse and the Isle of Dogs – carrying with me factual records from different times in the past, taking photographs and recording points of interest, the whole area coming alive for me and giving me contacts, picked up in museums, galleries and pubs along the way. I was amazed how much of the past is left or 'held' in the present by names and buildings. Where a refuge for the poor has been knocked down, the modern tower block that replaced it has been given its name. In spite of the planners, in spite of the stillness and emptiness of stretches of the Thames, there is still a clear sense of what-has-been – echoes of the past, which is, in the case of the East End, where inspiration for the future resides.

The past is held in signs, but also in the people, in the hearts of the people who speak to us in this book. Once, recently, the past was broken into, literally, as if it were a shadow-land that marches a whisper away from the present.

In 1980 someone opened a door of a room at No. 19 Princelet Street, the eighteenth-century Huguenot house, you will recall, which had been taken over by the Jews, when it was their turn to occupy the Brick Lane area a century later. This particular room had been leased to a reclusive Jew called David Rodinsky. In 1969 Rodinsky emerged from the room, locked the door and disappeared.

On opening the door almost eleven years later, his room was like a scene out of *Great Expectations* – a Miss Havisham room frozen in time, the dust and cobwebs of years, and the deathly absence of life, as in a tomb. Notebooks and diaries were found, strange 'Cabbalistic diagrams', and an *A–Z* marked with routes, everything apparently awaiting interpretation, explanation.[7]

Here was a time capsule within a house whose history is now generally known. 'Before it was used as a room, it was a silk weaver's garret,' says Susie Symes, curator of 19 Princelet Street today. 'That too is of interest . . . People always want to see whatever is hidden.'

Where more likely for this to happen than in London's East End, where so much of its history lies tantalisingly accessible, as if the whole area were itself a manuscript over-scored with successive texts, none ever erased, each one disappearing from view as the other is written, but, as with memory, awaiting something or someone – in the case of the East End, so often a migrant – to unlock its secrets.

Acknowledgements

I would like to acknowledge the contributions of the many people whose memories appear in this book, but my special thanks must go to Mary Lester, whose meticulous research bore all the hallmarks of the work of the scholar that she is, in an area she also understands through personal experience (it is a winning combination), and to my wife, Dee Dudgeon, who transcribed so much of the material and then brought so much of it to life on the page.

Among the interviewees, I would like to thank in particular, Shafiq and Pamela Uddin, David Bailey, Tony Burns, Alf and Edna Stuart, Bernard Kops,

Andrew and Barbara Newman, Martin Leonard, Emma Bennett and Jack Martin, whose characters make parts of this book their own. I am deeply indebted to all of them.

But there were many people without whom the book would not have been possible, and I list them here in no particular order: Minoo Bhatia, Bruce Flory, Abdul Azad, Susie Symes, Les Hearson, Hsiao Hung, Dr Kate Bradley, Julie Begum, Mukti Jaim Campion, Anna Chen, Emmanuel Amevor, PC 626, Michael Keating and Denise Jones.

My gratitude also goes to the many museums, libraries and societies that have gone out of their way to help, not least to Malcolm Barr-Hamilton at the Tower Hamlets Library on Bancroft Road; to Phil Mernicks of the East London History Society, for his permission to consult and quote from the *East London Record* and the Society Newsletters (an extraordinary resource: the society may be contacted at eastlondonhistory.org.uk @dsl.pipex.com); to Annette Day and Claire Frankland for their time and permission to quote from priceless interviews in the archives of the Museum of London and the Museum of Docklands; similarly to Ike Egbetola and Mary Stewart at the British Library Sound Archive, and Rickie Berman and Louise Asher at the Jewish Museum in London. Major work has also been done in this area by the Eastside Community Heritage and the Bethnal Green Museum of Childhood, and of course by Toynbee Hall, who opened their doors to me from the start. My thanks too to the Centerprise Trust

Ltd, 136–8 Kingsland High Street, London E8 2NS. Then there is the Museum of Immigration, the title under which that extraordinary time capsule, 19 Princelet Street, is now known.

Finally, I would like to thank the publishers who have granted permission for me to quote from the many East End histories on which I have drawn.

Every effort has been made to trace the holders of copyright in text quotations and photographs, but any inadvertent mistakes or omissions may be corrected in future editions.

Piers Dudgeon, May 2008

Sources and endnotes

Introduction
[1] Charlie Chaplin, *My Wonderful Visit* (Hurst & Blackett, 1922).

[2] See www.stmarylebow.co.uk for more information.

[3] Annie Besant, *An autobiography* (T Fisher Unwin, 1893).

[4] Today Toynbee Hall is probably most widely known as the place where Jack Profumo, the government minister caught up in the Christine Keeler prostitute-Russian-spy scandal, arrived as a penitent and volunteer in 1964. He was put straight to work in the most menial of tasks, but soon the value of his financial, political and social contacts were put to good use.

Part I

Chapter 1: The cockney spirit

[1] A resident of a Flower and Dean Street tenement, *East London History Society Newsletter*, January 1985.

[2] Walter Southgate, *That's The Way It Was. A Working Class Autobiography 1890–1950* (New Clarion Press, 1982), pp. 21–22.

[3] Kingsley Roydon, 'A Friend in My Retreat: Family Life in Bromley St Leonard between the Wars', *East London Record*, 1978 (1), 23–34, p. 23.

[4] Sally Worboyes, *East End Girl. Growing Up the Hard Way* (Hodder Headline, 2006), p. 17.

[5] Raphael Samuel, *East End Underworld. Chapters in the Life of Arthur Harding* (Routledge & Kegan Paul, 1981), p. 24.

[6] Ibid., p. 61.

[7] Kingsley Roydon, 'A Friend in My Retreat: Family Life in Bromley St Leonard between the Wars', *East London Record*, 1978 (1), 23–34, p. 24.

[8] Michael Young and Peter Willmott, *Family and Kinship in East London* (Routledge & Kegan Paul, 1957).

[9] George E. Bishop, 'Childhood Memories of Bethnal Green', *East London Record*, 1987 (10), 27–31, p. 27.

[10] Jack Banfield, Museum of Docklands interview transcript, 85/597, p. 2.

[11] George Renshaw, *Reflections of Changing Times*, East London History Newsletter, Vol. 1, Issues 2–5.

[12] Percy Clarke interviewed by Alison Turpin (1999). Millennium Memory Bank. British Library Sound Archive. C900/11578.

[13] Cyril Demarne, *The London Blitz: A Fireman's Tale* (Parents Centre Publication, c. 1980).

[14] Albert Corn.
[15] Charles Downes in Howard Bloch's *Canning Town Voices* (Tempus, 1998), p. 13.
[16] Charles Adams, pp. 25–6.
[17] Grace Blacketer, *Down the Nile in the East End*, East London History Newsletter, Vol. 1, Issue 17.

Chapter 2: Frontiers

[1] Ivy Alexander, 'Old Canning Town', *East London Record*, 1994–5 (17), 2–10, p. 7.
[2] Joyce Ayres, 'Memories of Bethnal Green', *East London Record*, 1983 (6), 2–5, p. 2.
[3] Jack Banfield, Museum of Docklands interview transcript, 85/597, p. 2.
[4] Sally Worboyes, *East End Girl. Growing Up the Hard Way* (Hodder Headline, 2006), p. 9.
[5] Bernard Kops.
[6] George Renshaw, *Reflections of Changing Times*, East London History Newsletter, Vol. 1, Issues 2–5.
[7] Joe Bloomberg, *Looking Back: A Docker's Life* (Stepney Books Publications, 1979), p. 2.
[8] Walter Southgate, *That's The Way It Was. A Working Class Autobiography 1890–1950* (New Clarion Press, 1982), p. 25.
[9] A resident of the Flowery, *East London History Society Newsletter*, January 1985.
[10] M. E. Carrington, 'Stepney Memories', *East London Record*, 1986 (9), 2–8, p. 4.
[11] Cyril Demarne, *The London Blitz: A Fireman's Tale* (Parents Centre Publication, c. 1980).
[12] Ibid.
[13] J. Monnikendam interviewed by Juliet Duff (1986). London Museum of Jewish Life Oral History Interviews.

British Library Sound Archive. C525/37/01. Copyright London Museum of Jewish Life.

[14] George Renshaw, *Reflections of Changing Times*, East London History Newsletter, Vol. 1, Issues 2–5.

[15] Emanuel Litvinoff, Museum of London interview transcript, 99.29, p. 19. See also www.emanuel-litvinoff.com

[16] Quoted in Venetia Murray, *Echoes of the East End* (Viking, 1989), p. 24.

[17] Henry Hollis & Dan Wooding, *Farewell Leicester Square* (Wm MacLellan (Embryo) Ltd, 1983), p. 29.

[18] George Renshaw, *Reflections of Changing Times*, East London History Newsletter, Vol. 1, Issues 2–5.

[19] Jack Banfield, Museum of Docklands interview transcript, 85/597, p. 26.

[20] Billy Scotchmer, *Memories of Bow*, East London History Newsletter, Vol. 1, Issue 7.

[21] Vicki Green, Museum of London interview transcript, 99.32, p. 5.

[22] Julie Hunt, Museum in Docklands interview transcript, DK/88/94/1, p. 12.

[23] Willy Goldman, *East End My Cradle. Portrait of an Environment* (Robson Books, 1988 [1940]), p. 10.

[24] Ralph Finn, *Grief Forgotten: The Tale of an East End Jewish Boyhood* (Macdonald, 1968).

[25] Renamed the Mayflower in the 1950s but renamed again since then.

[26] Stan Rose, Museum in Docklands interview transcript, DK/86/345, p. 7.

[27] A resident of the Flowery, *East London History Society Newsletter*, January 1985.

[28] Willy Goldman, *East End My Cradle. Portrait of an Environment* (Robson Books, 1988 [1940]), p. 17.

[29] Ralph L. Finn, *Grief Forgotten. The Tale of an East End Jewish Boyhood* (Macdonald & Co 1985 [1968]), p. 16.

[30] Joyce Ayres, *East London Record*, Issue 6, 1983.

[31] Emanuel Litvinoff, Museum of London interview transcript, 99.29, p. 4.

[32] Jim Stuart, *East London Record*, Issue 6, 1983.

Chapter 3: Cockney wide boys

[x] Stan Rose, Museum in Docklands interview transcript, DK/86/345, p. 7.

[2] Katherine Shellduck, *Dance For Your Daddy. The True Story of a Brutal East End Childhood* (Ebury Press, 2007), pp. 12–13. Reprinted by permission of the Random House Group Ltd.

[3] Walter Southgate, *That's The Way It Was. A Working Class Autobiography 1890–1950* (New Clarion Press, 1982), p. 68.

[4] Sally Worboyes, *East End Girl. Growing Up the Hard Way* (Hodder Headline, 2006), p. 147.

[5] George Renshaw, *Reflections of Changing Times*, East London History Newsletter, Vol. 1, Issues 2–5.

[6] Lilian Hine, 'A Poplar Childhood', *East London Record*, 1980 (3), 33–43, p. 35

[7] Raphael Samuel, *East End Underworld. Chapters in the Life of Arthur Harding* (Routledge & Kegan Paul, 1981), p. 60.

[8] Vi Short, 'A Childhood in Bow', *East London Record*, 1992 (15), 2–9, p. 2.

[9] Kingsley Roydon, 'A Friend in My Retreat: Family Life in Bromley St Leonard between the Wars', *East London Record*, 1978 (1), 23–34, p. 25.

[10] George A. Cook, *A Hackney Memory Chest* (Centerprise Trust, 1983), p. 34.

[11] *Littell's Living Age* (1888).

[12] Ivor Spencer, interviewed by Juliet Duff (1986). London Museum of Jewish Life Oral History Interviews. British Library Oral History Archives, C5252/23/01. Copyright London Museum of Jewish Life.

[13] Sam Clarke, *Sam: An East End Cabinet Maker. The Pocketbook Memoir of Sam Clarke, 1907–1979*, ed. Kedrun Ladurie (ILEA, 1982), p. 29.

[14] Vicki Green, Museum of London interview transcript, 99.32, p. 5.

[15] Martin Leonard.

[16] J. Monnikendam interviewed by Juliet Duff (1986). London Museum of Jewish Life Oral History Interviews. British Library Sound Archive. C525/37/01. Copyright London Museum of Jewish Life.

Chapter 4: Behind the scenes

[1] George A. Cook, *A Hackney Memory Chest* (Centerprise Trust, 1983), p. 23.

[2] Ibid., pp. 21–2.

[3] Grace Blacketer, *Down the Nile in the East End*, East London History Newsletter, Vol. 1, Issue 17.

[4] Jack Banfield, Museum of London interview transcript, 85/597/3, p. 4.

[5] Anne Griffiths, Museum in Docklands transcript, DK/88/66/1/A, p. 5.

[6] M. E. Carrington, 'Stepney Memories', *East London Record*, 1986 (9), 2–8, p. 4.

[7] Eileen Baillie, *The Shabby Paradise. Autobiography of a Decade* (British Book Centre, 1959), p. 39.

[8] Raphael Samuel, *East End Underworld. Chapters in the Life of Arthur Harding* (Routledge & Kegan Paul, 1981)

[9] Bernard Kops.

[10] Emanuel Litvinoff, Museum of London interview transcript, 99.29, p. 2.

[11] Michael Young and Peter Willmott, *Family and Kinship in East London* (Routledge & Kegan Paul, 1957).

[12] Jack London, *The Abyss* (1903).

[13] A resident of the Flowery, *East London History Society Newsletter*, January 1985.

[14] Metropolitan Police Instruction Book, 1973.

[15] Gilda O'Neill, *My East End. Memories of Life in Cockney London* (Penguin, 2000), p. 134.

[16] George A. Cook, *A Hackney Memory Chest* (Centerprise Trust, 1983), p. 4.

[17] Willy Goldman, *East End My Cradle. Portrait of an Environment* (Robson Books, 1988 [1940]), pp. 113–14.

[18] Henry Hollis & Dan Wooding, *Farewell Leicester Square* (Wm MacLellan (Embryo) Ltd, 1983), p. 40.

[19] Michael Young and Peter Willmott *Family and Kinship in East London* (Routledge & Kegan Paul, 1957).

[20] Stan Rose, Museum in Docklands interview transcript, DK/86/345/1, p. 6.

[21] Raphael Samuel, *East End Underworld. Chapters in the Life of Arthur Harding* (Routledge & Kegan Paul, 1981), pp. 28–9.

[22] Bernard Kops.

[23] Raphael Samuel, *East End Underworld. Chapters in the Life of Arthur Harding* (Routledge & Kegan Paul, 1981), p. 42.

[24] Henry Hollis & Dan Wooding, *Farewell Leicester Square* (London: Wm MacLellan (Embryo) Ltd, 1983), p. 18.

[25] M. E. Carrington, 'Stepney Memories', *East London Record*, 1986 (9), 2–8, p. 2.

[26] Melanie McGrath, Silvertown. *An East End Family Memoir* (London: Fourth Estate, 2003), pp. 62–3.

27 Raphael Samuel, *East End Underworld. Chapters in the Life of Arthur Harding* (London: Routledge & Kegan Paul, 1981), p. 25.

Chapter 5: Genesis

1 Louis XIV's Edict of Fontainebleau in 1685 revoked the Edict of Nantes originally issued in 1598 by Henry IV to grant the Huguenots substantial rights in a nation still considered essentially Catholic.

2 Roy Curtis in *East End Passport* (Guidebooks, 1969).

3 Michael Young and Peter Willmott, *Family and Kinship in East London* (Routledge & Kegan Paul, 1957).

4 Sydney Phelps.

5 Charles Booth.

6 Michael Young and Peter Willmott, *Family and Kinship in East London* (Routledge & Kegan Paul, 1957).

7 Jennifer Worth, *Shadows of the Workhouse* (Weidenfeld & Nicolson, 2008) p. 77.

8 Raphael Samuel, *East End Underworld. Chapters in the Life of Arthur Harding* (Routledge & Kegan Paul, 1981), p. 66.

9 Joe Morris, Museum of London interview transcript, 93.43, p. 14.

Chapter 6: Tailors, bakers and furniture makers

1 From the Russian word meaning 'to wreak havoc, to demolish violently'.

2 Fred Wright, 'The Ingles of Limehouse', *East London Record*, 1992 (15), 15–21, p. 15.

3 Goodman Schneider interviewed by Polly Rockberger (1988). London Museum of Jewish Life Oral History Interviews. British Library Sound Archive. C525/71/01 (Format F1966). Copyright London Museum of Jewish

Life.
4 Charles Poulsen, Museum of London interview transcript, 99.153.
5 Ralph L. Finn, *No Tears in Aldgate* (Cedric Chivers, 1963), p. 17.
6 Ralph L. Finn, *Grief Forgotten: The Tale of an East End Jewish Boyhood* (London: Macdonald & Co 1985 [1968]), p. 18.
7 Charles Poulsen, Museum of London interview transcript, 99.153.
8 Ibid.
9 Bernard Kops.
10 J. Monnikendam interviewed by Juliet Duff (1986). London Museum of Jewish Life Oral History Interviews. British Library Sound Archive. C525/37/01. Copyright London Museum of Jewish Life.
11 Andrew Newman.
12 M. Young and Peter Willmott, *Family and Kinship in East London* (Routledge & Kegan Paul, 1957).
13 Andrew Newman.
14 Willy Goldman, *East End My Cradle. Portrait of an Environment* (London: Robson Books, 1988 [1940]), p. 148.
15 Alf Stuart.
16 Sadie Herrera.
17 Anna Tzelinker, Museum of London interview transcript, 92.150.
18 Bill Belmont, 'As I Recall', in Venetia Murray, *Echoes of the East End* (Viking, 1989), 167–186, p. 167.
19 Ivor Spencer, interviewed by Juliet Duff (1986). London Museum of Jewish Life Oral History Interviews. British Library Oral History Archives, C5252/23/01. Copyright London Museum of Jewish Life.

[20] Ralph Finn, *Grief Forgotten: The Tale of an East End Jewish Boyhood* (Macdonald, 1968).

[21] Ralph L. Finn, *No Tears in Aldgate* (Cedric Chivers, 1963), p. 41.

[22] Vicki Green, Museum of London interview transcript, 99.32, p. 3.

[23] Jennifer Worth, *Call the Midwife. A True Story of the East End in the 1950s* (Weidenfeld & Nicolson, 2002), p. 33.

[24] Jack Miller, Museum of London interview transcript, 92.177, p. 2.

[25] Hannah, Eastside Community Heritage interview, Unit 8, 44 Gillender Street, E14.

[26] Martin Leonard.

[27] Ralph L. Finn, *No Tears in Aldgate* (Cedric Chivers, 1963), p. 41.

Chapter 7: Docklands

[1] Raphael Samuel, *East End Underworld. Chapters in the Life of Arthur Harding* (London: Routledge & Kegan Paul, 1981), p. 60.

[2] Eileen Baillie, *The Shabby Paradise. Autobiography of a Decade* (London: British Book Centre, 1959), p. 43.

[3] Maurice Pelter, 'Sliced From Life: A Stepney Tale', *East London Record*, 1982 (5), 13-21, pp. 17–18.

[4] Harry Salton, *Memories of Bow Common*. East London History Society Newsletters, Vol. 1, Issue 9.

[5] Ibid.

[6] Sally Worboyes, *East End Girl. Growing Up the Hard Way* (London: Hodder Headline, 2006), p. 23.

[7] Raphael Samuel, *East End Underworld. Chapters in the Life of Arthur Harding* (London: Routledge & Kegan Paul, 1981), p. 66.

8   Cyril Demarne, *The London Blitz: A Fireman's Tale* (Parents Centre Publication, c. 1980).

9   Tom Britton interviewed by Lynne Tucker (1999). Millennium Memory Bank. British Library Sound Archive. Catalogue No. C900/17053.

10   Jack Banfield, Museum of Docklands interview transcript, 85/597, p. 69.

11   Lucy Collard, Museum of Docklands interview transcript DK/88/96/1.

12   Jennifer Worth, *Call the Midwife. A True Story of the East End in the 1950s* (Weidenfeld & Nicolson, 2002), p. 19.

13   Sally Worboyes, *East End Girl. Growing Up the Hard Way* (Hodder Headline, 2006), p. 122.

14   Bill Abbott, Museum in Docklands interview transcript, DK 86/352, p. 83.

15   Stan Rose, Museum in Docklands interview transcript, DK/86/345, pp. 11–13.

16   Walter Dunsford, Museum of Docklands interview transcript, 85/593, pp. 9–10.

17   Joe Bloomberg, *Looking Back: A Docker's Life* (Stepney Books Publications, 1979), p. 16.

18   Bill Abbott, Museum in Docklands interview transcript, DK 86/352, p. 82.

Part II

Chapter 8: Rise of the working classes

1   'Bethnal Green: Building and Social Conditions from 1876 to 1914', *A History of the County of Middlesex: Volume 11: Stepney, Bethnal Green* (1998).

2   Maurice Pelter, 'Sliced From Life: A Stepney Tale', *East London Record*, 1982 (5), 13–21, p. 16.

3 'Bethnal Green: Building and Social Conditions from 1876 to 1914', *A History of the County of Middlesex: Volume 11: Stepney, Bethnal Green* (1998).

4 Raphael Samuel, *East End Underworld. Chapters in the Life of Arthur Harding* (London: Routledge & Kegan Paul, 1981), p. 275.

5 Horace Thorogood, *East of Aldgate* (London: George Allen & Unwin, 1935), pp. 83–4.

6 Sam Vincent, 'A Bethnal Green Childhood', *East London Record*, 1989 (12), 21–28, p. 22.

7 Sally Worboyes, *East End Girl. Growing Up the Hard Way* (London: Hodder Headline, 2006), pp. 4–5.

8 Maurice Pelter, 'Sliced From Life: A Stepney Tale', *East London Record*, 1982 (5), 13–21, pp. 16–17.

9 Anna Tzelniker & Philip Bernstein, Museum of London interview transcript, 92.150, p. 40.

10 Phil Piratin, *Our Flag Stays Red* [1948] (London: Lawrence & Wishart, 1978), p. 19.

11 J. Monnikendam interviewed by Juliet Duff (1986). London Museum of Jewish Life Oral History Interviews. British Library Sound Archive. C525/37/01. Copyright London Museum of Jewish Life.

12 Jim Wolveridge in Venetia Murray, *Echoes of the East End* (Viking, 1989), p. 140.

13 Phil Piratin, *Our Flag Stays Red* [1948] (Lawrence & Wishart, 1978), p. 25.

14 In July 1936, the fascist General Franco participated in a coup d'état against the elected left-wing Popular Front government in Spain. The coup failed and evolved into the Spanish Civil War. Many left-wing sympathisers took actively against him.

15 Jack Miller, Museum of London interview transcript, 92.177, pp. 12–13.

16 Jim Wolveridge in Venetia Murray, *Echoes of the East End* (Viking, 1989), p. 140.

17 Phil Piratin, *Our Flag Stays Red* [1948] (London: Lawrence & Wishart, 1978), p. 25.

Chapter 9: The Blitz

1 Frank R. Lewey, *Cockney Campaign* (Stanley Paul & Co., 1944), p. 41.

2 Ken Long, BBC WW2 People's War Archive, A2065402, 20th November 2003, http://www.bbc.co.uk/ww2peoples war/stories/02/a2065402.shtml.

3 Ibid.

4 Sam Vincent, 'A Bethnal Green Childhood', *East London Record*, 1989 (12) 21–28, p. 28.

5 Juliet Gardiner, *The Children's War* (Piatkus, 2005).

6 Stanley Keyte (1996), National life story awards. British Library Sound Archive. Catalogue No. C642/123/1–2.

7 Ibid.

8 Barbara Nixon, *Raiders Overhead* (Lindsay Drummond, 1943), p. 13.

9 Jim O'Sullivan, *The First Night of the Blitz.* East London History Society Newsletters Vol. 2, Issue 4.

10 Charles Chisnall, *Beyond the High Bob*, East London Record, 1993 (16), 2–6, pp. 2 & 4.

11 Anne Griffiths, Museum in Docklands transcript, DK/88/66/1/A, pp. 49–50.

12 Ivy Alexander, *Maid in West Ham* (Ivy Alexander, 2001), pp. 54–6.

13 Juliet Gardiner, *The Children's War* (Piatkus, 2005).

14 Jennifer Worth, *Shadows of the Workhouse* (Weidenfeld & Nicholson, 2008), p. 268.

15 Harry Willmott, *Memories of the Blitz*. East London History Society Newsletters Volume 1, Issue 18.

16 Sam Vincent, *A Bethnal Green Childhood*, East London Record, 1989 (12) 21–28, p. 28.

17 Barbara Nixon, *Raiders Overhead* (Lindsay Drummond, 1943), p. 19.

18 Phil Piratin, *Our Flag Stays Red* [1948] (Lawrence & Wishart, 1978), p. 73.

19 Michael Moorcock, *Mother London* (Simon & Schuster, 2000) pp. 156–7.

20 Ivy Alexander, *Maid in West Ham* (Ivy Alexander, 2001), pp. 65–6.

21 John Blake, *Memories of Old Poplar* (Stepney Books Publications, 1977), p. 42.

22 Charles Poulsen, Museum of London interview transcript, 99.153.

23 Barbara Nixon, *Raiders Overhead* (Lindsay Drummond, 1943), p. 120.

24 Clement Attlee, 'Introduction' to Frank R. Lewey, *Cockney Campaign* (Stanley Paul & Co., 1944), p. 1.

25 Ibid., p. 16.

26 Ibid., p. 75.

27 Jennifer Worth, *Shadows of the Workhouse* (Weidenfeld & Nicholson, 2008), pp. 268–9.

28 *The Stratford Express.*

Part III

Chapter 10: Broken, but not beat

[1] Toynbee Hall community group.
[2] Doreen M. Bailey, *Children of the Green* (Stepney Books, 1981), p. 31.
[3] John Blake, *Memories of Old Poplar* (Stepney Books Publications, 1977), p. 46.
[4] Lucy Collard, Museum of Docklands interview transcript, DK/88/96/1, p. 50.
[5] Joyce Ayres, *Memories of Bethnal Green*. East London Record, 1983 (6), 2–5, p. 5.
[6] Chandra Vansadia, Museum of London interview transcript, 99.84, p. 7.
[7] Daniel Farson, *Limehouse Days. Personal Experience of the East End* (Michael Joseph, 1991), pp. 121–2.
[8] Jennifer Worth, *Shadows of the Workhouse* (Weidenfeld & Nicholson, 2008), p. 273.
[9] Stan Rose, Museum in Docklands interview transcript, DK/86/345, p. 26.

Chapter 11: Changing faces

[1] Tarquin Hall, *Salaam Brick Lane* (John Murray, 2005), p. 46.
[2] Anna Tzelniker & Philip Bernstein, Museum of London interview transcript, 92.150, pp. 43–5.
[3] Former RAF serviceman, Martin Black.
[4] Daniel Farson, *Limehouse Days. Personal Experience of the East End* (Michael Joseph, 1991), p. 122.
[5] Jennifer Worth, *Call the Midwife. A True Story of the East End in the 1950s* (Weidenfeld & Nicolson, 2002), p. 180.
[6] Sir William Hunter, *Annals of Rural Bengal* (1868).

[7] Bengal and East Bengal, with Assam, was a huge area taking in the whole of the eastern side of the continent, bounded to the north by China and to the east by Burma.

[8] 'Lascar' meant soldier in seventeenth-century Urdu.

[9] Joseph Salter, *The Asiatic in England: Sketches of Sixteen Years Work Among Asiatics* (1873).

[10] Caroline Adams, *Across Seven Seas* (Eastside Books, 1987).

[11] Ibid.

[12] Ibid.

[13] Ibid.

[14] Ibid.

[15] Shafiq Uddin.

Part IV

Chapter 13: Violence and respect

[1] Interestingly, it is also the place where *EastEnders* star Barbara Windsor recently discovered one of her ancestors lived, while researching her lineage with TV's *Who Do You Think You Are?*

[2] C. A. Brown, *Memories of Mile End*, East London Record, 1979 (2), 28–33, p. 31.

[3] All public schools are registered charities; there are big tax advantages.

[4] The British and World Light Middleweight Champion up to 1982.

[5] Grievous bodily harm.

[6] Raphael Samuel, *East End Underworld. Chapters in the Life of Arthur Harding* (Routledge & Kegan Paul, 1981), p. 275.

[7] Sax Rohmer, *The Mystery of Dr. Fu Manchu* (1913).

[8] Daniel Farson, *Limehouse Days. Personal Experience of the East End* (Michael Joseph, 1991), p. 65.

[9] Ibid., p. 67.

[10] Iain Sinclair, *Lights Out for the Territory: 9 Excursions in the Secret History of London* (Granta, 1997).

[11] Years later, this proved the winning line for the famous Olympus camera advertisement in which Bailey appeared.

Part V

Chapter 14: Solidarity

[1] Ed Glinert, *East End Chronicles* (Allen Lane, 2005).

[2] George Renshaw, *Reflections of Changing Times*, East London History Newsletter, Vol. 1, Issues 2–5.

[3] Interview with Rebecca Taylor in *Time Out*, May 2007.

[4] Kuffar is Arabic for 'non-believers'. 'Dirty Kuffar' is a controversial 2004 Islamist extremist rap video.

[5] Martin Fletcher, *The Times* (November 3, 2007).

[6] Prafulla Mohanti, *Through Brown Eyes* (Oxford University Press, 1985), pp. 100, 167, 105.

[7] The find inspired a book, *Rodinsky's Room*, by Rachel Lichtenstein (Granta, 1999).

Index